LOST

DULUTH

Landmarks, Industries, Buildings, Homes,
and the Neighborhoods in Which They Stood

TONY DIERCKINS AND MARYANNE C. NORTON

Zenith City PRESS

Duluth, Minnesota

Zenith City Press
A Subsidiary of X-Communication
Duluth, Minnesota
218-310-6541
www.zenithcitypress.com

*Lost Duluth: landmarks, industries, buildings, homes,
and the neighborhoods in which they stood*

Text and research by Tony Dierckins and Maryanne C. Norton
Further research by Eric Faust, Carly Moritz, Mylii Pukema, and Dan Turner
Copy editing by Scott Pearson
Proofreading by Suzanne Rauvola, Hollis Norman, and Christopher Godsey
Additional editorial assistance by Camille Doom
Cover and interior design and maps by Tony Dierckins

A complete list of image credits appears on pages 204–205

First Edition, 2012

12 13 14 15 • 5 4 3 2 1

Library of Congress Control Number: 2012930089
ISBN: 978-1-887317-38-2

At left: The Duluth National Bank, 1890s
Opposite: Duluth Ship Canal's Original Wooden Pier, 1880s
Contents: (left) Scene at the Northern Pacific Docks, 1880s
Contents: (right) Manhattan Building, 1890s
Facing preface: Looking east from the hillside, 1890s
Preface: Duluth outer waterfront, 1871

The authors would like to thank…

Kent and Emily Aldrich, Patrice Bradley, Phil Bradley, Anthony Bush, Christine Carlson, Pete Dingels, Camille Doom, Doug Fairchild, Eric Faust, Chuck Frederick, Greg Grell, Alessandro Giuliani, Christopher Godsey, Heidi Bakk-Hansen, Charles Hanson, Wing Young Huie, Sandra Immerman, Andrew Krueger, Dennis Lamkin, Paul Lundgren, Rachael Martin, Greg Mattson, Carly Moritz, Nancy Nelson, Jon Niemi, Hollis Norman, Bryan Olson, Michelle Pearson, Scott Pearson, Mylii Pukema, Suzanne Rauvola, Lance Reasor, Leon Rohrbaugh, Joanne Sher, Dan Turner, Robin Washington…

and in particular…

Kris Ajo and David Ouse and the rest of the wonderful Duluth Public Library Reference Staff,
the incomparable Pat Maus of the Northeast Minnesota Historical Center,
Ellen Kriedler and the rest of the Duluth Building Safety Department staff,
the incredibly supportive Duluth Preservation Alliance,
and the history-curious posters on perfectduluthday.com.

Contents

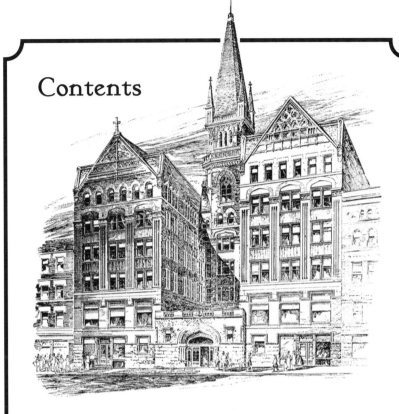

Preface

When Maryanne Norton and I first set out on this project, we thought it would be very similar to other "Lost City" books, primarily a cataloging of downtown commercial buildings that have come and gone. As we researched and encountered more and more information about homes, buildings, industries, even neighborhoods, we couldn't help but notice how they were intrinsically linked with one another. So we decided to widen our scope to include as much of what the Zenith City has lost as we could find. During our research of structures we uncovered stories of people—from hardscrabble pioneers to wealthy industrialists to impoverished immigrant laborers—whose ambitions and dreams built the Zenith City on a swamp and a rocky hillside at the westernmost point of Lake Superior.

Despite those ambitions, our work is certainly not a complete inventory of everything that has come and gone in Duluth. We focused on subjects from 1856, when Duluth was first established as a township, to 1939, a very symbolic year for Duluth. Samuel Frisbee Snively died in 1939. Duluth's longest serving mayor, Snively famously gave his own land and money—and convinced his friends and neighbors to do the same—to build Seven Bridges Road and finish Skyline Parkway, first envisioned when Duluth regained its city charter in 1888. It is also the year Enger Tower went up to commemorate Bert Enger, a Norwegian immigrant and furniture merchant who purchased the *Leif Erikson* replica Viking boat for Duluth and donated the land and money that created Enger Golf Course. Both men represented an era when the wealthy generously gave back to

their community, effectively helping to build the city. That year also saw the end of Duluth's streetcar system, which began operation in 1883, as the Seventh Avenue Incline Railway was dismantled and sold for scrap. The old was making way for the new, and World War II loomed just around the corner. Post-war Duluth would see a loss of many industries, a population drop, and a shift in architectural sensibilities that would change the town's character and economy. So the most recent building you will find in these pages is the Halvorson House, built in 1939 (in architectural terms, it is also the book's most modern building).

While most of the words herein have sprung from my keyboard, Maryanne executed the lion's share of the research, and together we formulated the entire book. We had a lot of help in our research, especially from David Ouse, Kris Aho, and the rest of the Duluth Public Library's reference staff, as well as from Pat Maus at the Northeast Minnesota Historical Center. We could not produce a well-researched book without the DPL and the NEMHC. And thanks to the University of Minnesota Duluth's English and Composition Departments, more research and editorial help came in the form of interns Eric Faust, Carly Moritz, Mylii Pukema, Dan Turner, and Camille Doom. Together we combed through the public library's Minnesota Collection, its publications clippings files, microfilm editions of old newspapers, slide collection, insurance maps, and city directories. Maryanne in particular poured over building records filed at the Duluth Building Safety Department, where Ellen Kriedler provided assistance. Maryanne also used Geneaologybank.com to find information in newspaper archives from across the nation. (Our collective research will be donated to the Duluth Public Library to become part of its publications clippings archives.)

Many others helped over the five years Maryanne and I have been assembling this book. They provided subject ideas, images, family stories, editorial needs, suggestions for content, and support. We are eternally grateful to these folks, whose names you will find on this book's acknowledgements page.

Readers of some of my previous works about Duluth

PICTURESQUE DULUTH, A SAMPLE OF THE BOOSTER BOOKS THAT INSPIRED THIS BOOK'S DESIGN—AND THE TEMPLATE FOR ITS COVER.

promote the developing city to outside investors or convince industrialists to move their operations to the Zenith City. These books are packed with both beautiful images of Duluth's emerging architecture and natural landscape as well as information that has proved invaluable to us as researchers. So influenced by these works was I that with few exceptions this book's design reflects the typography and graphic sensibility prominent in these works, many of which were published at the height of the Arts & Crafts movement. The cover de-

may recognize some material from two earlier books created with the help of Maryanne's research: *Zenith: A Postcard Perspective of Historic Duluth* and *Crossing the Canal: An Illustrated History of Duluth's Aerial Bridge*. We have paraphrased, revised, updated, sometimes corrected, and either expanded upon or condensed that material for use in the context of this book. The introduction is greatly informed by Anne Stuntz Bailey's "The Towns that Became Duluth" from *Duluth: Sketches of the Past*, June Drenning Holmquist's *They Chose Minnesota: A Survey of the State's Ethnic Groups*, Richard Hudelson and Carl Ross's *Down by the Ore Docks: A Working People's History of Duluth*, and A. B. Horwitz's *Land Platting History of Duluth, Minnesota, 1856–1939*.

This book would hardly be complete without the work of photographers long dead, many unknown, who first made the images that explain so much more than do our words. Included among these are Duluth's two great historic photographers, Hugh McKenzie and Louis "Perry" Gallagher, who together shot Duluth from 1895 through the 1940s. Our work would also be lessened without the efforts of those who wrote and published Duluth booster books popular from the 1880s to the early 1920s, designed to

sign is an homage (or outright thievery, depending on your perspective) to *Picturesque Duluth* (pictured above) published by the Northwestern Lithography and Publishing Company at the turn of the last century.

For those who lament the lost buildings, industries, and neighborhoods of old, we urge you to keep in mind that cities—like languages—are always adapting to our needs as we ourselves evolve. Despite being made of timber, stone, and steel, architectural landscapes are not static; cities are living, breathing things. Change keeps a community alive. But just as languages include many old words that perfectly serve their users today, not every old building has an expiration date that renders it useless to a community. It is our hope that in the future, Duluthians will pause before they accept the demolition of a sound, culturally significant structure and ask, "Can this building still serve the community?" Maryanne and I also hope that readers will find the information we have gathered here as fascinating as we have, and that it helps put Duluth's history in better perspective for all of us who want to see the Zenith City thrive in the twenty-first century and beyond.

— Tony Dierckins | March, 2012

Introduction: Duluth's Development from 1856–1939

The city we now know as Duluth began developing in 1856, after the 1854 Treaty of LaPointe opened land north of Lake Superior for settlement by Americans of European descent. Superior, Wisconsin, pioneer George Stuntz famously set up the first structure—a trading post on the southern end of Minnesota Point—four years earlier. Between 1856 and 1859, pioneers established eleven townships from Fond du Lac in the west to Belville in the east. Many townships involved the same people: Orrin Rice of Rice's Point was also a settler of Duluth, and Duluth's first mayor, J. B. Culver, was also a trustee of Fond du Lac Township. These townships and others established in the 1880s would come together—most between 1888 and 1896—to form the City of Duluth.

1850s

Prior to European settlement the entire area familiar to us as Duluth and Superior, was known as Fond du Lac, French for "bottom of the lake." The name was also used for an Ojibwe settlement eighteen miles up the St. Louis River from Minnesota Point. In 1816 John Jacob Astor built the American Fur Post at Fond du Lac; the Ojibwe, who partnered with Astor in the fur trade, occupied an island adjacent to the fur post. The fur post was out of business by 1839, but a few people stayed, including Reverend Edmund Ely, who had established a missionary school for the Ojibwe. When the land opened to development in 1854, the previous infrastructure made it an ideal spot for a townsite, and in 1857 the township of **Fond du Lac** was incorporated.

THE MINNESOTA POINT LIGHT HOUSE, AND LIGHTHOUSE KEEPER'S HOUSE, BUILT ON THE SOUTHERN TIP OF MINNESOTA POINT IN 1858 TO GUIDE MARINERS THROUGH THE SUPERIOR ENTRY AND ON TO SUPERIOR, WISCONSIN, WHERE MANY OF DULUTH'S PIONEERS FIRST ARRIVED—AND LIVED—WHEN THEY REACHED THE HEAD OF THE LAKES.

Three years before Fond du Lac's incorporation, Reverend Ely relocated to Superior. That same year, 1854, he crossed the bay, landed near today's Forty-Second Avenue West, and envisioned a townsite. Shortly thereafter, he contacted Henry Wheeler in St. Paul, who in 1855 walked from St. Paul to today's West Duluth to set up a sawmill. Nearby, Lewis Merritt of Ashtabula, Ohio, and his son Napolean had struck a claim. They started calling the area **Oneota**, a word taken from a local Ojibwe legend meaning "the rock from which the people sprang." Ely moved his family to the site in 1856, the same year the rest of the Merritts arrived from Ohio—and the year the town was surveyed, so goes the legend, with a "carpenter's square and level." The small community survived the Financial Panic of 1857 and a scarlet fever epidemic in 1859, the same year its citizens elected the first town council.

Orrin Rice, another Superior pioneer, moved his family across the bay in the spring of 1854 and filed a claim on the peninsula that jutted into the bay west of Minnesota Point and east of Oneota. Rice then operated a ferry service between Superior's Conner's Point, Minnesota Point, and the peninsula he had claimed, which in 1858 would be platted as **Rice's Point**. The township stretched from the end of the point north to Point of Rocks and included a great deal of what would later be called Duluth's West End. Rice had big ambitions for his township, and attempted to have Rice's Point made the St. Louis County Seat—even temporarily changed its name to "Port Byron" to give it a more glamorous appeal. His efforts failed, but the Territorial Legislature did give him the sole rights to run his ferry service across the Bay—and state lines—to Connor's Point for fifteen years.

East of Rice's Point and west of Minnesota Point stood a tract of marshy land along the northern shore of what was then called Superior Bay (essentially below today's Michigan Street between Minnesota Point and Rice's Point). In 1856 C. P. Huestis and C. A. Post platted a township atop the muck and named it **Fremont**. Much of the township actually consisted of floating islands of "accumulated vegetable matter," and few structures were built there.

As for Minnesota Point itself, several communities were established. (Pinpointing the precise original borders of these claims has been a source of frustration for researchers, as there is little written evidence, no maps, and plenty of contradictory anecdotal evidence; the following is the most logical summation at which the authors could arrive.) Beginning at Oatka (today's Thirty-Ninth Street South) and running north to a point south of where the Duluth Ship Canal runs today, Robert Reed and T. A. Markland platted a community called **Middleton**. Directly north of Middleton, Englishman William G. Cowell purchased a tract stretching north to today's Buchanan Street, called **Cowell's Addition**. The land north of Cowell's

Addition to the base of the point was owned by pioneer brothers George and William Nettleton, who arrived in 1852 and staked a claim at the base of the point east of Third Avenue East that stretched west to Eighth Avenue West, corresponding to much of today's downtown. John Pendergrast of New York platted the land immediately north of the Nettleton claim—essentially today's Central Hillside. As the Nettletons would name their stake **Duluth**, Pendergrast called his **North Duluth**. Pendergrast lost much of his land when a false claim he made against the Nettletons backfired on him; he forfeited all but eighty acres to the Nettletons. By the time Duluth was incorporated by George and William Nettleton, Joshua B. Culver, Orrin Rice, and Robert Jefferson, it included North Duluth, the Nettleton property, Cowell's Addition, and Middleton, stretching from today's Central Hillside to Oatka. At Buchanan Street the township split into **Upper Duluth** and **Lower Duluth**.

Platted in 1856 by seven men led by James D. Ray and Clinton Markell, **Portland** stretched roughly from Third Avenue East to Twelfth Avenue East. Sidney Luce built the first warehouse at Portland's southeastern corner, where Third Avenue East meets Lake Superior. It stood three stories tall, with half of its foundation carved into rock on its north side and the other half perched atop cribbing submerged in the lake on the south.

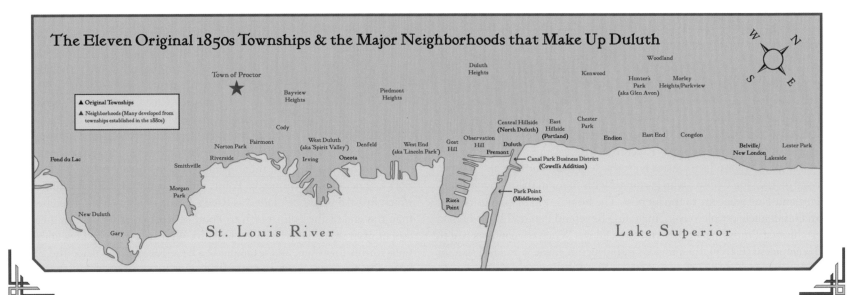

The Eleven Original 1850s Townships & the Major Neighborhoods that Make Up Duluth

▲ Original Townships

▲ Neighborhoods (Many developed from townships established in the 1880s)

Town of Proctor

Woodland

Duluth Heights

Kenwood

Hunter's Park (aka Glen Avon)

Morley Heights/Parkview

Bayview Heights

Piedmont Heights

Cody

Central Hillside (North Duluth)

East Hillside (Portland)

Chester Park

Fairmont

West Duluth (aka 'Spirit Valley')

Norton Park

Denfeld

West End (aka 'Lincoln Park')

Goat Hill

Observation Hill

Duluth

Endion

East End

Congdon

Belville/ New London

Lester Park

Fond du Lac

Riverside

Irving

Oneota

Fremont

Lakeside

Smithville

Canal Park Business District (Cowell's Addition)

Morgan Park

Rice's Point

Park Point (Middleton)

New Duluth

Gary

St. Louis River

Lake Superior

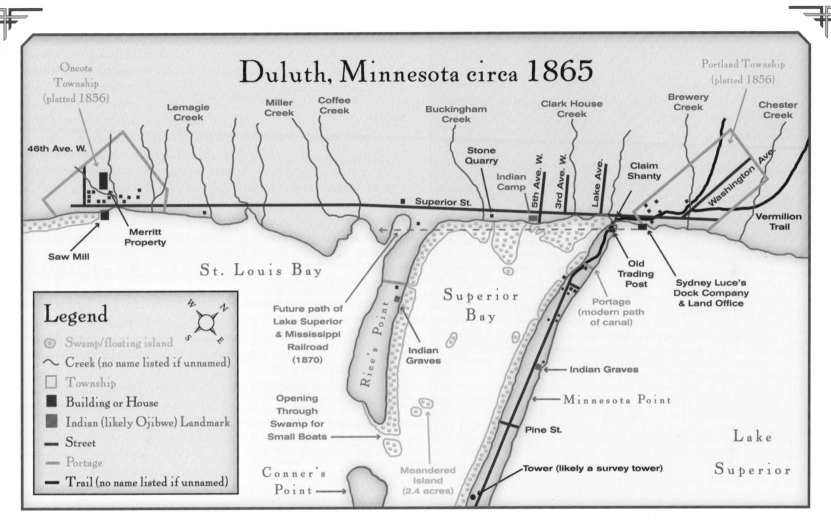

Duluth, Minnesota circa 1865

Oneota Township (platted 1856)

Lemagie Creek

Miller Creek

Coffee Creek

Buckingham Creek

Stone Quarry

Clark House Creek

Indian Camp

Brewery Creek

Chester Creek

Portland Township (platted 1856)

46th Ave. W.

5th Ave. W.

3rd Ave. W.

Lake Ave.

Claim Shanty

Washington Ave.

Superior St.

Vermilion Trail

Merritt Property

Saw Mill

St. Louis Bay

Old Trading Post

Sydney Luce's Dock Company & Land Office

Legend

- ⊚ Swamp/floating island
- ∼ Creek (no name listed if unnamed)
- ☐ Township
- ■ Building or House
- ■ Indian (likely Ojibwe) Landmark
- ━ Street
- ━ Portage
- ━ Trail (no name listed if unnamed)

Future path of Lake Superior & Mississippi Railroad (1870)

Rice's Point

Indian Graves

Superior Bay

Portage (modern path of canal)

Indian Graves

Minnesota Point

Opening Through Swamp for Small Boats

Pine St.

Lake Superior

Conner's Point

Meandered Island (2.4 acres)

Tower (likely a survey tower)

THE MAP ABOVE IS BASED UPON A PERIOD MAP DRAWN BY ROBERT CAREY, SON OF JUDGE JOHN CAREY (SEE PAGE 15). THE ORIGINAL IS LARGE AND DETAILED AND INCLUDES A KEY TO IDENTIFYING ALL OF THE LANDMARKS PLOTTED. IT IS AVAILABLE AT THE DULUTH PUBLIC LIBRARY.

Portland was established as a residential area, and most of its incorporators and residents had business interests in Duluth.

East of Portland stood **Endion**, platted by Captain T. A. Markland as a quiet suburb for "capitalists doing business at Superior," which at the time looked to be the region's city of destiny. The township—named after the Ojibwe word for "my, your, or his home"—stretched from Fourteenth Avenue East to about Twenty-First Avenue East. East of Endion in 1856 J. B. Bell platted a township between Fortieth and Forty-Third Avenues East from Lake Superior to today's McCullough Street and named the town **Belville** after himself.

In 1857 the Minnesota State legislature incorporated all eleven townships, in which about 1,500 souls lived and worked. That same year a financial panic struck the nation, putting the pioneers' dreams on hold. Most left before the decade ended.

1860s

Few stayed behind to oversee the young townships after the Panic of 1857, and the Civil War further decimated the population, as many pioneers set off to fight for the Union. In 1860 the three largest townships—Duluth, Oneota, and Fond du Lac—had a total population of just 353. No deliveries were made to the Minnesota townships; all goods had to be purchased in Superior, and the pioneers had little to eat outside of fish pulled from Lake Superior. Those who rode out the financial panic in Duluth called themselves the "Ancient and Honorable Order of the Fish Eaters."

The mid 1860s brought hope in the form of Philadelphia's Jay Cooke, who set out to build the Northern Pacific Railroad from Duluth to Seattle's Puget Sound and the Lake Superior & Mississippi Railroad from St. Paul to Duluth. Cooke's ambitious plans brought prosperity to Duluth: to build railroads, you need manpower and materials. Soon the townships were teeming with people and activity, nearly all living off Cooke's pocketbook in one way or another, either building his railroad (or working any number of jobs in support of that effort) or housing, feeding, and outfitting the flow of newcomers.

Cooke's investment also coincided with what turned out to be a false gold rush at Lake Vermilion. The prospectors came in droves, and when their plans went bust, many found work in the Minnesota townships. Building that had stalled in 1857 picked up again after 1866. The newcomers not only built Cooke's depots, docks, and a grain elevator, but also the buildings that would house and serve the growing population. By 1869 the Lake Superior & Mississippi Railroad approached Duluth and the local population neared 3,000. The Fish Eaters called the newcomers "Sixty-Niners."

The townships were all growing, but Portland had a problem. When first platted, its streets ran directly north and south. The other townships had platted their streets more or less parallel to the lake, essentially tipping the traditional north/south compass points on a 45 degree angle. In order to follow suit with the other townships, in 1869 every house in Portland was temporarily vacated, the streets replatted to align with other townships, and the house placements adjusted. Washington Avenue remained a north/south road, but only a half-block remnant of it exists today.

1870s

In the 1860s the townships adjacent to Minnesota Point had gone from near extinction to boomtowns. On March 6, 1870, Duluth became a city, at the same time annexing Fond du Lac, Rice's Point, Fremont, Portland, and Endion. It stretched from Twenty-First Avenue East to Fortieth Avenue West, from the top of the hillside to the end of Minnesota Point—plus all of Fond du Lac. That year Duluth's population reached 3,130.

Duluth's booming population was about sixty percent foreign-born laborers. The other forty percent was American-born, mostly professionals and businessmen from New England, Maryland, Michigan, Illinois, and Wisconsin. Many of the original pioneers had connections in Ohio, and Jay Cooke's agents hailed from Philadelphia. Most of these were of British or German ancestry and nearly all were practitioners of some Protestant religion: Methodists, Episcopalians, Presbyterians, Congregationalists, and even a few Baptists.

Duluth's foreign-born majority came for the most part from western and northern Europe. Half were Scandinavian (Swedes, Norwegians, and Danes), the rest primarily Irish, German Catholics, and Canadians (many of French heritage). Over one hundred were English or Scottish, followed by a handful of Swiss, French, Luxemburgers, Belgians, and one Australian. Austrians Bernard and Nettie Silberstein were two of Duluth's first four immigrants of Jewish descent.

The West End would welcome most of Duluth's immigrants for the next forty years, although many would also begin to populate the ramshackle "No Man's Land" in what is today's Canal Park Business District. Upon first arrival, many of these people found temporary housing in the Immigrant Houses established by Northern Pacific Railroad.

All the promise of Duluth anticipated by early pioneers was finally starting to materialize. In 1871 the initial cut of the Duluth Ship Canal—which would allow the land west of the point to develop into the world's largest inland port—was completed. With a railroad, a canal, and a safe port, Duluth sat poised to become a major center of commerce in the

An 1870 view of "No Man's Land" along St. Croix Avenue—later South First Avenue East and today's Canal Park Drive. In the 1890s the area would be known as Finn Town.

Duluth's Immigrant Patterns, 1880~1920

During the 1880s waves of immigrants began to pour into Duluth and would continue doing so for the next thirty years. Some were recruited for specific skilled jobs, such as Norwegian and Swedish fishermen. Some were well-educated western Europeans—Protestant English, Scots, and Germans, mostly—and came to Duluth, as did Yankees from the eastern U.S., with letters of introduction to help establish them in their professions.

But most of Duluth's immigrants were unskilled laborers, escaping the problems of their home lands, from famine to poverty to political strife. During the 1880s Duluth saw mostly Scandinavian (Norwegian, Swedish, and Danish) immigrants, along with Irish, Germans, Austrians, and Canadians with a few French and Italians mixed in. Over seven hundred Russians had arrived by 1890. The 1890s saw more of these same groups arrive, along with a smattering of others: Belgian, Bohemian, Dutch, Hungarian, Spanish, Turkish, and even a few Asian immigrants. The French and Swedish populations increased while the Russian was cut in half. Beginning in 1896 Finns were recruited to build the concrete piers along the Duluth Ship Canal; by the turn of the century, they were here in large numbers. After 1900 the population of Italians, Germans, Turks, and Russians took a significant leap upward.

The Russian population included a number of Orthodox Jews. Duluth had long included Jewish residents, but the majority of them were considered "German" Jews: those from Germany, or Hungarians and Bohemians who spoke German. Most lived on the East Hillside—close to their synagogue, Temple Emanuel—and practiced Reform Judaism. The Russians were Orthodox and lived further west on the Hillside, near Tifereth Israel, which was first located at Third Avenue East and Fifth Street. A group of Lithuanian Jews lived on St. Croix Avenue, between Buchanan Street and the ship canal. They relocated to the Hillside after building Adas Israel Congregation in 1899, just down the hill from Tifereth Israel. The area became known as "Little Jerusalem." By 1900 Duluth had four synagogues; the Jewish population peaked in the 1930s at 4,000. (See page 74 for more about Duluth's Jewish population.)

While many skilled and professional transplants to Duluth mostly found places to live north and east of downtown, families of unskilled laborers settled in undeveloped areas, mostly found in the West End, close to the mills and docks where they would find work. The Finns took over "No Man's Land," the shanty town along Minnesota Point in today's Canal Park Business District. Swedish-speaking Finns found a home on Grass Island near Rice's Point and along Garfield Avenue; the community was referred to as Swede Town. The French first inhabited The Glenn below Point of Rocks, and after they moved deeper into the West End the Italians turned The Glenn into the lower half of Little Italy. A portion of today's West End business district was once called Corktown because of its heavy Irish population. Many Poles, who farmed on their properties and raised geese, lived in a corner of the West End called Goosetown (many also lived on the Central Hillside). By 1910 Third Street in the West End had a French Catholic Church, a German Catholic Church, and a Polish Catholic Church all within the space of a few blocks. Despite this, the West End has been called "heavily Scandinavian," as Norwegians and Swedes still dominated the landscape throughout Duluth.

After the turn of the century immigrant populations began to level off or even decline. Outside of a jump in Austrians and Romanians (and a continued flow of Finns) in 1900, existing immigrant populations stabilized. A wave of Serbs arrived in 1905 to build Thompson Dam, and another wave in 1913 to build U.S. Steel and Atlas Cement, where many of them would find steady work as unskilled laborers. But they could not live in Morgan Park, which was reserved for families of management, foremen, and skilled laborers. Instead, they lived in Gary and New Duluth in substandard housing.

United States. Giant warehouses began popping up along the waterfront and, now that the canal had cleared the way, on Rice's Point.

In the spring of 1873 came the loss of an entire township in a single day. A large storm had hit the region, and the St. Louis River swelled. The two-year-old canal had shifted currents in the bay, and much of the loose vegetation that made up Fremont broke loose and floated out through the canal. This included a large portion of Fremont Island, 1,200 feet long by 400 feet wide when platted. Fremont township was no more.

The loss of Fremont was of little consequence compared to what happened that September: Jay Cooke ran out of money, and all of his businesses failed. This sent the entire nation into a depression known as the Panic of 1873; no community was hit as hard as Duluth. With no money, much of the business in the Zenith City came to a screeching halt and building stopped. The population dropped, and debts mounted. By 1877 Duluth had lost its city charter. Endion, Portland, North Duluth, Duluth, Middleton, Rice's Point, and Fond du Lac all reverted to independent townships. While records are unclear, Middleton's border may have moved north to the canal at this time.

1880s

The 1880s turned things around for the area, in no small thanks to the ship canal

Looking eastward down Third Street from west of Mesaba Avenue in 1887.

and railroads, which allowed Duluth to turn itself into a major grain trading center. Grain elevators and flour mills sprang up on Rice's Point. The lumber industry also picked up, and soon mills stretched from Minnesota Point to Oneota.

Not everyone was pleased. The folks in Middleton were none-too-happy that the canal had essentially cut them off from the rest of Duluth, turning their community into an island, and that Duluth had done nothing in ten years to bridge the canal. In 1881, Middleton residents changed the township's name to something its citizens preferred and had been calling it for years: **Park Point**. Despite this, most of the townships got along fine, and divisions continued to blur. Those Fish Eaters who had developed both Portland and Duluth—many of whom had connections with Ashtabula, Ohio—finally saw their investments pay off and began building themselves elaborate Queen Anne Victorian homes in a neighborhood they called Ashtabula Heights (covering today's lower Central Hillside).

In the early 1880s, immigrant laborers began building homes west of Mesaba Avenue, an area that would evolve into Duluth's West End.

At this time not much had developed west of Rice's Point outside of Oneota. The only way to get to Oneota was by Michigan Street: Superior Street west of Point of Rocks wouldn't be graded until 1886. In 1885, pretty much everything west of Twenty-Eighth Avenue West was, according to land developer C. E. Lovett, "covered with bushes, underbrush, stumps, and logs…. Grand Avenue was a country road cut through the alder bushes."

Lovett was part of a group of men who speculated in land development west of the West End. As Duluth was booming, many were speculating that it would become a great distribution center, which would attract a variety of industries, all of which would need a place to build factories and warehouses. With a "syndicate" of investors he purchased land west of Oneota hoping to bring that new industry west and make a fortune from real estate.

In 1888 they incorporated their land—along with Oneota Township—as the **Village of West Duluth**. West Duluth's founders widely believed it promised to become the "new Pittsburgh" after gaining a blast furnace and rolling mill from the Duluth Iron and Steel Company. While

Immigrant Sentiment in the 1890s

Many in the "servant class," who tended to the needs of the wealthy, were Irish Catholic. Anti-Catholic sentiment ran high among Prohibitionist Protestants of the day, who considered the Irish Catholics prone to alcoholism. The fact that (for the most part) the Protestants were wealthy and the Catholics were not, further divided the two groups. This combined religious, ethnic, and social prejudice ran rampant throughout Duluth as people from a variety of cultures who rarely understood or appreciated other culture tried to come together as a community. According to historians Richard Hudelson and Carl Ross, groups throughout Duluth—from Northland Country Club to the Kitchi Gammi Club to high school fraternities—"specifically refused to accept Jews, South Slavs, and Italians."

Anti-immigrant sentiment certainly wasn't isolated to Duluth. Hudelson and Ross's *Down By the Ore Docks* reminds us that throughout the country Americans were divided by their ethnicities and religions: the melting pot was still heating up, and old differences still made a big difference to many, creating a pecking order of classes. At the top were the Yankees, those usually of English and Scottish descent who had been born in the eastern U.S. and were seeking a fortune in the burgeoning "Northwest" as the entire region west of Chicago was called. Next came Protestant British and German immigrants, then the Protestant Scandinavians—Norwegians, Swedes, and Danes. After them came the "godless" socialist Finns (in 1918, a vigilante group tarred, feathered, and hanged Finnish laborer Oli Kinkkonen in Lester Park, reportedly because of his anti-war sentiments). Then came the Catholics in descending order: Poles and Germans, Irish, South Slavs, and Italians. Below the Italians came the Eastern European Jews, mostly Russian. Apparently Reformist Jews of Western European descent, like Duluth merchant Bernard Silberstein, were more welcome. African Americans, not yet thirty years free from slavery, pulled up the rear.

People were fractured further within these factions. The histories of many of Duluth's churches and synagogues involve splitting off from earlier congregations. Even the northern Italians felt that their southern cousins were an inferior people; southern Italians were not considered Caucasian by many of the day, and the Irish despised them. When the new Sacred Heart Cathedral's primarily Irish and Polish congregation opened the church's doors in 1896, they threw a grand celebration, inviting Catholics from all over the city— French, Poles, Germans, Irish, and others—but Catholics of southern Italian descent were not welcomed. Later the Catholic Poles would split off and open their own parish because of an argument with Bishop James McGolrick, who was Irish, over cemetery locations. At the same time, in neighborhoods like The Glenn and Slabtown, French, Italian, and Norwegian children played together even if, as reported by historian Jacqueline Rocchio Moran, the Norwegian mothers forbade their kids to go into the Italian grocery stores, where the scent of garlic and oil smelled "menacing."

that vision didn't materialize, West Duluth did become the industrial center of town, particularly near the river by the old Oneota settlement.

The empty spaces of what is now Duluth began to fill in as well, as a larger population required more housing. As the newer arrivals filled in neighborhoods in Duluth, Portland, and Endion, further east developers were attracting those who now found the city too crowded. In 1871 Hugh McCollough had purchased much of Belville and land stretching east to the Lester River. He platted the area and called it **New London**, giving many of the streets and squares British names, including his own (McCollough would never see his township, as he did all the work from his London office). McCollough sold his property to George Sargent. When Sargent died in 1875, the property went to his son, William. William and a few friends organized the Lakeside Land Company and divided New London into **Lakeside** and **Lester Park**. In 1889 the entire area became the **Village of Lakeside**.

While all this growth was occurring in new village sites and in the west, the Village of Duluth continued to pay off the defunct city's debts, clearing the books in early 1887 to once again become a city.

As the decade came to an end, Duluth stretched eastward from roughly Fortieth Avenue West to Twenty-First Avenue East and again included many of the townships that once hoped to become grand cities all their own: Endion, Portland, North Duluth, and Rice's Point. Fremont, of course, had floated away in 1873. Duluth did not include Park Point. The village refused to rejoin the newly sanctioned city until a bridge was built connecting Minnesota Point to the rest of the city. Duluth promised a bridge, and Park Point became part of Duluth in 1889. Park Pointers had to exercise patience: it would take Duluth another fifteen years to build that promised bridge, which would become the symbol of the entire city.

1890s

Duluth's expansion continued into the 1890s. In 1891 Duluth acquired **Hunter's Park, Woodland, Kenwood, Duluth Heights**, and **Piedmont Heights**, all primarily residential developments served by streetcar lines installed by developers and operated by the Duluth Street Railway Company—Duluth's infamous Seventh Avenue West Incline was built to help Duluth Heights develop.

The **Hunter's Park** neighborhood took off in the early 1890s when it was reached by streetcar line. Angus MacFarlane and his brother-in-law, Ronald Hunter, purchased the land that would become Hunter's Park in the early 1880s. A portion of Hunter's Park became known as Glen Avon, the name used for the neighborhood's school, church, playground, and other facilities. When the neighborhood was platted in 1891, MacFarlane and Hunter named the streets for English and Scottish place names, patron saints, and prominent people. One stretch of Waverly Avenue was known as "Oatmeal Hill."

They then began a recruitment campaign, offering Duluth's well-heeled and well-respected Protestant families lots at a reduced cost—or for free—in order to give the neighborhood instant prestige. Soon they drew many of the residents from Ashtabula Heights, which was then beginning to grow out of fashion with Duluth's elite. Hunter's Park also included several families of Italian heritage—in fact, a small enclave of houses along Carlisle Avenue was kindly called "Little Italy,"

pejoratively "Dagoville." Most of the Italian men worked in the neighborhood as gardeners for their wealthier neighbors; the Italian women worked as domestics.

In 1892 Duluth attempted to annex the Village of Lakeside, which had become another "streetcar suburb," but the city would have to make the village a promise. More than a few of Lakeside's Protestant leaders were involved in the growing Prohibition movement, and when it became a township the charter prohibited the sale or manufacturer of alcohol within its borders. When Lakeside Village became part of Duluth, the city had to make a promise to the village, and it did so with this piece of state legislation:

> "The common council of the city of Duluth is hereby prohibited from ever granting any license to sell or dispose of any wines, spirituous or malt liquors within the limits of the territory hereby constituted as the city of Lakeside, after the same shall have been annexed to the said city of Duluth in accordance with the provisions of this act."

THOUSANDS OF FINNISH IMMIGRANTS ARRIVED AFTER 1895 TO HELP BUILD THE DULUTH SHIP CANAL'S CONCRETE PIERS.

Downtown Duluth circa 1905. The elevated roadway is the Lake Avenue Viaduct.

Besides the wealthy who primarily built their homes along London Road, Lakeside's growing population included many members of Duluth's professional class: fairly well-to-do but far-from-rich merchants, medical professionals, and other "white collar" professionals. Most of these were Yankees of English and Scottish descent and almost uniformly Protestant. Others were of the "servant class": those who cooked, cleaned, laundered, and cared for the properties and livestock of the affluent. Most of these domestics were of Irish Catholic or Scandinavian descent. A few actually lived in modest homes in Lakeside, but thanks to the convenience of the streetcars, domestics living west of Mesaba Avenue could get from home to work and back with ease. The streetcars also helped them reach the homes of a fast-growing breed of wealthy Duluthians: lumber barons, grain commissioners, shipping magnates, mining executives, and various industrialists as well as physicians, lawyers, and other highly paid professionals. They had been building grand homes in Lakeside and Hunter's Park and, beginning around 1900, in the growing developments east of Endion that would become known as the **East End** and **Congdon Park**.

On the other end of town, West Duluth was becoming the industrial center its founders had anticipated, although it wasn't immune to national economics. The Panic of 1893 didn't slow Duluth down as much as it did the rest of the nation, but it had enough influence to force the hand of several local communities that Duluth had been trying to coax into annexation. In 1894, as West Duluth neighborhoods including **Cody, Fairmont, Irving**, and what would later be called **Denfeld** were already taking shape, the Village of West Duluth became part of the City of Duluth.

The next year Duluth annexed **Bayview Heights** and the land that would become **Riverside, Morgan Park**, and **Smithville**, although those names did not appear until some time later. All this land was platted in the 1880s when C. E. Lovett and other developers anticipated incredible growth. The Ironton Land Company was to develop **Ironton**, which became Riverside, and the St. Louis Bay Land Company (which included Lovett) would develop land south of Spirit Lake. The expected industrial boom never happened, and the land sat idle until 1913.

During the late 1880s a community later called **Smithville** quietly grew on the banks of Spirit Lake, a widening of the St. Louis River sacred to local Ojibwe. The neighborhood developed in part as a tourist retreat. But outside of the lake, its only attraction was the Spirit Lake Hotel, advertised in 1892 as the "finest summer resort at the head of the lakes." It was built in 1888 by brothers Edward and Albert Swenson. That same year the neighborhood got its own post office, which served the community for eighteen years. By 1895 enough people lived in the community to justify the construction of its own elementary school. The Smithville School was the first recorded use of the name "Smithville." But the hotel sat empty through most of the 1890s and in 1903 became the Finnish Theological Seminary (later called the Finnish Work People's College).

Duluth also annexed Bayview Heights in 1894. Located six hundred feet above West Duluth, Bayview is more often associated with the nearby town of Proctor—even the elementary school serving the neighborhood is affiliated with Proctor's school district. Bayview Heights had been platted in the 1880s, and an incline railway was developed to help make the neighborhood more attractive to potential residents. Despite this effort, the neighborhood did not become a major population center, and the railway was gone by 1916.

The New Duluth Land Company had platted the land that would become **New Duluth** in 1889, boasting that it was the "largest body of level land on the Minnesota side of the St. Louis Bay." It attracted many businesses to the area, including established Duluth outfits such as Atlas Iron and Brass Works and W. P. Heimbach

Native and African Americans in Duluth

Long before European settlement–perhaps thousands of years–the head of the lakes was home to several Native American tribes. When the 1854 Treaty of La Pointe opened what is now Duluth for settlement, the Ojibwe had already forced the Dakota west and had established settlements at Spirit Island, Spirit Mountain, Indian Point, Rice's Point, and Minnesota Point.

The treaty ceded all of what would become Duluth except for 682 acres negotiated by Chief Buffalo to serve as a reservation. He chose land in the heart of Duluth, known later as the "Buffalo Tract," which included an existing Indian village and burial grounds on Rice's Point that Chief Buffalo wanted to protect. But within two years Benjamin G. Armstrong wrestled the tract from Buffalo. The land was subdivided and sold time and time again, and no Ojibwe reservation developed in Duluth.

Until the late 1860s, more Ojibwe lived in Duluth than Europeans. As new settlers arrived, the natives were pushed aside. Although they lived peacefully among the settlers, the Ojibwe were often feared by those of European descent, an attitude fueled primarily by the media's portrayal of Native Americans as savages. They were further marginalized by whites who refused to hire Native Americans for even the most basic labor. Instead they recruited European immigrants.

The Ojibwe population declined dramatically over the years, as many relocated to reservations or became assimilated by marriage. By 1928 Duluth held fewer than two hundred Native Americans. That number would slowly increase, to 402 in 1960, 615 in 1970, 1,344 in 1980. The 2010 census showed 2,134 Native Americans living in Duluth.

Duluth's earliest African American residents were also part Ojibwe. In the 1850s, seven of Duluth's eleven African American residents were members of the George Bonga family. Bonga was the son of Pierre Bonga, a free Black fur trader, and his Ojibwe wife. Bonga, who legend says was born on Minnesota Point in either 1799 or 1802, also became a fur trader. In the 1870s there were just twenty-two Blacks in all of St. Louis County, and each one lived in Duluth; nearly every African American lived in The Glenn or on Rice's Point.

That number grew slowly. In the 1880s most of Duluth's African Americans lived in the Central Hillside, establishing St. Mark's African Methodist Church at 530 North Fifth Avenue East in 1890 when just 220 people of African descent lived in the Zenith City. In those early decades most worked as porters, waiters, messengers, janitors, and valets. One, Alexander Miles, was considered the richest Black man in the region (see page 106). At the turn of the century, less than 400 Black people lived in Duluth.

Duluth's Black population was bolstered after U.S. Steel opened. In 1916 U.S. Steel recruited a number of Blacks from southern states who would work for less pay than laborers in Duluth. Like the Southern Serbs, they lived in substandard housing in Gary, not in Morgan Park. Despite the recruitment, Duluth's Black population failed to grow. Researchers have speculated that this is likely due in part to an increased anti-Black sentiment in the U.S. following World War I, which led to the lynching of three innocent Black men in Duluth in 1920. Many of Duluth's established Black families left after the tragedy. By 1940, the population had dropped to 314. The 2010 census reported 1,988 Blacks living in Duluth. Together, Blacks and Native Americans make up just under 5 percent of Duluth's current population. Roughly 1,800 Duluthians (just over 2 percent) consider themselves mixed race of white and either African or Native American ancestry.

Lumber. Their land sale was a tremendous success, but when Duluth's Bell & Eyster Bank failed, the company lost much of its capital, which frightened investors, who refused to pay. All further sales were stopped. The financial panic of 1893 scared away any other potential investors. Duluth annexed New Duluth (and what would become **Gary**) in 1895, but neither would see significant growth until 1913.

Meanwhile Fond du Lac, which had been part of the first City of Duluth back in the 1870s, also rejoined the Zenith City in 1895.

1900 – 1939

Duluth's western environs had been platted in the 1880s and 1890s, but not greatly populated until U.S. Steel built Morgan Park in 1913 on land between Riverside and New Duluth. Named for U.S. Steel's J. P. Morgan, Morgan Park was a carefully planned company town for the families of the steel firm's managers, foremen, and skilled laborers—Germans, Scandinavians, and native-born Americans of European descent. Most unskilled laborers, recent eastern and southern European immigrants and Blacks, populated New Duluth, a portion of which had been purchased by U.S. Steel and renamed Gary in honor of Elbert H. Gary, a co-founder of U.S. Steel. Gary contained a faction of Orthodox Serbs, who were recruited to Duluth in 1905 to build the Thompson Dam (which provides Duluth with electricity) and stayed to work at U.S.S. and its affiliate, Atlas Cement.

In 1917, as World War I was tearing apart Europe, the McDougall-Duluth shipbuilding company—flush with government contracts to build naval vessels—developed Riverside along the St. Louis River between Morgan Park and West Duluth. The community provided housing for workers employed at the shipyards. Riverside had its own clubhouse, hospital, and theater. By 1918 nearly one thousand people called Riverside home, and many more shipyard workers moved to nearby Smithville.

By 1920 most of Duluth's major neighborhoods had taken shape. In 1920 a section east of Hunter's Park was developed as Morley Heights. Named for Albert Morley Marshall of Duluth's Marshall-Wells Hardware, Morley Heights was created for employees of the Marshall-Wells Hardware company. It was not a company town, as Duluth provided all of its utilities; instead, it was considered part of a benefit plan. In 1919 Marshall Wells purchased over eighty houses from the DuPont company in Barksdale, Wisconsin. The houses were dismantled, placed on packing freighters, and shipped to Duluth over Lake Superior. They were then hauled up Woodland Avenue on sleds and reassembled along Spear Avenue and Morely Parkway. The idea didn't go over very well with Marshall-Wells employees, however, and the neighborhood opened to anyone who wished to live there.

By the time Morley Heights was developed, Duluth was home to about 100,000 people from backgrounds as diverse as any city in the U.S. Its neighborhoods had developed and divided on lines financial, religious, and ethnic. Its most ambitious period of growth had come to an end, and the city was filled with examples of its development: homes both impressive and modest; commercial buildings simple and grand, many towering exclamations of native brownstone; and public buildings that spoke loudly of Duluthians' commitment to their government, their children's education, and their varied faiths. And behind it all the hum of industry kept the city at work.

While Duluth's population would not hit its peak until 1960, it didn't grow much in the 1920s and 1930s. By the twenties the great immigrant waves had subsided. The 1930s brought the Great Depression, retarding growth throughout the country. (The post-war housing boom that swept the nation in the 1950s and into the 1960s was seen in Duluth primarily in Piedmont and Duluth Heights, with Duluth Heights growing further in the 1970s with the construction of Miller Hill Mall and surrounding developments.)

The Great Depression and World War II would help the immigration pot to finally start melting in earnest. It took many years, but as the decades rolled on ethnic, religious, and financial lines blurred further and further. The middle class emerged, and people moved out of the neighborhoods of their youth. Others moved to town without the need for the ethnic communities that had been so important to an immigrant's adjustment just decades before; now they were simply looking for a neighborhood that provided comfort and convenience. The congregations of churches divided along ethnic lines began to decline in numbers, and many eventually merged. Duluth would change in other ways as well, as most of the industries that helped shape the city and drove its economy would be dead or dying by the 1950s. Its population would peak at 104,000 in 1960; today about 85,000 people live in the Zenith City.

PART ONE

LOST HOMES & NEIGHBORHOODS

Bell House (1887 – Extant) & Forbes House (1886 – 1966)

Lost Homes & Neighborhoods

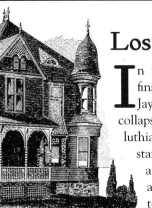

In the 1880s, when Duluth finally began to recover from Jay Cooke's 1873 economic collapse, a large number of Duluthians started to build substantial homes designed by architects, mostly in the area now considered downtown.

A number of Duluth's pioneers came to the Zenith City from Ashtabula, Ohio, and when the risk they took developing a frontier town at the head of the Great Lakes finally paid off, many of them built homes in the same area of town, roughly from Second Avenue East to Sixth Avenue East and from First Street to Fourth Street in much of what was originally Portland Township. In the 1880s, the neighborhood was the center of Duluth's socially and politically elite. They called it "Ashtabula Heights."

At the turn of the century, development began east of Twentieth Avenue East, where Duluthians who made their fortunes in the 1890s began to build the stately mansions of Duluth's East End and Hunter's Park. By the 1920s most original residents of Ashtabula Heights had either died, moved back East, or moved to Hunter's Park or the East End. Many of their old homes, too expensive for upkeep by individual families, were subdivided into boarding houses. As St. Mary's and Miller Memorial hospitals developed and grew, more of theses homes were destroyed to make room for the expanding health care campuses. Few Ashtabula Heights homes survive today. Fortunately, a number of Duluth's grand old homes remain throughout the city, most clustered in Duluth's East End and Congdon neighborhoods as well as some along London Road and others scattered in other neighborhoods, such as Woodland, Hunter's Park, Lakeside, and Lester Park.

Affluent Duluthians also dwelled in townhouses designed for upscale living. As with the Ashtabula Heights homes, the charm of "downtown living" wore off for the wealthy as real estate opened in the East End, and these too were subdivided into apartment buildings, allowed to deteriorate, and many were destroyed. Examples still exist, such as the Munger Terrace (405 Mesaba Avenue), Salter Terrace (301–307 East Third Street), and Chester Terrace (1210–1232 East First Street).

Few Duluthians could afford the mansions the city's major architects designed. Upon arrival, many European immigrants found temporary lodging in immigrant houses built by the Northern Pacific Railroad before finding ethnic enclaves that developed into somewhat unplanned communities, with houses—mere shanties for the most part—being built rather haphazardly. Finn Town developed on the lake side of what is today the Canal Park Business District, Little Italy and The Glenn above and below Point of Rocks, and Rice's Point once included a community called Swede Town. A portion of the West End called Slabtown, centered on Twenty-Seventh Avenue West from Superior Street to the bay, did not develop because of the ethnicity of its population but because of its inexpensive housing and proximity to its inhabitants' workplaces.

Most of these communities are gone, in part because of the rise of the middle class, the demolition of derelict buildings, urban renewal and highway expansion, or the demise of ethnic divisions within neighborhoods. Some of the neighborhoods still stand, although they are no longer known by their colorful names. Corktown, for instance, was centered around Twentieth Avenue West and Superior Street and named for its heavy Irish population. The upper portion of Little Italy is now referred to as Observation Park, and while the population is now homogenized, much of the neighborhood stands as it did one hundred years ago. Similarly, Goosetown, found west of Lincoln Park approximately where the 2012 Lincoln Middle School was built, no longer includes the Polish farming families whose geese gave the area its name, but most of their homes still stand.

The house shown in the sketch above was the E. P. and Agnes Alexander House at 1508 East Superior Street. Alexander was the son of a celebrated Confederate Civil War General from Virginia, and his daughter Agnes, when nine years old, saved a four-year-old playmate from drowning in an icy Chester Creek. A Queen Anne Victorian built in 1887, the house was demolished in 1954. A parking lot now occupies the site.

Robert E. Jefferson House

430 Lake Avenue South
Architect: UNKNOWN
Built: 1856 | Lost: CA. 1920

The 1856 Jefferson House may well have been the first frame house built in what would become Duluth, but what at the time was a township called Cowell's Addition. (Although George Stuntz and William Nettleton had both built on Minnesota Point by 1853, the results were mere shanties.) Robert Jefferson, born in 1836 in Illinois, was just twenty years old when he came to Duluth from Minnesota's Ramsey County in about 1855 and made the first claims on land in what became Duluth Township. He built this large house on Minnesota Point the following year. The building's most interesting feature was its entrance, with porthole windows and castellations on the entrance tower. The building served as Jefferson's residence as well as a boarding house during Duluth's early years, and Duluthians often referred to it as the town's first hotel, although that honor technically belongs to the Bay View House.

Jefferson married in 1859 and a year later his wife gave birth to a daughter, Harriet, the first child of European descent born in the township. When the Civil War began in 1861, he and his wife and infant daughter left Duluth for Fort Snelling where he enlisted in the Union Army. He died in the early part of the war, and his wife died shortly thereafter; their daughter was raised by his parents near St. Paul.

(A common misconception holds that Duluth's Jefferson Street was named for Robert, but that honor actually goes to his brother Ernest, another pioneer who opened a harness shop in Duluth in 1869. Ernest Jefferson had fought in the Civil War with the storied First Minnesota Regiment, losing a leg at Gettysburg. While in Duluth he also worked as a lighthouse keeper and served on the Duluth City Council and St. Louis County Board of Commissioners.)

With its owner dead, the Jefferson House stood empty until 1865 when Oneota's John Carey, a native of Bangor, Maine, found it "unoccupied, unlocked, and unclaimed" and moved in, needing "no key, no burglar tools to enter it." Carey became one of St. Louis County's first judges, and the Jefferson House hosted the first session of the St. Louis County District Court.

After moving to Duluth in 1866 to edit and publish the city's first newspaper, *The Minnesotian*, Dr. Thomas Preston Foster took possession of the Jefferson House in 1869 and set up his newspaper's headquarters there. Foster famously gave an 1868 Independence Day speech on Minnesota Point during which he made bold predictions about the fledgling city's future and first called Duluth "The Zenith City of the Unsalted Seas."

The building (shown below, date unknown) was demolished some time around 1920; its site is now part of a parking lot across Lake Avenue from Grandma's Sports Garden and Bellisio's Restaurant.

Roger S. & Olive Munger House

405 – 407 Mesaba Avenue

Architect: UNKNOWN

Built: CA. 1870 | Lost: CA. 1955

Roger S. Munger was born in North Madison, Connecticut, in 1830 and married Olive Gray in Maine in 1858. A year before he wed he and his brothers Russell and William opened a music store in St. Paul and performed as "The Munger Brothers Orchestra."

Munger (pictured at left) became an early Duluth pioneer, his family being the twelfth to settle in Duluth Township. Partnering with other Duluth settlers, Munger built the first flour mill, first coal dock, first sawmill, and first opera house, and served on the first board of trade, first school board, and first city council. He would later become president of Duluth's Imperial Mill and the Duluth Iron & Steel Company. Munger also took charge of a task that changed Duluth forever, the 1870–1871 digging of the Duluth Ship Canal. Although Munger himself hired the W. W. Williams & Co. and their dredging tug *Ishpeming* in September, 1870, years later Munger himself would perpetuate the false legend that Duluth citizens dug the canal by hand. Munger's brother Gilbert was a noted painter; his 1871 depiction of Duluth hangs in the Duluth Public Library's North Shore room. Olive Munger died in 1894 and Roger Munger left the house in 1899. He lived for another fourteen years.

The Munger House (shown here in 1887) had many characteristics of the Italianate-style, which was uncommon in Duluth: a low pitched roof with overhanging eave, a cupola on the roof, and tall and narrow arched windows. Munger built a gazebo on the front lawn and a carriage house east of the house. In 1889 Oliver Traphagen remodeled the house, removing the cupola and extending the second floor front pediment. A porte cochere was added on the east side, as was a third floor. In 1909 architects Starin and Melander "modernized" the house by removing its porches, balconies, porte cochere, and gingerbread trim.

Later converted to apartments, the house was razed in 1955, replaced by a parking lot for nearby Munger Terrace. Today's widened Mesaba Avenue runs over the former gazebo location. The carriage house still stands but has been so severely remodeled that it is almost unrecognizable from its original form.

George B. & Mary Sargent House

4500 London Road
Architect: UNKNOWN
Built: 1872 | Lost: CA. 1915

When the Sargents built this house on London Road in 1872, the neighborhood was considered part of the "forest primeval." As one of the first homes in what would become Lakeside, it was a landmark during the early days and the Sargents customarily kept a light burning all night during stormy weather as a beacon for ships approaching the Duluth harbor. In June 1876, twenty-seven steamers became stuck in the ice off the Lester River. Many crew members and passengers came ashore by jumping from ice floe to ice floe, and supposedly Mrs. Sargent—then already a widow—served over three hundred cups of coffee to those who took refuge in her home. The house (right, date unknown) also provided a welcome respite for woodsmen returning late to Duluth from lumber camps along the North Shore.

The Sargent House—with its square footprint, Mansard roof, dormer windows, and wide eaves with brackets—was a good example of Second Empire architecture, popularized in Paris in the nineteenth century. It was not a common style in Duluth. When the Sargents held a party there in 1873 after returning from a trip to Europe, over two hundred guests attended the soiree.

George Sargent (pictured above) was born in Boston in 1852. After he married Mary Perin he served as a Union Army general in the Civil War and was later appointed federal surveyor for Iowa, Wisconsin, and Minnesota. Sargent left Iowa for Duluth in 1869 to work as Jay Cooke's financial agent and is credited as being the prime driving force behind Duluth's early commercial success. He opened Duluth's first bank, oversaw the construction of Duluth's first hotels (Clark House and Bay View House), and helped finance St. Paul's Episcopal Church, Duluth Township's first church. He and Mary also had a summer home on Minnesota Point, later the property of their son, William.

General Sargent died in 1875 in Germany, where he had gone for his health. Sargent Creek, between Gary-New Duluth and Fond du Lac, is named for him. Mary Sargent continued to live in the house until her death in 1896. Hotel owner W. A. McKay purchased the house in 1915; he razed it to make room for another home, which still stands.

Lost Duluth | Part One: Lost Homes & Neighborhoods | Houses — 17

Charles F. & Mary Johnson House

120 North 4th Avenue West
Architect: UNKNOWN
Built: 1881 | Lost: 1907

In 1871, barely two years after arriving in Duluth, Charles F. Johnson wrote in his diary, "I have hung myself on the future prosperity of this young city, and it is not pleasant to think that I may be destined to hang here like a scarecrow on a bean pole, a warning to young adventurers…and as for failing, I will not fail, and be it through thick or thin, I will have a castle on Lake Superior yet!" Johnson (picture) indeed thrived in Duluth, and in 1881 built his "castle" along Fourth Avenue West in downtown Duluth: a clapboard-sided house standing two stories tall with two porches, clipped roof gables, finials on the roof, decorative bargeboards, and carved wood panels.

Johnson was born in Stockholm, Sweden, in 1843 and immigrated to Minnesota in 1853. During the Civil War Johnson served with the Ninth New York Volunteers, which saw action in several major battles, including Antietam, where he was wounded. He wrote a book about his war experience titled *The Long Roll*; it included sixty of his sketches.

In 1869 he moved to Duluth with his wife, Mary, and their children, Frederick and Emma, and set up shop as a stationer and bookseller in his Pioneer Bookstore. He continued to sketch (and later photograph) Duluth; perhaps his most famous sketch is that of the temporary suspension bridge used to cross the Duluth Ship Canal before it was permanently bridged (below). He also sketched a notorious event in 1873. After heavy rains, part of Fremont Township—a swampy area found where the Duluth Entertainment and Convention Center stands today—floated out through the canal and into Lake Superior. Johnson and three others gave chase in a rowboat. The next day the "island" broke up along Minnesota Point.

Johnson established the town's first free circulating library in 1870, acted as the town's first comptroller, and served in Duluth's first volunteer fire department, first parks commission, and city council. He remained in the book trade until 1889 when he became Duluth's federal customs collector. Johnson died of tuberculosis in 1896. Christie Printing purchased the house in 1907 and razed the building to construct an office; today the Government Services Center Building occupies the site. (By the way, the dog in the undated photo is Johnson's English Setter, Snap.)

James D. & Caroline Ray House

Another example of the Astabula Heights neighborhood's many homes designed in the Queen Anne style, the Ray House stood three stories high and featured gables, ornamental wood panels, a six-sided corner tower, and patterned brick chimneys, with one of the chimneys protruding through the tower's roof. Construction of the house (right, 1891) cost the Rays $20,000 in 1887, which would be over $470,000 today.

403 East 2nd Street
Architects: McMillen & Stebbins
Built: 1887 | Lost: 1944

Born in Massachusetts, James Ray (pictured above) came to Duluth in 1855 by way of Ashtabula, Ohio, but left after five years. He returned in 1864 to open a real estate office. He was involved in digging the ship canal in 1871 and had large mining holdings on the Mesaba Range from the Rouchleau-Ray Iron Land Company, a partnership with Louis Rouchleau. An active Mason, Ray strongly influenced construction of the Temple Opera Block and Opera House at Second Avenue East and Superior Street; newspapers reported that it may not have been built without his efforts.

When Ray died in 1894 the city hall flag was lowered to half staff. Caroline Ray lived in the house until 1900; by 1930 it had been converted to a boarding house. Demolished in 1944, its site is now occupied by Essentia Health, the former St. Mary's Duluth Clinic.

Robert C. & Helen Ray House

226 North 4th Avenue East
Architects: McMillen & Stebbins
Built: 1887 | Lost: 1953

Robert Ray made his living working in real estate with his father, James, and after his father's death in 1894, with his mother, Caroline. Robert and Helen Ray built their home in Ashtabula Heights just north of his parents', James and Caroline, on the same block. It too was a Queen Anne design by the same architects and built in the same year. This Ray house (shown at left in 1891) had a large veranda, patterned shingles in the gables, and a round corner tower.

The younger Rays lived in their house for just four or five years, as records indicate that by 1899 they had moved in with Caroline. By 1910 Robert and Helen Ray had moved to Palo Alto, California. Their house suffered almost the same fate as that of his parents' home: it served as a boarding house from about 1930 until 1952, then was demolished in 1953 for apartments that have since been torn down to make way for the former St. Mary's Duluth Clinic.

Clinton & Kate Markell House (aka the Whiteside House)

325 East 2nd Street

Architect: OLIVER G. TRAPHAGEN

Built: 1890 | Lost: 1961

This Ashtabula Heights Queen Anne, like many of its neighbors, sported a round corner tower, four patterned brick chimneys, a brownstone foundation and porch posts, wood ornamentation in the gables, and a porte cochere. Construction of the house (shown here in 1891) cost $30,000, well over $700,000 today.

Clinton Markell served as the city of Duluth's second mayor, elected to a one-year term in 1871. He was born in Ohio, married Katherine Watrous of Ashtabula in 1855 and arrived in Duluth in 1869. He and other future Ashtabula Heights residents, including J. D. Ray and Sidney Luce (Duluth's third mayor), founded the township of Portland within today's East Hillside. Markell was one of the founders of the grain trade and built several grain elevators, one with his business partner Roger Munger. Together Munger and Markell built Duluth's 1883 Grand Opera House (see page 92).

On January 6, 1872, Mayor Markell's carriage was famously stopped by a police officer named Thompson for speeding. Duluth had recently passed a law against horses traveling in town "faster than the walking gait of a man." The driver, teamster William Trowbridge, who worked for Pratt & Co., was fined five dollars. In the carriage with Markell were former Mayor J. B. Culver and William Nettleton, whom Markell had defeated in the mayoral race. Together the three of them covered the fine by taking donations from patrons in local taverns.

The Markells moved to 2215 East First Street in 1907 and sold their Ashtabula Heights home to Robert and Sophia Whiteside. Whiteside's wealth came from timber and iron mining. As a founder of the town of Ely, he helped open both the Pioneer and Chandler mines, platted an addition that is now the center of town, and also built Ely's first hotel, the Pioneer, in 1887. He was a partner in the Zenith Dredge Company and purchased the first ticket to ride on the Duluth and Iron Range Railway. In 1899 Whiteside optioned to purchase Calaveras Grove, a redwood forest in California, to exploit its timber. This spurred groups like the Sierra Club into action to stop the sale. Whiteside did purchase the land, but he agreed that he would not cut down a single tree for sale as lumber. In 1931, the year Whiteside died, the Grove became the Calaveras Big Trees State Park.

Sophia continued to live in the house until her death in 1950. Other members of the Whiteside family lived here until 1961 when the Duluth Catholic Diocese purchased the house and demolished it to build St. Anne's Residence and St. Anne's Nursing Center.

William C. & Amelia Sherwood House

Wisconsin native William Sherwood arrived in Duluth in 1880 when he was twenty-five years old and began to work in real estate and insurance. The Sherwoods lived in their Superior Street home (shown here in 1888) from 1886 to 1892, after which they moved to another Traphagen-designed house on Woodland Avenue in Hunter's Park. Sherwood (pictured at left) died in 1933, Amelia a year later.

1125 East Superior Street
Architect: OLIVER G. TRAPHAGEN
Built: 1886 | Lost: 1956

A Mansard roof usually indicates a Second Empire–style house, but this Oliver Traphagen creation includes Queen Anne characteristics such as patterned shingles and iron cresting on the roof and a round corner tower with balconies.

Other families lived in the house after the Sherwoods; it eventually became a boarding house before being demolished in 1956. The lot has since held a gas station, a pizza parlor, and last an office building, demolished in 2011 along with the Loeb House (below) and two historic Traphagen-designed duplexes to make room for a new Walgreens Pharmacy. The Walgreens replaced an existing Walgreens, built on the site that once held the Hartley House, less than two blocks away.

Louis S. & Cecelia Loeb House

This large Neo-Classical Revival–style house featured a two-story-high porch that spread across the full width of the house and was supported by six classical columns topped with Corinthian capitals; the house also featured a porte cochere and a matching carriage house. Louis Loeb worked in the real estate industry and also operated a wholesale wine and liquor business; he also owned the Metropole Hotel. He sat on the board of directors of Duluth's Northern National Bank. In 1921 the Loebs moved to Lester Park; later, Loeb would donate some of his property for Seven Bridges Road. After the Loebs moved the house became the residence of Duluth's Roman Catholic bishop until 1941. It served as a boarding house until the 1980s when Silver's Dress Shop—which Ida Silver opened in her apartment in the late 1930s—took occupancy. Silver's closed in 2001 and the house was demolished in 2011 (see the Sherwood House, above).

1123 E Superior Street
Architect: JOHN J. WANGENSTEIN
Built: 1900 | Lost: 2011

Edward L. & Lucrecia Bradley House

Edward Bradley (pictured in sketch) and his brother Alva were the sons of Henry Bradley, a lumberman who helped turn Bay City, Michigan, into a lumber center. Henry Bradley

701 West 2nd Street
Architect: UNKNOWN
Built: 1887 | Lost: 1971

was heavily involved with the development of Bay City's Methodist church and school system. When the Bradley Mill went bust in 1877, he became a timber cruiser and iron ore speculator in northern Minnesota. By 1880 he had teamed up with Heber H. Hanford to form the Bradley-Hanford Lumber Company, and two years later Edward and Alva moved to Duluth to operate the firm. (Henry himself retired from the firm in 1883 and didn't move to Duluth until 1890; besides lumber, Henry's investments in the Vermillion Iron Range's Chandler Mine had made him wealthy.) Edward resigned from Bradley-Hanford in 1888 and worked by himself until 1898, when he organized the Duluth Log Company. All three Bradleys contributed heavily to the construction of Duluth's 1893 First Methodist Church.

The Bradley House was a two-and-a-half story Queen Anne with a tower and verandas. It was demolished in 1971 to make room for an apartment complex.

Archibald B. & Annie McLean House

3 East 4th Street
Architect: OLIVER G. TRAPHAGEN
Built: 1888 | Lost: 1939

Archibald and Annie McLean had their two-and-a-half-story Queen Anne home (left), with its prominent corner tower, built on the northeast corner of Lake Avenue and Fourth Street in 1888. Architect Traphagen designed the clapboard house with fish-scale shingles on the corner tower, a half tower with an open porch on the front façade, and a profusion of decorative wood panels.

Archibald McLean was another pioneer of Duluth, a true Sixty-Niner who came to Duluth when he was about twenty-eight years old. He partnered in the town's first foundry and machine shop, A. B. McLean and Co., on Lake Avenue in today's Canal Park Business District. The firm specialized in making engines, boilers, and wood and iron-making machinery. It eventually merged with Clyde Iron Works, after which McLean worked as a blacksmith for the city. Archibald died in 1917, but Annie continued to live in the house until 1936; the McLeans' daughter, Sarah Grant, occupied the house until 1938. The McLean House was demolished in 1939. The lot, which remained empty for over sixty years, is now the site of a modern townhouse.

William W. & Electra Spalding House

rchitects Charles M. McMillen and Edwin S. Radcliffe designed the Spaldings' grand Queen Anne home with a corner tower, shingle-covered gables, tall patterned-brick chimneys, and a veranda. Construction of the house cost the Spaldings about $15,000, over $350,000 today.

> 504 West 2nd Street
> Architects: McMillen & Radcliffe
> Built: 1888 | Lost: 1908

Spalding, born in Pennsylvania in 1820, traveled the nation as a young man, eventually working the copper trade at Octonagon, Michigan. There he he married Electra Wilkinson in 1854. Like many pioneers, Spalding came to Duluth in 1869. He purchased the lower 400 block of West Superior Street and built a store at the southeast corner of Fifth Avenue West and Superior Street. He then dismantled his Octonagon home and rebuilt it at 504 West Second Street. In 1888, the same year he built the grand Spalding Hotel, the old house was replaced by their grand Queen Anne home. Spalding served as an early Duluth alderman, president of the Duluth and Iron Range Railroad, and president of the St. Louis County Agricultural Society. He died in 1901, Electra in 1920. Their home (shown at left, date unknown) was torn down in 1908 to make way for the St. Louis County Courthouse.

Matthew B. and Lucy Harrison House

atthew Bland and Lucy Harrison came from families steeped in American politics. He was related to U.S. Presidents William Henry and Benjamin Harrison, and Lucy was a descendant

> 2605 Greysolon Road
> Architect: Oliver G. Traphagen
> Built: 1889 | Lost: 1935

of patriot Patrick "Give-Me-Liberty-Or-Give-Me-Death" Henry. Born in Virginia in 1854, Harrison moved to Duluth in 1886 and built the largest real estate business in the city. When Harrison died in 1892, Lucy returned to her native Virginia.

The house (shown at right in 1891) became a college preparatory school from 1896 to 1900. Albert and Julia Marshall—for whom the University of Minnesota Duluth's Marshall Performing Arts Center is named—lived here from 1901 until 1932. The house was demolished in 1935 and three houses were built on the large lot in the 1930s. Built for $11,000 (about $260,000 today), it was a good example of a Shingle-style house: patterned shingles covering wall surfaces, a large half tower whose roof line blended into the house, and an open, arched porte cochere.

Guilford G. & Caroline Hartley House

1305 East Superior Street
Architect: OLIVER G. TRAPHAGEN
Built: 1889 | Lost: 1954

One of the Zenith City's most distinctive Romanesque Revival mansions, the Hartley's brick-and-stone home stood poised on the banks of Chester Creek. It had arched windows trimmed in stone, four patterned brick chimneys, gables, porches, and triangular dormers bursting from its red tile roof. Inside, the twenty-one room house boasted ten fireplaces and was the first home in Duluth wired for electricity. It also had a primitive air conditioning system which carried fresh air to every room and a telephone-like intercom system—and a telephone as well. According to Mrs. Hartley, once during a visit by the Congdon family, Hartley "ripped the telephone off the wall" after it rang incessantly.

When built in 1889, the house stood at the eastern end of the horse-drawn streetcar line; a turntable rotated the streetcar for its return trip. Property across Superior Street, where a bank and a shopping center parking lot now stand, was used as pasture for Hartley's cows and horses.

The estate included a stable with an elevator to reach the second floor, where John Valin, the Hartley family coachman for fifty years, kept his residence. The back of the estate (actually located on First Street), housed a small cedar cabin Hartley used as a respite from the activity of the busy Hartley household.

Guilford Hartley (pictured) was born in New Brunswick, Canada, in 1853. As a teenager he moved to Brainerd where he worked in the timber industry and set up his own logging business. In 1883 he married Caroline Woodward of Minneapolis, and the couple later moved to Duluth. He served in the Minnesota Legislature and was a delegate to the 1888 Republican presidential convention. Hartley also helped develop the western Mesaba Iron Range. Throughout his life he had interests in lumbering, mining, farming, real estate, the newspaper business, and almost every major industry in Duluth. Hartley helped establish the Northland Country Club and built Duluth's Orpheum Theatre. His Allendale Farm in the Woodland area of Duluth is now Duluth's Hartley Park, and his office building still stands at 740 East Superior Street.

After Guilford's death in 1922, Caroline Hartley continued to live in the house until her death in 1939. Hartley's daughter Jessie and her husband, Walter Congdon, lived here until she died in 1953. The house (shown here in 1885) was razed in 1954. The site became a Walgreen's pharmacy and parking lot.

DeWitt Clinton & Sarah Prescott House

4831 West 5th Street
Architect: UNKNOWN
Built: 1890 | Lost: CA. 1944

While Duluth's East End is known for its mansions, one of the most striking Victorian homes in Duluth, the Prescott House, was built in West Duluth. The house (shown here in 1895) exemplified the exuberance of the Queen Anne–style, sporting three towers, an encircling veranda, stained-glass windows, gables with bargeboards, a third-story balcony, patterned-brick chimneys, finials, brackets, and many decorative wood panels. Prescott outfitted the interior with hand-carved panels of South American hardwoods, elaborate staircases, five fireplaces, inlaid floors, imported English earthenware plumbing, stained-glass windows, and zinc bathtubs. Even the closets boasted hand-carved wood panels. The house's third floor was a grand ballroom, and in the first floor reception room a gold-plated, flower-engraved wash basin awaited guests arriving by horse-drawn carriages after traveling dusty roads.

D. Clinton Prescott was born in Illinois in 1841 and lived in northern Wisconsin, where he founded the Marinette Iron Works to manufacture sawmill machinery. In 1890 he moved the plant to West Duluth, which was then being developed as a large industrial center.

The Prescott family lived in the spectacular house until 1896, when they moved to Chicago; Marinette Iron Works closed two years later. Hansen Evesmith, one-time president of the Duluth Chamber of Commerce, moved in afterward and occupied the house until about 1910. In 1914 it was purchased by Thomas F. Feigh, who in turn offered it to the Duluth Catholic Diocese as a children's hospital. It is unclear whether the house ever held the Thomas Feigh Hospital for Crippled Children. By 1916 the hospital operated within a new building at the head of Twelfth Avenue East, on the site of a former Catholic cemetery.

Thereafter the house remained vacant and became known to area residents as "The Haunted House." St. Louis County then took over the home, placing it on the delinquent tax list.

Elmer J. Woefler bought the deserted house from the county in 1944 for $1,500 and dismantled it. Many parts of the house—including three of its fireplaces—were used in a house Woefler built for himself along Highway 61 in Duluth at Rest Point. He also built some tourist cabins at that site with materials salvaged from the Prescott House, and Mrs. Woefler kept the gold-leaf basin. By the 1950s, other homes had sprung up on the Prescott lot.

Alonzo J. & Julia Whiteman House

2732 London Road
Architect: OLIVER G. TRAPHAGEN
Built: 1890 | Lost: 1894

Alonzo James Whiteman was born in 1860 in Dansville, New York, to parents of considerable wealth. In 1881, after he had graduated law school, his father sent him to Duluth to manage the family's timber interests. In Duluth he took a job as a teller at the Bell and Eyster Bank for a year before starting his own business buying and selling timber property. He married Julia Nettleton, daughter of a prominent Duluth pioneer family, and at age twenty-six the popular young attorney represented Duluth as its Minnesota state senator. After his later reelection, his father presented him with a gift of $1.5 million (well over $35 million today). In 1892, after a narrow defeat in a run for Congress, Whiteman was named a delegate for the Democratic national convention, where he was instrumental in helping Grover Cleveland win the party's nomination. He hoped to parlay those efforts into an ambassadorship.

But Whiteman (pictured in sketch) had a darker side. A skilled forger of signatures, Whiteman would become known as "Jim the Penman." While he became a successful timberman and the president of two banks, Whiteman also developed a taste for poker and the stock market, both of which he played poorly. During one night at the Duluth City Club, Whiteman lost fifteen straight hands trying to fill flushes, losing over $500 each hand. His entire fortune was wiped out when he invested in Joseph Leiber's failed 1898 plan to corner the Chicago Wheat Market.

After he and his partner R. B. Knox were caught cheating at a Duluth City Club card game, he skipped town for New York, where he fell in with Knox's gang of criminals and began forging checks and carrying out various confidence schemes throughout the eastern half of the United States. A known and wanted man, Whiteman long eluded prison despite several arrests. In 1904 he famously escaped the Pinkerton Detectives by diving out a window of a moving train, but they caught up with him just a few weeks later at his parents' home. He spent eight years in a New York prison, emerged a broken man, and turned back to his criminal ways. From 1917 to 1919 he served two years in the Atlanta Penitentiary for "violating federal statutes." After his release Whiteman lived his last years in a poor house in Dansville. After Whiteman left Duluth, Julia Nettleton moved to Washington state, where she obtained a divorce and remarried.

Built on a promontory on the Lake Superior shore, the Whiteman house (left, date unknown) was covered with shingles, had a stone foundation and piers for the porte cochere, and prominent gables so common in Shingle-style homes. The Whiteman house was vacant by 1894 and burned on December 24 of that year, a total loss. Another house occupies the site.

Jed L. & Alma Washburn House

101 Oxford Street
Architect: UNKNOWN
Built: 1892 | Lost: CA. 1946

The Hunter's Park neighborhood was platted in 1891 and attracted many of Duluth's resident professionals, particularly after streetcar service began in 1892. This Queen Anne home (below, date unknown) was built a short distance from Woodland Avenue amid other Victorian-style homes. It featured a round corner tower, patterned shingles on the third floor walls, and an encircling veranda. Arthur and Lillian Holgate originally owned the house, but lived in it for less than two years.

Jed Washburn (pictured above) was born in 1856 in Indiana and was brought to southern Minnesota by his family when he was an infant. He practiced law in Mankato where he met and married Alma Pattee in 1882. In 1889 the couple moved to Duluth, where he continued to practice law.

Washburn was notably involved in education as a member of the Duluth School Board and a director of the Duluth State Teachers College, now the University of Minnesota Duluth. Duluth's Washburn Elementary was named for him, as was Washburn Hall, the first dormitory for women at the teachers college. He also played a key role in the development of Jay Cooke State Park. Always civically and socially active, Washburn held memberships in the Kitchi Gammi Club, the Northland Country Club, and the Duluth Curling Club.

His business interests outside of his law firm were varied, as he invested in the Spalding Hotel, Union Match, Northern Shoe, Oneida Realty, Northern National Bank, Minnesota and Oregon Land and Timber Company, and many others.

Alma Washburn was born in Wisconsin in 1856. By the time she met Washburn, she had already established a reputation as a prominent figure in education and charity work throughout the state. She was a founder of the Duluth Women's Club and also served as both state and national president of the Federation of Women's Clubs.

Jed Washburn died in 1931, Alma in 1943. Their home stood vacant until demolition in about 1946. Another house was built on the lot.

Townsend W. & Grace Hoopes House

2206 Woodland Avenue
Architect: TRAPHAGEN & FITZPATRICK
Built: 1892 | Lost: 1938

Francis Fitzpatrick moved to Duluth in 1890 to join Oliver Traphagen's architectural firm, and together the two designed some of Duluth's most impressive buildings, including the Hoopes' home in Hunter's Park. A classic example of Shingle-style architecture, shingles covered the house's roof and walls and even wrapped around porch posts; its steeply sloped roofs featured large dormers.

Pennsylvania native Townsend Hoopes spent his early adulthood trying his hand at farming. He settled in Duluth in 1882, when he was twenty-five years old, and established himself as a real estate developer and business pioneer. Working with the Duluth Street Railway, Hoopes helped plan and construct Duluth's first street car line, a narrow-gauge line which eventually ran from Twenty-First Avenue West to Sixth Avenue East along Superior Street. The streetcar was drawn by a single horse. Hoopes would oversee the construction of the Fourth Street Line on behalf of the Motor Line Improvement Company in 1909.

He and Mendenhall then established a real estate and insurance company eventually named Hoopes-Kohagan Company, from which he retired in 1923. Hoopes belonged to the Duluth Boat Club, the Kitchi Gammi Club, and Northland Country Club, which he helped organize.

He also invested in several early Duluth businesses, including the Spalding Hotel, the Duluth Dry Goods Company, the Duluth Shoe Company, and Sagar Drug (which became Northern Drug). Grace and Townsend Hoopes lived in their Hunter's Park Home until 1935; the house was demolished in 1938. Townsend passed away in 1937, and Grace followed him ten years later. The photo at left shows the Hoopes family enjoying their backyard gazebo, date unknown. The house photo was taken in 1907.

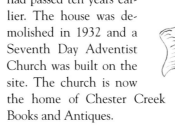

Hamilton M. & Martha Peyton House

1329 East Superior Street
Architects: TRAPHAGEN & FITZPATRICK
Built: 1893 | Lost: 1932

The Peyton name has been noteworthy in Duluth banking since since Hamilton Peyton moved to Duluth in 1873 and later established the American Exchange Bank, one of Duluth's early commercial banks. Born in New York in 1835, Peyton moved to Superior, Wisconsin, in 1858. He opened a private bank and operated a sawmill until moving across the bay to Duluth in 1873. Peyton was the first president of the American Exchange Bank—shown in the sketch and on page 108—and remained in that position until he died in 1928. A year later his bank merged with First National Bank.

The Peytons had their Shingle–style house (shown below in 1909) built in 1893 for $16,000. Its second- and third-story walls were covered with shingles while the first floor had a brownstone entrance and porte cochere with a long, sloping roof over the entrance. It also featured striking porches, balconies, and gingerbread trim. Chester Creek ran between the Peyton House and the Hartley House, shown in the photo below. After Peyton died the house stood empty—Martha Peyton had passed ten years earlier. The house was demolished in 1932 and a Seventh Day Adventist Church was built on the site. The church is now the home of Chester Creek Books and Antiques.

Marshall H. & Nellie Alworth House

1928 East 1st Street

Architect: UNKNOWN

Built: 1893 | Lost: 1935

Marshall and Nellie Alworth's house exemplified the typical homes built in the 1880s and '90s by Duluthians gaining wealth in lumber, mining, real estate, the grain trade, and various white-collar professions. Alworth made his fortune in mining and real estate investments. This late Queen Anne–style house (below left, date unknown) had decorative shingles in the gables, spindlework ornamentation, a patterned-brick chimney, a variety of wall projections, and at least three porches (the Alworth family is shown on one of the porches, below right).

Marshall Alworth (pictured above) was born in Oneida County, New York, in 1846. He left home at age fourteen to work on the Great Lakes and eventually became a land and timber explorer in Michigan's Upper Peninsula, Wisconsin, and Minnesota. He was in Duluth as early as 1873 but left after the financial crisis of that year. He married Nellie LaVeigne in Saginaw, Michigan, in 1878 and they moved to Duluth in 1882. Together they raised seven children, including Royal Alworth, who also rose to prominence in the Zenith City.

Alworth purchased extensive mining lands on Minnesota's Iron Range and formed the Alworth Mining and Development Company in 1893, the same year the house was built. Mining wealth followed, and Alworth invested in real estate in Duluth, including the Alworth Building on Superior Street—then and now the tallest building in Duluth—which he financed for $500,000 in 1910. The sixteen-story building took just nine months to build, and most of that work took place over the winter. When it was complete, the *Duluth News Tribune* called it "a cosmopolitan office building, one that dwarfs the Tower of Babel" and "an epoch in the architectural history of Duluth."

The Alworths moved from their First Street house by 1913; the house was demolished in 1935 and another home was built on the lot eleven years later. Alworth died in 1931 in Florida, leaving an estate worth over $6 million; Nellie died in 1947.

John U. & Susan M. Sebenius House

4000 London Road

Architect: UNKNOWN

Built: 1907 | Lost: CA. 1933

A native of Wermland Province, Sweden, John Uno Sebenius (pictured at left) graduated Stockholm's Royal Technical Institute and School of Mining in 1886 and emigrated to the United States two years later. In 1892 he turned thirty years old and moved to Minnesota's Iron Range, where he developed a cross-sampling technique and a concentrating process for iron ore mining. He eventually became chief mining engineer and superintendent of exploration for the Oliver Mining Company. He would stay with the firm, which later merged with U.S. Steel, until his retirement in 1930.

The Sebenius property along London Road boasted a one-thousand-foot frontage on Lake Superior. Built in 1907, the imposing brick house stood two-and-a-half-stories tall, featured two corner towers, and was capped with a tile roof. The house (below, date unknown) sat on a very large lot, which enabled Sebenius to experiment with his hobby, raising farm crops and cattle. According to the *Duluth News Tribune*, his cows were considered "some of the finest dairy stock in the country."

Susan Sebenius, who married John in 1895, died in 1918. Sebenius continued to live in the house and remained socially active—he belonged to the Kitchi Gammi Club and the Minnesota Historical Society—until his death in 1932. The Lake Shore Lutheran Home purchased the Sebenius property the next year and demolished the house to make room for what is now The Shores, an independent, assisted-living, and memory-care facility for the elderly.

Roy & Edythe Halvorson House

2628 Branch Street
Architect: HAROLD ST. CLAIR STARIN
Built: 1939 | Lost: 1994

Native Duluthian Roy Halvorson, son of Norweigan immigrants, founded Halvorson Trees with his wife, Edythe, in 1929. From a factory at 389–391 Lake Avenue South they produced and sold three-foot tall colored Christmas trees, actually the tops of black spruce trees that grew in northern Minnesota peat bogs. Halvorson (pictured above) developed a chemical coloring process that enabled the company to produce green, silver, white, and pink holiday trees. The trees sat in a metal base filled with a synthetic sap called Liquid Life, which gave the trees longevity. By 1960, the Halvorsons annually sold over 1.5 million trees throughout the United States. Besides the family tree business, Halvorson was a pioneer snowmobile dealer, operating what was at one time the largest Ski-Doo dealership in the world.

The Halvorson house exemplifies a shift in architectural trends, from Traditional to Modernist. Executed in the International style, a subset of Modernism, the house (shown below ca. 1993) had a flat roof, smooth wall surfaces, a horizontal orientation of the walls and windows, and no external ornamentation. When first built the house was noted for its many automatic devices and gadgets which controled heating and cooling, watered plants, and turned on cupboard lights when a door was opened. Twenty-six thermostats regulated temperatures throughout the house. When the doorbell was pushed, a front door speaker announced the residents' location.

Edythe passed away in 1988, and Roy sold the house the next year. It was demolished in 1994—the same year Halvorson died—for construction of another house built on the lot in 1996.

Ashtabula Flats

218–228 North 5th Avenue East
Architect: UNKNOWN
Built: 1893 | Lost: 1987

Ashtabula Flats was built on the southeast corner of East Third Street and Fifth Avenue East in 1892 by Ray T. Lewis and Charles R. Haines. A native of Maine, Lewis had been a ship captain and sailed the world on clipper ships. He came to Duluth in 1884, worked in real estate, and served as Duluth mayor from 1894 to 1896. Haines also worked in real estate and served as president of the Lakeside Land Company from 1896 to 1900. Neither Lewis nor Haines ever lived in Ashtabula Flats. Haines and his wife, Amanda, lived just across Third Street from the Flats at 501 East Third Street. Lewis died in 1912 and Haines left Duluth in 1916 after Amanda's death. A true Duluth pioneer, Amanda Randall Haines came to Duluth from Philadelphia in 1870 as a young woman, staying with Luther Mendenhall's family until she married Charles in 1873.

The massive, four-story apartment building in the Romanesque Revival–style, shown here in 1901, was made of brick and stone with two rounded half towers on the Fifth Avenue side and rounded stone arches over entrances and some windows. In 1930 there were twelve apartments in the building. It survived until 1987 when it was demolished for an SMDC parking lot.

Traphagen & Fitzpatrick: Duluth's "Representative Architects"

Oliver Greene Traphagen (1854–1932, pictured), a native of Tarrytown, New York, moved to St. Paul in about 1880 and worked as a carpenter for prominent architect George Wirth. By 1882 Traphagen had moved to Duluth to supervise construction of buildings designed by Wirth. They became partners in 1884, but Wirth returned to his native Germany in 1886. (Traphagen would redesign many of Wirth's buildings.) Traphagen worked alone until 1890 when Francis Wilford Fitzpatrick joined the practice. Fitzpatrick (1863–1931), a Canadian from Montreal, worked in Minneapolis from 1884 until 1890 when he joined Traphagen. From 1890 until 1896 Traphagen and Fitzpatrick designed more than thirty of Duluth's most significant structures, including Chester Terrace (1890), Incline Pavilion (1892), First Presbyterian Church (1891), Hardy School (1891), the Lyceum Theater (1891), the second Board of Trade Building (1894), and many homes for Duluth's financial elite, including several in Ashtabula Heights. They were called "Duluth's representative architects."

Both men left Duluth in 1896, Fitzpatrick first to Washington D.C. to work for the federal government and later to Chicago. He became internationally known as an authority on fire prevention and originated October's National Fire Prevention Day. Traphagen moved to Hawaii where he was responsible for at least thirty-five buildings constructed in Honolulu and Hilo between 1898 and 1907. He moved to San Francisco after the 1906 earthquake and fire, but designed only one building there before retiring.

O. G. TRAPHAGEN.   F. W. FITZPATRICK.

Traphagen & Fitzpatrick,
Architects,
DULUTH.

510, 511, 512, 513
FIRST NATIONAL BANK BUILDING,

Gray Terrace

410–416 West 4th Street
Architect: AUSTIN TERRYBERRY
Built: 1889 | Lost: 1973

Gray Terrace's four townhouses stood three stories high and each was outfitted with a small front porch and separate entrance, brick walls, and patterned wood shingles on the top floors. As shown in the 1891 photo at left, some windows were arched and others featured stone trim or stained glass. It featured modern conveniences such as electric lights and bells, speaking tubes, gas fixtures, and hot and cold water. The *Duluth Daily News* called the townhouse "one of the finest buildings in the city."

Charles M. Gray was born in Maine; he moved to Duluth in the early 1880s with his wife, Ida, and children to work as the secretary of North-western Loan and Investment Company. The Gray family lived in a house a block away from the Terrace. They left Duluth in 1896 and moved to Detroit, Michigan. Gray Terrace was eventually divided into apartments and was used as such until it was demolished in 1973 when Mesaba Avenue was widened.

Bradley Townhouses

218 & 220 West 3rd Street
Architects: PALMER & HALL
Built: 1889 | Lost: 1968

Alva Bradley (pictured at left) hired Emmet S. Palmer and Lucien P. Hall to design his three-story Romanesque Revival double townhouse built of brick with brownstone trim, gables, roof dormers with finials, half towers, arched windows, and several porches (shown here in 1891). Palmer and Hall designed many schools in Duluth, including the city's grand 1892 Central High School.

Bradley, born in Ohio in 1849, came to Duluth in 1882 after spending many years in the lumber business in Newark, Ohio. In the Zenith City he joined his father Henry's firm, the Bradley-Hanford Lumber Company. They were wholesalers: they did not own any yards or mills. The Bradleys and several relatives lived in the townhouses until he left Duluth for Denver, Colorado, in 1908. The following year the Bradley townhouses were divided into apartments and furnished rooms. The building served as an apartment house until 1968, when it was demolished. The site is now part of a parking lot for San Marco Apartments.

Park Terrace

801 West 1st Street

Architects: CHARLES & EARL BARBER

Built: 1890 | Lost: 1936

Poised on a rather steep hill on the northwest corner of Eighth Avenue North and West First Street, overlooking downtown Duluth and the harbor, Park Terrace was a grand example of a Victorian townhouse. Some of the units were two stories tall, others three, and residents had to climb a steep set of stairs to get to their homes.

The complex, which stood northwest of the present Duluth Bethel, was built by the Myers Brothers Company, a Duluth real estate business. Owners Benjamin, Henry, and Jacob Myers and their families all lived in Park Terrace until 1895. Jacob left Duluth for Texas and Benjamin moved to a house on London Road—and later to St. Paul—but Henry stayed in Duluth and worked in real estate and investments until he died in 1931. The Myers brothers were of Jewish descent, which they symbolized by mounting a large Star of David weather vane atop the building's central tower. By 1935 Park Terrace (shown above in the 1890s) sat vacant and had fallen into disrepair; it was demolished in 1936. The site is now overgrown with trees and bushes; the staircases and nearly all the foundations survive. The city has labeled the site "Myer's Park."

Philadelphia Terrace

1412–1420 East Superior Street

Architects: TRAPHAGEN & FITZPATRICK

Built: 1890 | Lost: CA. 1984

Philadelphia Terrace stood two-and-a-half stories tall along Superior Street between Fourteenth and Fifteenth Avenues East. The building (left, date unknown) housed five family residences, each with a separate entrance, roof dormers, and finials. Architect Frances Fitzpatrick and his family lived here at 1420 East Superior Street until they moved from Duluth in 1896. In the 1930s Philadelphia Terrace became the Hamilton Hotel and served as such until 1981 when it was subdivided into thirty apartments. About three years later the building was vacated and demolished for an auto dealership. The site is now a parking lot serving the Duluth Detoxification Center.

Northern Pacific Immigrant Houses

5th Avenue South & Railroad Street
6th Avenue South and Michigan Street
Architect: UNKNOWN
Built: CA. 1871 | Lost: CA. 1880s & 1890s

Beginning in 1871, the year after its lines first reached Duluth, the Northern Pacific Railroad began encouraging immigrants, mainly from northern Europe, to settle in Minnesota and what would become North and South Dakota. Northern Pacific conducted recruiting campaigns in Europe, including Germany, Sweden, Great Britain, Norway, and Denmark. To house these recruits upon arrival, the railroad built "reception houses" in Minnesota at Duluth, Brainerd, and near Moorhead. At one time Duluth had several immigrant houses which mainly catered to single men. Unmarried immigrants stayed in individual bedrooms and had access to furnished kitchens and parlors. But these large boarding houses, in which residents stayed rent free until they found homes or moved on, could also house entire families. Both of Duluth's immigrant houses were located within half a block of the original Union Station, where immigrants would have gotten off the train as they first entered Duluth.

One of these immigrant houses, built on Fifth Avenue South alongside the railroad tracks, was known as the Colonists' Reception House (pictured, top). A simple white-frame building erected in 1871, the establishment was run by Allen M. Longstreet for the Northern Pacific. It reportedly housed up to seven hundred men per day. By 1885 the Fifth Avenue building had become the Bartlett Hotel; three years later the hotel changed its name to the New Commercial Hotel. It was demolished in the early 1890s. The first immigrant house's lot is currently occupied by a parking ramp.

In either 1871 or 1872 (records are not clear) Northern Pacific Railroad built a second immigrant house in Duluth. The building (pictured, bottom) sat along Sixth Avenue South at Michigan Street and featured a handsome corner tower offering splendid views of the bay. It was not used for long and disappeared from Duluth maps by 1880. Today the building's site is a parking lot.

Finn Town

Finnish immigrants came to Duluth as early as 1868, and in the 1870s and '80s began arriving in greater numbers. During this period the base of Minnesota Point to the canal (today's Canal Park Business District) was made up of two divisions called Cowell's Addition and Industrial Addition, known collectively as Uptown—at least on the western or bay side of the Point. The eastern or lake side along St. Croix Avenue (later First Avenue South, today Canal Park Drive) and north of Buchanon Street was called "No Man's Land" in the 1870s, and there many immigrants set up shanties.

By 1895 this area had become known as Finn Town and was primarily populated by Finnish (and some Swedish) laborers and their families, many of whom were at work building the canal's concrete piers, earning two dollars a day for their efforts. Locals began calling St. Croix Avenue "Finlander Avenue"; Finns called it *Rottakatu* or "Rat Street" due to the large number of rats who lived among the outhouses. Near their homes (pictured right, along St. Croix Avenue in the 1890s) they built a Finnish church, a Finnish school, a large Finnish bathhouse, Finnish restaurants, and Finnish boarding houses. Finn Town later became home to other minority groups, and other boarding houses (that's the Soumalainen Boarding House, below) and cheap residential hotels hosted sailors and migrant workers.

The area south of Buchanon Street was populated by a community of Lithuanian Jewish immigrants who established the Adas Israel congrega-

tion, which later built a synagogue on East Third Street. This community included Weiland Flats, an apartment complex built by Ernest Weiland behind the site of his tannery on Lake Avenue South, the current site of parking lots for the Lake Superior Marine Museum and Grandma's Restaurant. It was a three-story vernacular structure facing Lake Avenue on ground created by filling in the lake shore. Weiland and several of his relatives lived there in the 1890s, but it soon became low-income housing. The flats were occupied until 1942, when the building was demolished.

Uptown could be a rough and rowdy place, and some of the city's seedier citizens spent their free time in its many saloons and brothels. Children passing through the area to get to and from Park Point were warned by parents to "stay away from the pretty ladies dressed in kimonos." From the the 1880s to the 1930s housing units occupied by prostitutes were labeled "female boarding houses" on insurance maps and were clustered together in Duluth's own red light district: either side of the St. Croix alley south of Railroad Street and north of Sutphin Street. The red light district was "cleaned up" in the late 1930s, and illegal activity shifted to the Bowery, west of Fifth Avenue West between the railroad yards and Superior Street, where that behavior had been going on since at least the 1890s.

Fewer and fewer people chose to live in the Finn Town area over the years, and it fell into decay. By the late 1960s wrecked cars, broken appliances, and other abandoned items lay strewn among the ruins of Finn Town. Today the site of Finn Town is populated by luxury hotels.

Little Italy & The Glenn

Many of the Italians who immigrated to Duluth beginning in the 1880s settled from Tenth Avenue West to roughly Fourteenth Avenue West, from Michigan Street up to about Fourth Street, forming a community known as Duluth's "Little Italy." Those from Northern and Central Italy settled above Point of Rocks. Several of these northern Italians worked as stonemasons and constructed much of the brick and stone work that still graces Duluth (see page 73). ("Goat Hill," west of Central Park and East of Piedmont Avenue, was also a chiefly Italian neighborhood, and an enclave of Italians and Southern Slavs lived along West Duluth's Raleigh Street.)

Duluth's Southern Italians, many of whom worked the railroad yards and coal docks, settled below Point of Rocks in an area also known as The Glenn (also "Glenn Place," "Glenn Rock," and, derogatorily, as "Skunk Hollow"). Prior to the Italians, this had been a French settlement. Most of the homes, built not along streets but on the hillside tucked among the rocks, were little more than shanties. When the French moved to the West End in 1905, Italians purchased their church, St. Jean-Baptiste, at 1100 West Superior Street (see pages 72 and 73). The church, now called St. Peter's, became the center of the community and helped change "The Glenn" to "Little Italy." St. Peter's remained a "personal parish," not owned by the Catholic Diocese until 1967.

In 1926 another St. Peter's was constructed atop Point of Rocks at 818 West Third Street, east of the Darling Observatory, and the new church became the community's center (see page 50). The "upper" portion of Little Italy was also home to a variety of Scandinavian immigrants, and as the years went by fewer and fewer Duluthians of Italian descent remained there. As in other Duluth neighborhoods, the ethnicity of its residents became more and more homogenized. Today the area is known as Observation Hill, in commemoration of the former Darling Observatory, and in 2010 the Duluth Catholic Diocese closed St. Peter's.

Meanwhile, the ramshackle housing of The Glenn (shown on this page in the 1890s) was dismantled and its streets realigned. Ruins of foundations remain, including those of Duluth's first water reservoir, which operated from 1883 to 1899. They can be seen rising from the hill above First Street between Tenth and Eleventh Avenues West.

Lower Oneota

Essentially established by the Merritt, Wheeler, and Ely families, Oneota Township developed along St. Louis bay at about today's Forty-Second Avenue West. Edmund Ely arrived here first, then soon asked St. Paul's Henry Wheeler to come north and set up a sawmill near Forty-Fifth Avenue West. By 1856, when development opened for Europeans on the northern half of Lake Superior, Oneota Township was ready to incorporate. That fall Hepzibah Merritt and five of her seven sons arrived to set up a homestead with her husband Lewis, who was already there with their two oldest boys. Among the buildings they constructed was the Merritt Hotel (shown at right, date unknown, with much of the Merritt family). The Merritts would become famous for gaining and losing a fortune in iron mining. The Wheeler family remains prominent in Duluth business, and we have them to thank for the Wheeler Field softball complex, once known as the Wheeler Race Track and Oneota Park.

Oneota stretched from about Thirty-Ninth to Forty-Seventh Avenues West, from the bay all the way up to Oneota Cemetery, just below today's Skyline Parkway. The first school in what would become Duluth was built here (see page 51). The lower portion near the bay became industrialized over the years, home to blast furnaces and other smokestack industries. Oneota became part of the newly incorporated town of West Duluth in 1888, and part of Duluth when West Duluth merged with the Zenith City in 1894. By the 1950s, about 1,600 people lived in the area below Grand Avenue, considered "Lower Oneota."

It took a while for all of Lower Oneota to disappear. It started in the early 1960s, as houses were purchased and demolished to make way for the Interstate 35 extension to downtown. Everything between Michigan Street and Oneota Street—homes, schools, warehouses, manufacturing plants—was destroyed. Twenty-five more homes and other properties were lost in the late 1970s, from Fortieth to Forty-Seventh Avenues West between Michigan and First Street, to make way for the Oneota Industrial Park. The city also created Mike Colalillo Drive at this time to connect the new industrial park to Interstate 35. Unhappy residents—one family called Mayor Robert Beaudin and the Housing and Redevelopment Authority "a bunch of land grabbers"—filed a petition to request an environmental impact study, hoping to derail the project. Other residents, pleased to get a fair-market value for their unsellable homes, started a counter petition. The effort to stop the process failed.

More homes were lost in 1980 and 1981 when the Richard I. Bong Memorial Bridge was constructed. In 1984 the last of the Lower Oneota homes were purchased for demolition. These were in what was termed the "Oneota Isolation Pocket," a two-block area containing twenty-five houses bounded by the Bong Bridge, Superior Street, railroad tracks, and industrial yards. Tom Black, a lifelong Oneota resident, had moved his entire house to the area in 1962 so that it wouldn't be lost to the initial Interstate 35 construction. He lost his Oneota house in this final wave of demolition.

Slabtown & Below the Tracks

Duluth's Slabtown neighborhood, actually a subsection of the West End, housed a variety of low-income families from varied ethnic backgrounds, including Finns, Norwegians, Germans, Swedes, Poles, and French. The neighborhood stretched from roughly Twenty-Sixth to Thirtieth Avenues West and from Michigan Street to St. Louis Bay, centered on the Twenty-Seventh Avenue West Bridge (shown at right). Immigrants came to the area to find work on the ore and coal docks and in the lumber mills and other smokestack industries that lined the bay, and they built their houses and churches as close to their workplaces as they could.

Slabtown's name comes from the area's historical background. This spot along the St. Louis River long served the timber industry and was lined with lumber mills. At these mills, the outer layer of bark was removed from logs before they were milled into lumber. These leftover "slabs" were then tossed into the bay, where they floated. The local residents gathered this surplus wood and used it to heat their homes. Hence, the neighborhood whose residents used slabs of bark-covered wood as heating fuel

became known as "Slabtown." An enclave of Slabtown west of Twenty-Seventh Avenue was called "Below the Tracks" because it stood south of the railroad tracks that run between Michigan and Superior Streets.

Everyone worked, even the children. In a 1998 *Duluth News-Tribune* story, former residents explained that the ore docks hired teenagers to steam-thaw frozen iron ore so it could load better. To save money, coal was delivered in the street, and youngsters spent their after-school hours shoveling it into basement storage bins. They played hard, too, facing off against one another at broomball and hockey on the frozen bay, where they sometimes raced homemade single-masted ice boats.

Urban renewal doomed Slabtown. As early as the 1950s, the city purchased, condemned, and demolished houses and other neighborhood buildings such as corner grocers and filling stations. By the time Interstate 35 pushed through the area in the 1960s, 232 homes had been destroyed and the families that lived in them displaced. The new post office replaced Below the Tracks, and businesses such as the Duluth Grill and several gas stations have replaced homes east of there. Below the highway the Western Lake Superior Sanitary District occupies the rest of Slabtown.

Both photos on this page came from brothers Sylvester and Dick Yagoda, who grew up in Slabtown and helped organize reunions of former Slabtown residents in the 1990s.

Swede Town (aka the Garfield Avenue Neighborhood)

While most of Duluth's early Finnish immigrants set up housing on Minnesota Point, in the 1880s Swedish-speaking Finns or "Swede-Finns" first settled in Duluth on Rice's Point along what was platted as Garfield Avenue—merely sand dunes at the time—and on nearby Grass Island in St. Louis Bay. The area became known as Swede Town.

Residents included such immigrants as August Signer or "Water August," a bartender who tried his hand at the fresh-water delivery business, using an ox to haul fresh water drawn from St. Louis Bay from Rice's Point to the West End and charging his customers a nickel a pail.

By 1910 residents had moved off of Grass Island to make room for the Peavey Grain Elevator. By the 1920s, most Swede-Finns had relocated to the West End. Many low-income families continued to live on Rice's Point, and the enclave became known as the "Garfield Avenue neighborhood." One native Duluthian recalls that children from the area were known as "Garfield Avenue Kids," a moniker that indicated poverty (the houses shown at right were photographed in 1955).

Businesses serving the neighborhood included Hellman Grocery, Kayo's Hotel and Apartments (top, 1955), The Tip-Top Tavern (also called Fritz's at one time) and the Vi-Kar Diner, a classic eatery housed

in old trolley car (top right, 1955). Garfield Avenue was also the home of Goldfine's Department Store (now the Goodwill Building), Madison School (now the Seaway Building), Garfield Welding and Machine Works, Mesabi Iron Works, and other industrial concerns.

Because it was the only road leading to the Interstate Bridge between Duluth and Superior, from 1897 to 1962 Garfield Avenue was one of Duluth's busiest streets. With the end of the bridge came the end of the neighborhood. When construction of Duluth's High Bridge (later renamed the Blatnik Bridge) was approved in the late 1950s; most of Rice's Point was rezoned to prohibit residential housing and razed. By the time the bridge opened December 8, 1961, the neighborhood was gone. The Interstate Bridge ceased operations just over a year later (see page 194).

Park Point's Cabins

Since Superior *and* Duluth pioneer George Stuntz famously established a cabin, trading post, and dock on the southern end of Minnesota Point in 1852—before Europeans were even allowed to settle in what would become the Minnesota side of Lake Superior—wealthy citizens of both Duluth and Superior built summer dwellings there. Lakeside pioneers George and Mary Sargent built the cabin pictured at right, later the property of their son William.

After the township of Park Point established a trolley car on Minnesota Avenue in the 1880s, entrepreneurs established cabin enclaves called "Hay Fever Havens," clusters of cabins inhabited by those who could afford to summer in Duluth to avoid allergens in their own towns. In the postcard below (circa 1900, text enhanced for readability) Minnesota Point is advertised as "Duluth's Far Famed Hay Fever Haven and Summer Resort."

In the early 1900s Minnesota Point residents Charlotte and John Harry Peabody ran a ferry service near Stuntz's old trading post, and their dock was called Peabody's Landing. Most of the surrounding cabins were owned by Superiorites who used Peabody's ferry to cross the harbor; it took

longer to get to the end of Minnesota Point from Duluth than it did from Superior.

The last remaining cabin at Peabody's Landing, Pine Knot, was reportedly built in 1900 by Superior Mayor Charles O'Hehir. In 1927 it was acquired by the Pollock family, who donated it to the city of Duluth in 1999. Once four feet from the bay, dredging waste dumped at the landing widened the point in the 1930s, "moving" the cabin much further from the water. Some believe the original Pine Knot may have been destroyed by fire and replaced at an unknown date. It was demolished in 2010.

The only remnants of the old community at the southern end of Minnesota Point that remain today are the ruins of the 1858 Minnesota Point Lighthouse and the United States Lighthouse Station Depot (see page 191). The area is now part of Duluth's park system and home to the Minnesota Point Hiking Trail.

9119, Minnesota Point "Duluth's Far Famed Hay Fever and Summer Resort." A Strip of land seven miles long forming our wonderful harbor, Duluth, Minn.

PART TWO

LOST PUBLIC BUILDINGS

Franklin Elementary School (1888 – 1979)

Lost Public Buildings

Public buildings, for the purposes of this book, are those structures erected to serve the public good, whether publicly or privately funded, for profit or nonprofit. These include buildings that serve city, county, and federal governments as well as public and private schools, houses of worships, and nonprofit charitable organizations such as children's homes and other social facilities, some with religious affiliations. Most of these are nonprofit entities.

Duluthians are fortunate to have an abundance of these old buildings still intact and serving the community, although not always for their original purposes. Many of our historic public schools still stand, some still serving the school district; others that have transferred to private hands, like Emerson, Endion, Irving, and Jefferson elementary schools, have been converted to housing complexes. Churches as well have been put to reuse as private

homes, community centers, and performance spaces such as the Sacred Heart Music Center at the 1896 Sacred Heart Cathedral. Many others, such as 1891's First Presbyterian Church, 1913's St. Paul's Episcopal Church, and 1917's Pilgrim Congregational Church, still serve their original purposes.

Duluth's government buildings at the Civic Center are masterpieces of the City Beautiful architecture movement. The St. Louis County Courthouse was designed by Daniel Burnham, father of the movement. Duluth City Hall and the adjacent Gerald W. Heaney Federal Building were designed with Burnham's plan in mind. So was the historic St. Louis County Jail, which was almost lost to demolition until developer Grant Carlson stepped in to purchase it in 2010. Carlson plans to restore the building's damaged façade and convert the jail's interior into multiuse space.

Other government buildings continue to grace Duluth, such as the 1897 Lakewood Pumping Station, the 1902 Public Library, and several old fire houses. The 1915 National Guard Armory is undergoing restoration and a portion of it is ready for tenants.

Two significant former government buildings continue to serve downtown Duluth long after completing their service to the city. The former jail at 126 East Superior Street still features its original brownstone façade and is now home to Architectural Resources. Next door at 132 East Superior Street stands Old City Hall. The owners have renovated the building to hold offices and a restaurant with a Duluth-history theme. The building's original façade, lost in the 1960s, was restored in 2010 to replicate its original sandstone construction.

The odd little building at left, apparently constructed in the middle of Third Avenue West below Superior Street, is the U.S. Thrift Stamp Sub Treasury. It was erected to sell war bonds during the first World War. In 1917 the United States Treasury Department began selling War Savings Certificate Stamps in two denominations, twenty-five cents for thrift stamps and five dollars for war savings stamps. They matured after five years and gave investors about a four percent return on their investment. There is little information available on the Duluth Sub Treasury, but it was likely made of wood and designed as a temporary structure.

Duluth Township's 1857 Post Office

The first post office in what is now Duluth was established in Oneota Township on May 13, 1856, with Reverend Edmund F. Ely presiding as postmaster. The first in Duluth Township went up just over a year later with Joshua B. Culver, Duluth's first mayor, acting as postmaster. Earlier post offices had been located in the homes of the postmasters. The 1857 building also served as the Duluth Village Council's first meeting place. (The person in the photo is likely Theodore Helinski, postmaster in 1895 when the photo was reportedly taken.)

409 East Superior Street
Architect: NONE
Built: 1857 | Lost: 1936

The building was a small, one-story frame structure with a false second-level façade. By the early 1930s the building had been moved to the alley behind its original location; it was described as "ramshackle and dilapidated" and considered a fire hazard. Duluth historians attempted to save the building, proposing it be moved to Leif Erikson Park as a civic monument. That effort failed, and it went down in 1936. The Amendola building now stands on the site.

1889 County Jail

614 East 3rd Street
Architect: OLIVER G. TRAPHAGEN
Built: 1889 | Lost: 1954

The first St. Louis County Jail served double duty, with its sixteen jail cells housed in the rear and a home for the sheriff and his family in front. The red brick building had carved brownstone trim, several arched windows, Palladian windows in the gables, and iron cresting atop the roof. The doors, windows, and columns featured carvings. The sheriff and his wife lived in the building (shown in 1895) and she prepared meals for prisoners.

The jail held Charles Henderson after his 1902 murder conviction until he was hanged at the courthouse next door on March 6, 1903; he was the last man legally hanged for murder in St Louis County. When the jail closed in 1923, it was remodeled as Hearding Hospital, which served the county's poor until 1947, after which it became a rooming house. At one time sixty-seven tenants called the building home; only seven had to move when the condemned building was razed in 1954. The site now hosts St. Luke's Hospital's Hillside Center.

1892 U.S. Federal Building & Post Office

431 West 1st Street

Architect: H. G. LINDERMAN

Built: 1892–94 | Lost: 1935

For years this building's design was credited to Duluth architects Oliver Traphagen and Francis Fitzpatrick, but more recent research indicates that the architect was actually H. G. Linderman, who sold the blueprints to the U.S. Treasury Department for $1,100 in 1889. It's possible that Traphagen and Fitzpatrick were credited with the design because its Romanesque Revival–style was often employed in their designs and because Traphagen supervised the building's construction.

Masons set the building's cornerstone on June 25, 1892, but construction was slowed because local brownstone was determined too weak for the three-story building. Eventually Bedford limestone was purchased and delivered from Indiana for the building, which cost $250,000 when completed in October, 1894—over $6 million today. The building contained the customs house, courtrooms, and the main branch of the Duluth Post Office. Most Duluthians referred to the building as simply "the post office." (The photo shows the building ca. 1930.)

The Federal Building featured a square tower with turrets, arched second floor windows, and terra cotta trim on its windows and doors, all of which contributed to the heavy, massive feel of the building's Romanesque style. On the second story of the western façade workers carved an eagle onto an eight-ton square piece of sandstone.

In 1930, construction completed on the new Federal Building anchoring the west end of Duluth's Civic Center, and offices moved from the old federal building into the new. Soon Duluthians began calling the old landmark an "eyesore." Demolition took nine months, from December, 1934 to August, 1935. Workers dismantling the building found a bottle within its walls; it contained a cloth written with the message "goodbye, Friends." It was dated November 11, 1892, and signed by "James Peterson, 14th Ave. E. and Charles Bowman, 465 23rd W." Officials hoped to relocate the eagle carving to the Naval Reserve Station on Park Point, and it was safely removed from the second floor façade with a six-ton crane. Unfortunately the Navy had to reject the offer because of the stone's immense weight.

After demolition the site of the old Federal Building was seeded as a park. Since that time the area has developed into a circular driveway with parking serving today's Federal Building, Court House, and City Hall. In its center stands fountains and statues, including the Soldiers & Sailors Monument designed by architect Cass Gilbert and sculptor Paul Bartlett.

West Duluth Public Library

701 North Central Avenue
Architect: WILLIAM J. SULLIVAN
Built: 1912 | Lost: 1992

While West Duluth had no official library until 1912, beginning in 1882 the Women's Christian Temperance Union operated reading rooms in several different West Duluth locations. The Duluth Public Library took over in 1896, sponsoring the West Duluth Reading Room with $105.

In 1910 the library board purchased a lot on Central Avenue and Elinor Street. Duluth architect William Sullivan drew up plans for a one-story brick building with terra cotta trim, and in 1912 the library (shown below, date unknown) was constructed with a $20,000 grant from Andrew Carnegie, who also helped fund Duluth's 1902 public library.

More than just a book depository, the West Duluth Public Library served as a community center, even offering a weekly "baby clinic" in 1920. As early as the 1930s the facility felt the pinch for more space. In 1936 the Duluth Business Men's Club offered $23,000 to see through a planned expansion of the facility, but the addition was never built. The library continued to serve West Duluth until the 1991 construction of the West Duluth Community Center, which includes a branch library. The old library was then demolished; its lot was used as a playground for the 1957 Laura MacArthur Elementary School until that school's 2011 demolition.

Darling Observatory

910 West 3rd Street

Architect: Richard Schmidt

Built: 1912 | Lost: CA. 1970

When John H. Darling retired as an engineer for the Army Corps of Engineers in 1913, he turned his full attention to his hobby: astronomy. He privately funded the Darling Observatory on West Third Street atop Duluth's Point of Rocks, roughly 325 feet above the lake. The stucco building (below, date unknown) featured a nineteen-foot dome. Its telescope (right, date unknown), mounted on solid bedrock, had a nine-inch, 261-pound refracting lens with a focal length of 130 feet; Darling designed some of its components himself. The observatory included a lecture room that seated up to twenty, and Darling regularly conducted public sessions lasting up to three hours. Over 16,000 people visited the observatory in 1930.

Darling died in 1942. His will gave the observatory to the city of Duluth with a trust fund of $20,000 to continue operation. Public viewing continued until 1956 under the direction of Darling's assistant, noted UFO enthusiast Frank A. Halstead. In 1965 the University of Minnesota Duluth took control of the observatory. The telescope was moved to the UMD campus and the building, which had been repeatedly vandalized, was demolished. The land on which the observatory stood is now Observation Park and the telescope is on display at UMD.

1857 Oneota Township School

4300 Oneota Street

Architect: UNKNOWN

Built: 1857 | Lost: UNKNOWN

Oneota Township was just a year old when its citizens built their first schoolhouse to teach the children of the founding Merritt, Ely, and Wheeler families. The one-room wood frame building (right, date unknown) was built with lumber milled by Henry Wheeler's sawmill, and Jerome Merritt first performed teaching duties within its walls (four of his pupils were his brothers). The small, rustic building had few windows, its door faced the bay, and historic photos indicate it may not have been painted. It had no furnace, electricity, or plumbing, but it did have a belfry. Early Oneota residents noted that the bell rang for school classes and Methodist church services, which were held in the building until 1869. The Oneota Town Council also met at the school. No records indicate when the building was demolished; the building's site is now a greenspace within an industrial park south of Interstate 35.

1888 Oneota Elementary

4420 West 1st Street

Architect: OLIVER G. TRAPHAGEN

Built: 1888 | Lost: 1973

The second Oneota School (shown at left in 1888), a three-story Romanesque Revival–style building constructed of red brick, featured a tall square tower and a smaller round tower, both topped with iron finials. (That's architect Oliver Traphagen's sketch of the school at right.) The school had six classrooms when it opened for students on November 26, 1888. Built by the newly incorporated Village of West Duluth, it became part of the Duluth School District when West Duluth merged with Duluth in 1894. Just as the Oneota Village Council had done with the first Oneota School, the West Duluth Village Council met in the second Oneota School until it became part of Duluth. In 1901 a seventh classroom was added to better fit the school's 159 students. It closed in 1946 and was used by the school district for storage until 1973 when it was demolished to make room for an industrial park.

Adams Elementary

1721 West Superior Street
Architects: McMillen & Stebbins
Built: 1885 | Lost: 1968

Adams School, built to serve the West End neighborhood, was perched on a granite hill overlooking Rice's Point. The school was named for a President Adams, but records do not indicate if the namesake was John Adams, the second president, or John Quincy Adams, his son and sixth president, or both. The brick school stood three stories high and featured a square tower and some arched windows and entrances. Originally Adams had eight classrooms, but an 1891 addition designed by McMillen and Radcliffe increased it to fourteen. When the building closed in 1951 its 280 students transferred to Lincoln School.

In 1962 excavation contractor Harvey Grew purchased the building from the school district for $100, planning to raze the building and create a parking lot. Three years later he regretted the purchase and offered the building and land for free if a new owner would use the property for a public purpose. There were no offers. In 1965 the *Duluth Herald* called the building "the city's No. 1 eyesore." Adams (shown below in 1886) remained vacant until 1968 when it was demolished. Its rock retaining wall remains.

Duluth High School (aka Washington Elementary)

226 North 1st Avenue East

Architect: CHARLES M. McMILLEN

Built: 1886 | Lost: 1976

Although students graduated from high school in Duluth as early as 1879 (Duluth's first two graduates were girls), the first building specifically constructed for use as a high school went up in 1886 and opened in January 1887 on the southeast corner of First Avenue East and Third Street. Prior to that, high school students were taught among elementary students in a wooden schoolhouse at the southeast corner of Lake Avenue and Third Street.

The school board built a brick structure adjacent to the wooden school in 1881. Named Washington School, it served students from kindergarten through the eighth grade. While records remain unclear, apparently the wooden building was used for the high school from 1881 to 1886.

The 1886 high school (right, date unknown) was three stories of red brick with a square tower which rose above the arched entrance on the front façade. Classrooms occupied the first and second floors while the third—with a high-domed ceiling—housed a combined gymnasium and auditorium. The building cost $33,000 in 1886, about $750,000 today.

As Duluth boomed through the 1880s, the new high school soon became inadequate for the city's growing population. The massive sandstone Central High School opened across the avenue from Duluth High School in 1892. Both older schools on that lot would have had to have been razed before that time to make room for it. At this time Duluth's old high school became an elementary school and was renamed in honor of George Washington. When Washington Junior High opened in 1911 at 315 Lake Avenue North, Duluth had two Washington schools. In 1919 another building was constructed just behind Washington Elementary and named Liberty Elementary.

In 1921 Washington Elementary closed and the building became home of the Duluth Board of Education and was renamed accordingly. Liberty closed in 1930, reopening briefly from 1944 to 1946 before becoming the Duluth

Board of Education Annex. Both buildings served the school board until 1975 when the Board of Education offices moved into the vacated 1892 Central High School, whose students relocated to a brand new Central High School set atop the hillside. (In 2010 the 1975 Central High School was abandoned by the Duluth School District as part of its Long Range Facilities Plan.) Duluth's first high school was demolished in 1976. A parking lot now occupies the space.

1888 Franklin Elementary

Built in 1888 and opened in January 1889, Franklin School took the place of an earlier wooden school of the same name that stood on the same lot. That first Franklin School (both were named for Benjamin Franklin) was moved to Minnesota Point and took on the name Cleveland Elementary. The 1888 Franklin School (left, date unknown) contained twelve classrooms designed to support 650 students. In 1907 fire severely damaged the school, and the city had it rebuilt. A new wing was added in 1939, when Franklin became a junior high school. Duluth Junior College held classes there from 1946 to 1950. The Duluth School Board's 1972 decision to close Franklin (as well as Munger Elementary) brought strong opposition from parents of Franklin students, who fought to have the school—called "the only racially segregated school in Duluth" by the *Duluth News Tribune*—converted to an "open school." The parents won, but the Duluth Open School closed in 1977 due to lack of enrolment. Two years later the building came down; the lot is now used as the Hillside Sports Court.

1893 Jackson Elementary

Like the 1888 Franklin Elementary, the 1893 Jackson School (right, date unknown) replaced a wooden facility of the same name on the same lot. Constructed in 1884, the first Jackson Elementary was a ten-room wood-frame building veneered in brick and designed by McMillen and Stebbins. By 1890 overcrowding led to its obsolescence, and it was demolished to make room for a new building. During construction, Jackson students took classes at Central High School. A wing was added in 1895, increasing the classrooms to seventeen. Jackson—named for President Andrew Jackson—served the Downtown Hillside neighborhood until 1962 when students transferred to Emerson and Nettleton Schools. The building was sold to St. Louis County for its Social Service Department, which remained here until 1983 when the building was razed and replaced with a parking ramp.

Longfellow Elementary

6015 Elinor Street

Architects: PALMER & HALL

Built: 1891 | Lost: 1959

Slated to open in the fall of 1891, Longfellow Elementary didn't see a student until April 1892 due to a Scarlet Fever epidemic. After that its twelve classrooms served West Duluth for over a half century. Named for American author Henry Wadsworth Longfellow, the facility sat on a hill on Elinor Street in West Duluth. The brick school (shown here in 1891) featured many architectural details, including arched windows and corners dressed with quoins, but its most distinctive feature was its tower, which held neither bell nor clock. Private sources raised the $3,000 needed to add the tower, which served as a landmark in West Duluth. In 1949 the *Duluth News Tribune* reported that mothers would tell their children, "if you ever get lost, just walk to the tower and all will be well." The school's most celebrated teacher, Laura MacArthur, arrived in 1896 to teach Latin, algebra, and civics to ninth graders. The elementary school closed in 1956 and stood empty; it was vandalized repeatedly, and a 1959 fire forced its demolition. The lot today remains vacant; only the stairs leading from Elinor Street remain.

Ely Elementary (aka the first Robert E. Denfeld High School)

West 6th Street & Central Avenue

Architect: AUSTIN TERRYBERRY

Built: 1906 | Lost: 1956

This West Duluth school took its name from pioneer and educator Reverend Edmund Ely, who established a mission at Fond du Lac before heading downriver to start Oneota Township. The two-story building of "thoroughly modern construction" held ten classrooms designed for up to five hundred students.

West Duluth's first high school, Duluth Industrial High School, was housed inside Irving Elementary from 1905 to 1913. Most West Duluthians called the school "Irving High School" or "West Duluth High School." In 1915 the first Robert E. Denfeld High School was built at 725 Central Avenue North (right next to Ely Elementary) and served 150 students. Irving Elementary became a junior high, and Laura MacArthur (see above) became its principal. By 1925 over eight hundred students were crammed into the first Denfeld. When today's Robert E. Denfeld High School opened in 1926, old Denfeld was rechristened West Junior High. That same year Laura MacArthur was named principal of both West Junior High and Ely Elementary.

Ely Elementary (left, date unknown) was destroyed in 1956, the same year Longfellow closed. Both schools were replaced by Laura MacArthur Elementary in 1957, and West Junior High became the west wing of Laura MacArthur in 1983. Both schools are scheduled to be demolished in 2012 to make room for a new Laura MacArthur Elementary as part of the Duluth School District's Long Range Facilities Plan.

Lincoln Elementary

2427 West Fourth Street

Architects: PALMER & HALL

Built: 1889 | Altered: REPEATEDLY

Lincoln Elementary was one of several schools Duluth built and named after prominent Americans, including Washington, Jefferson, Adams, Franklin, Madison, Monroe, Bryant, Grant, Emerson, and Longfellow. When first built, Lincoln was a two-and-a-half-story Romanesque building with a central bell tower made of brick and sandstone from the Flag River Quarry. Its design was nearly identical to that of Franklin School, and its main entrance faced Fourth Street. By 1904 the building's twelve classrooms had become cramped, so an addition was made—one of many that would occur over the next one hundred years. A junior high school, facing Fifth Street, was constructed behind Lincoln in 1915 and connected to the elementary school through a simple corridor. A 1930 addition added a wing east of the main building that housed shop classes and music programs. In 1951, Lincoln was severely remodeled: the tower was removed, the pitched roof flattened, and two three-story wings were added. Today the work of architects Palmer and Hall has either been removed or completely hidden. Lincoln closed in 2011 as part of the Duluth School District's Long Range Facility Plan. Originally slated for demolition, the building received a new lease on life when Sherman & Associates purchased it for $1 in 2011. The firm plans to work with the Housing and Redevelopment Authority of Duluth and Duluth Local Initiatives Support Corporation to find ways to adapt the building so it can continue to serve Duluth's West End.

Bryant Elementary

Named for American poet William Cullen Bryant, the West End's original 1893 Bryant School was a modest,

3102 West Third Street

Architects: McMILLEN & TENBUSCH

Built: 1895 | Lost: 1974

wooden structure with few rooms. It was replaced in 1895 with a two-and-a-half-story building containing sixteen classrooms. The brick building was adorned with brownstone trim, featured a double-arched brownstone entrance, and sat on a brownstone foundation. Several dormers allowed the smaller top floor to be utilized. Bryant was active in the formation of early labor unions, so it seems fitting that a West End school would carry his name: it was the stronghold of Duluth's early labor and socialist movements. Bryant School served the West End until June, 1974; it was razed in December of that year. The lot where it stood remains empty.

Monroe Elementary

2502 West First Street

Architect: JOHN J. WANGENSTEIN

Built: 1900 | Lost: 1992

Duluth's first Monroe School, built in 1884, stood at the southeast corner of Twenty-Fifth Avenue West and West First Street. Run by Annie Hicken, the wooden structure (all four rooms of it) stood "farthest west of all the schools." In 1900 the tiny building was replaced, but not destroyed; it was moved to Eleventh Avenue West and Piedmont Avenue and renamed the Horace Mann School (see below).

The 1900 Monroe School, two stories of brick trimmed in brownstone, contained eight classrooms. It opened in January 1900 and served the West End until 1951. While most Monroe students attended the new building, others were sent to Bryant School. When Monroe closed, local students attended Lincoln Elementary. After closing as an educational institution, the building was used as a storage facility by several Duluth firms, including Central Sales and Garon Knitting Mill. A suspicious fire in 1992 ravaged the building, which had been vandalized the day before the blaze. Monroe had to be razed for safety reasons; the site is now a parking lot.

Ensign Elementary

1013 Piedmont Avenue

Architects: RADCLIFFE & PRICE

Built: 1908 | Lost: 1981

Horace Mann School, the former Monroe Elementary, proved insufficient for its new location, and it was poorly insulated, making it very cold. In 1908 Ensign Elementary replaced Horace Mann, and the former was sold for its lumber.

The new school took its name from beloved Duluth pioneer J. D. Ensign, who joined the school board soon after arriving in Duluth in 1870 (see page 31). The new school stood three stories tall and was wrapped in brick; rubble stone adorned the first story, which featured a decorative column entrance and quoins at each corner. It contained ten classrooms and even had its own library.

The school underwent remodeling in 1929 and served the upper West End for the next fifty years, closing in 1979. Arsonists set the building ablaze in 1981. Several houses now occupy the site.

1892 Lester Park Elementary

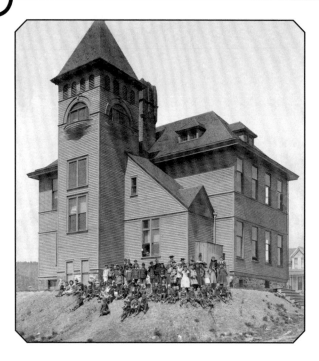

5410 Otsego Street

Architects: German & de Waard

Built: 1892 | Lost: 1925

Duluth's eastern neighborhoods—New London, Lakeside, and Lester Park—developed in the 1880s and 1890s as residential townships. The New London School was built on the northeast corner of Regent Street and Forty-Sixth Avenue East in 1889 but closed five years later. The school was sold to Bradford C. Church, who had the building dismantled and reconstructed at 5217 London Road as a private home; it stands there today. The New London students moved to Lakeside School at 4628 Pitt Street. In 1993 that school was sold to St. Michael's Catholic Church and now serves as the church's school.

In 1892, Lester Park School was built at 5410 Otsego Street. The two-story frame building (shown at left in 1898) featured a three-story tower. Later images indicate the building was remodeled at some time, and the tower was lost. When New London, Lakeside, and Lester Park merged with Duluth in 1893, the school became part of the Duluth School District and served grades one through six until 1918. It was sold to the City of Duluth, which demolished it in 1925 to make room for the Lester Park branch of the Duluth Public Library, which later became the Lakeside and Lester Park Community Center.

1918 Lester Park Elementary

315 North 54th Avenue East

Architects: de Waard & Staudahar

Built: 1918 | Lost: 2011

Architect John de Waard, who helped Frederick German design the first Lester Park School, teamed up with Francis X. Staudahar to plan the school that would replace it just a few blocks away. Built of multicolored bricks trimmed in stone, the rectangular 1918 Lester Park School (right, date unknown) stood three stories tall, capped with three parapets across the front; the middle parapet carried the school's name. Tall twin pilasters framed its stone entrance. In 1954 a wing was added to the school's north side, but it featured none of the architectural details of the original building. In 2010 a new Lester Park School, the third of that name, was built as part of the Duluth School District's Long Range Facilities Plan. The 1918 Lester Park School was demolished in 2011 for the new school's recreational field.

1892 Whittier Elementary

1140 Minnesota Avenue

Architects: McMillen & Radcliffe

Built: 1892 | Lost: CA. 1923

Named for influential Quaker poet and abolitionist John Greenleaf Whittier, Whittier Elementary stood two-and-a-half stories tall at the corner of Minnesota Avenue and South Street on Minnesota Point. The six-room frame building (right, date unknown) opened in 1892 to serve students living on the northern half of Minnesota Point (Radisson School, later renamed Lafayette Elementary, served the southern half). In 1895 Whittier boasted an enrolment of 242 students, but by 1901 that number had dropped to just 103. The school closed in 1919 and was demolished about four years later; a house now occupies the lot. Note the ladder at the left side of the school, extending down from a second-story window to the ground; that was the school's fire escape.

1893 Glen Avon Elementary

In 1887 the patriarch of Glen Avon and Hunter's Park, Angus MacFarlane, built a one-room school on his own property between Lewis and St. Andrew's Streets, right on the bank of Tischer Creek (the "Avon" of the Glen Avon name). The building itself had two rooms; the other served as the MacFarlane family's ice house.

St. Andrews Street & Roslyn Avenue

Architects: Palmer & Hall

Built: 1893 | Lost: 1910

MacFarlane also donated the land upon which a second Glen Avon school was built in 1893. The school was a small, two-story frame building with four classrooms and no architectural decoration, save for two interesting oval windows shown in the undated photo at left. Glen Avon closed in 1905 when Washburn Elementary School opened nearby. It was demolished in 1910; houses now occupy the lot.

Hardy Hall (aka Maynard School and Craggencroft School)

2000 Woodland Avenue
Architects: TRAPHAGEN & FITZPATRICK
Built: 1891 | Lost: CA. 1905

Hardy Hall, a college preparatory school for young women, opened in Eau Claire, Wisconsin, in 1887 and moved to Duluth in 1891, lured here by Hunter's Park developers. Traphagen and Fitzpatrick designed the school in the Shingle style with dark red shingles on the upper stories and an olive-colored roof. The school (shown below in 1895) had steeply sloping roofs, many dormers, a Palladian window in the front gable, and a balcony. The entire first floor was encased in field stone with stone pillars supporting the front porch.

Kate Hardy, director and founder of the school, claimed that a certificate from her school would admit graduates to "Smith, Wellesley and other Colleges of Like Grade." But as Hardy Hall's reputation as a fine school grew, Miss Hardy herself became the center of a scandal. She became the love interest of Duluth pioneer Luther Mendenhall, who had come to Duluth from Philadelphia in 1869 to build Jay Cooke's Lake Superior and Mississippi Railroad. Mendenhall became president of the Duluth National Bank and served many years on Duluth's park board.

The trouble with Mendenhall's courtship of Kate Hardy was that he was already married, and Mrs. Mendenhall didn't appreciate all the time her husband spent at Hardy Hall. The divorce proceedings—which were jury trials at the time—played out in the local newspapers, with witness after witness telling tales of Mendenhall's many visits to the private school. At a banquet in honor of Proctor Knott, namesake of nearby Proctor, Minnesota, one witness described how Mendenhall "turned his back on his wife" and "talked with Miss Hardy the entire evening." Mendenhall survived the divorce (he won the jury's sympathy, and the case) and lived with Hardy, whom he married in 1898, until his death in 1929 at age ninety-three. He ascribed his long life and health to the fact that he was a Quaker and had led a Quaker's calm and temperate life. (Oddly enough, that "Quaker" was a founding trustee of Duluth's First Methodist Church.)

In 1895, before the dust of scandal settled, Hardy Hall became the Maynard School, still a college prep school for women but with an affiliation with the University of Chicago. By 1897 the school had been sold again, its name was changed to Craggencroft, and another administrator, Reverend John Mason Duncan, was put in charge. Duncan stressed his school's "Choice Christian Faculty" and called Craggencroft the "Leading Classical Institute in the Northwest for Young Ladies." Craggencroft survived only until 1902 when the building was vacated. The origins of the Maynard and Craggencroft names remain unclear.

In 1905 Mendenhall purchased the building and had it disassembled. The couple hired Duluth architects Frederick German and A. Werner Lignell to build three houses on the land occupied by Hardy Hall at 2000, 2010, and 2020 Woodland Avenue. Most of the stones were used in the house at 2000 Woodland Avenue, which the Mendenhalls used as their own, and today you can still see some similarity between that property and the original school.

Duluth Normal School (aka "Old Main")

2205 East 5th Street

Architects: PALMER, HALL & HUNT

Built: 1898 – 1901 | Lost: 1993

Construction of the Duluth Normal School began in 1898, but a 1901 fire gutted the unfinished building. Rebuilding and completion of the Renaissance Revival–style school was delayed until 1901 at a final cost of $80,000. The school, whose mission was to train local students to become teachers, opened in September 1902 with ninety-one students and ten faculty members. The original brick building was enhanced by two wing additions designed by William A. Hunt in 1909 and 1915. (The photo below, date unknown, shows both wings in place.) The Normal School became the Duluth State Teachers' College in 1921 and, in 1947, the University of Minnesota Duluth.

Most classes were moved to the newly developing upper campus in the 1950s. Old Main, as the building had then come to be called, served as the university's theater and was also used for office space. In 1985 the building closed and was vacated, awaiting renovation into apartments. On February 23, 1993, vandals broke into Old Main and set it on fire, completely gutting the building. Except for the three arches of its main entryway, the school was demolished. The arches are now part of Old Main Park.

The former campus' other two buildings, Torrence Hall and Washburn Hall, remain. Torrence, built as a dorm, is now an apartment building.

Palmer, Hall & Hunt: Designers of Duluth's Boomtown Schools

The firm of Emmet Palmer and Lucien P. Hall—later joined by William Hunt—designed the majority of Duluth's public schools built from the late 1800s through the early twentieth century, as the city experienced a financial boom and the population increased dramatically. Perhaps their most famous academic design is Duluth's historic 1892 Central High School, a Richardsonian Romaesque masterpiece designed after the Allegheny County Courthouse in Pittsburgh, Pennsylvania; it still stands along the upper side of Second Street between Lake Avenue and First Avenue East.

Indiana native Emmet Palmer (1848–1935) cut his architectural teeth working in New York City before settling in Duluth in 1886. He and Lucien Hall were working together by 1888 when they designed Franklin Elementary. Hall (1854–1933) also worked in New York City in his native state before moving to Duluth. William A. Hunt (1859–1930), a native of Cincinnati, Ohio, studied architecture in his home town and then worked in Minneapolis before moving north to join Palmer and Hall in 1892.

Hall retired in 1903 and moved to Minnesota's Crow Wing County. Two years later Palmer moved to Seattle, Washington, and later to Fresno, California, where he died. Hunt stayed in Duluth and went on to design many of the city's important homes and buildings, including the William & Mina Prindle house (2211 Greysolon Road), the A. L. Ordean House (2307 East Superior Street), the Wolvin Building (227 West First Street, now the Missabe Building), the Lonsdale Building (306 West Superior Street), and the Sellwood Building (202 West Superior Street), which he is shown holding in the sketch.

Hunt moved to Hibbing, Minnesota, in 1916 to work as the supervising architect for Oliver Mining Company and lived there until his death in 1930.

The 1888 Duluth Bethel

246 Lake Avenue South

Architect: UNKNOWN

Built: 1888 | Lost: 1948

Reverend Doctor Charles Cotton Salter of New Haven, Connecticut (Yale, class of 1852), came to Duluth in 1871 and organized the Pilgrim Congregational Church (see page 68). In 1876 poor health sent him abroad for a cure, but he returned to Duluth and his church in 1881. In 1887 he rented a small store on Lake Avenue South adjacent to Sutphin's Dock, where for a few months he conducted gospel meetings and a Sunday School. He later moved services into a tent. In 1887 he organized the Duluth Bethel, a religious and social service organization for sailors on leave in Duluth. The main purpose was to keep these transients out of saloons, gambling houses, and brothels, plenty of which could be found at the time along Lake Avenue South, the heart of today's Canal Park Business District. It was Salter's strong belief that "no soul is too low to be received or ministered unto at the Bethel."

In 1888, through Salter's vigorous leadership, the Bethel constructed a clapboard building with a corner tower on Lake Avenue and Sutphin Street in today's Canal Park Business District (shown here, date unknown). It held reading rooms, a chapel, a cooking school, a restaurant, and furnished rooms for sailors, lumberjacks, and miners. Salter held a religious service each evening. In 1894 the Bethel opened a branch along the 500 block of West Superior Street, the eastern end of Duluth's Bowery, which at that time included over twenty-five saloons.

In 1893 workers raised the Lake Avenue building and added a third floor; six years later a fourth floor was built to increase space for a growing demand of lodgers. By 1910 the Lake Avenue Bethel again needed more space—and a great deal of repairs. The Bethel raised funds for a larger building at 23 Mesaba Avenue. The old Bethel's last service was held on April 29, 1911. The building became the People's Hotel and Tavern until it closed and was demolished in 1948. Today the KDLH and KBJR television studios occupy the Bethel's original site.

1892 Bethany Lutheran Children's Home (aka Alfred & Jane Merritt House)

Oneota pioneer Alfred Merritt and his wife, Jane, built their West Duluth home (as well as a barn) on a six-acre lot just above the railroad tracks (right, date unknown). Alfred Merritt was a member of the Merritt family who settled Oneota Township in the 1850s and later helped develop the Mesabi Iron Range. Oneota became part of West Duluth when it incorporated in 1888. Just two years after this house was built, West Duluth joined Duluth, and the Merritt family lost their iron mining holdings to John D. Rockefeller. In 1916 the Merritts sold their home to the Swedish Lutheran Church of West Duluth, who adapted it for an orphanage. The Merritt house served as the Bethany Lutheran Children's Home until fire struck on October 10, 1920. The building was a total loss.

> 4000 West 9th Street
> Architect: UNKNOWN
> Built: 1892 | Lost: 1920

1922 Bethany Lutheran Children's Home

Soon after the first Bethany Children's Home was reduced to ashes, construction began on a new facility on the same site. Children were housed in other buildings until the new home opened in 1923. The brick building (left, date unknown) stood three-and-a-half stories high with roof dormers and a cupola. The facility was later converted to a home for troubled teens; in 1965 it suffered major fire damage, but remained in use until it was demolished in 1974. A new building on the site became part of Northwood Children's Center, which evolved from the "Ladies Relief Society" begun by Sara Stearns in the 1880s. That organization became the Duluth Home Society in 1887, the Children's Home Society in 1904, and the Northwood Home in 1956.

> 4000 West 9th Street
> Architect: UNKNOWN
> Built: 1922 | Lost: 1974

The 1881 St. Luke's Hospital

12 North 3rd Avenue East

Architect: UNKNOWN

Built: UNKNOWN | Lost: UNKNOWN

When an outbreak of typhoid fever threatened Duluth in 1881, Reverend J. A. Cummings of St. Paul's Episcopal Church responded by furnishing an abandoned blacksmith shop along Third Avenue East (left, date unknown) with a few chairs, three beds, and a stove donated by British officials at the Duluth emigrant station. Church leaders chose St. Luke's as the hospital's name because they first met to plan the facility on October 18, 1881, St. Luke's Day (in his letter to the Colossians, the apostle Paul calls Luke "our beloved physician"). Cummings' first patients were a railroad worker with a broken leg and a destitute old man who received typhoid treatment without charge. Cummings placed an ad in local papers and within a week the tiny hospital had filled its twelve beds. Records do not indicate when the hospital was demolished; the Hotel Duluth now stands over its location.

Typhoid would also prompt the creation of St. Mary's Hospital and remained a problem until the creation of the Lakewood Pumping Station in 1897. The bacteria that cause typhoid, *typhus bacillus*, develops in tainted water supplies, and before the Pump House Duluth used a very primitive system to deliver fresh water to its residents: a hogshead barrel filled with Lake Superior water and transported to homes and businesses in a horse-drawn cart.

The 1883 St. Luke's Hospital

323 2nd Avenue East

Architect: GEORGE WIRTH

Built: 1883 | Lost: CA. 1920

When the first St. Luke's proved too small to meet the needs of Duluth's ill and injured just a year or two after it opened, St. Luke's constructed a new thirty-eight bed facility on the corner of Fourth Street and Second Avenue East (right, date unknown). The simple two-story frame building featured a gabled roof, a porch overlooking the city and harbor, many windows, and an entrance on Second Avenue. The *Duluth News Tribune* congratulated the management for providing a hospital "with everything necessary for the caring of the sick and wounded." By 1900, caring for those sick and wounded again called for a larger building. When the new St. Luke's opened at Ninth Avenue East and First Street in 1902, the Second Avenue hospital became a rooming house until about 1920, when it was demolished; no other structures have been built on the site. The 1902 building still stands, but is hardly recognizable amidst the sprawling campus of facilities owned by St. Luke's.

2002 West 3rd Street
Architect: FATHER GREGORY
Built: 1888 | Lost: 1958

In 1892 Dr. John B. Murphy, in Duluth for a medical convention, performed the first appendectomy in Minnesota at St. Mary's. Witnesses to the surgery that day included Drs. Charles and William Mayo, founders of the Mayo Clinic. Three years later St. Mary's own Dr. Magie performed the state's first gastroenterostomy.

By 1896 overcrowding forced the sisters to build a new facility at 404 East Third Street; the hospital moved there in 1898. The old hospital in Lincoln Park became the first St. James Catholic Orphanage, also run by the Benedictine nuns. In 1911 the building became the first St. Ann's Home for the Aged. St. Ann's moved to East Third Street in 1958 on the former site of the Clinton Markell House (see page 22). That same year the West End building was demolished to make room for a parking lot serving a low-income high-rise apartment. The 1898 hospital has grown and more buildings have been added. St. Mary's later merged with the former Duluth Clinic and Miller-Dwan Medical Center, and its buildings and parking lots sprawl over much of what was once Duluth's Ashtabula Heights neighborhood. Today it is part of the Essentia Health system.

The 1888 St. Mary's Hospital

Monks from St. John's Abbey in Collegeville built this structure next to St. Clement's Catholic Church in the West End, intending to use it as a boys' school and seminary (the next door St. Clement's Church can be seen in the sketch, date unknown). When that plan did not materialize, they rented the building to Benedictine nuns who used the handsome four-story brick building with arched windows and a Mansard roof for a hospital they named St. Mary's (right, date unknown). The hospital opened with one hundred beds but no running water or electricity. St. Scholastica's Mother Alexia Kerst and six other nuns, along with surgeon Dr. William H. Magie, comprised the hospital's staff.

St. Mary's was innovative in its early years, when the timber industry reigned in northern Minnesota. Long before medical insurance, St. Mary's own Sister Amata sold those who worked the lumber camps "lumberjack hospital tickets." The cards cost seventy cents a month and guaranteed the jacks—who performed dangerous work and were rarely flush with money—medical care and a bed. It was one of the first plans of its kind in the nation and helped the young hospital stay financially afloat. (The program ended in 1913 with Minnesota's Workman Compensation law.)

Morgan Park Hospital

Falcon Street
Architects: GEORGE & ARTHUR DEAN
Built: 1916 | Lost: 1934

Like many of the homes and buildings in Morgan Park, its hospital was built of concrete mixed by the Portland Cement Company, part of the U.S. Steel complex. Overlooking the St. Louis River, the four-story building (right, date unknown) offered thirty-two patient beds on the second and third floors. Its first floor had a kitchen, laundry, and a garage for an ambulance; solariums faced the south. A planned expansion in 1917 was canceled when fire destroyed the fourth floor nurses' dormitory. Twenty-four patients escaped the blaze. Unfortunately, a patient awaiting emergency surgery died when he finally reached St. Luke's Hospital. The building was repaired, but expansion plans were shelved. By 1927, with improved road conditions to Duluth and its larger hospitals, Morgan Park no longer needed its own medical facility. That year it closed and was converted into an employment office for the steel plant. It was demolished in 1934. A house now occupies the site.

Dean & Dean's Other Great Lost Morgan Park Building

Chicago architects George and Arthur Dean—or at least their firm—designed many of the buildings in Morgan Park. Dean & Dean played an active role in shaping the nation's Prairie School architectural theory and national movement led by well-known architects Frank Lloyd Wright and Louis Sullivan. In 1916 Larry Franklin Robinson left Wright's offices and went to work for Dean & Dean, where he was put in charge of two U.S. Steel projects, including Morgan Park. So Robinson, not one of the Dean brothers, likely drew the actual plans for the Hospital and the Good Fellowship Club (shown at right, date unknown).

U.S. Steel built the Good Fellowship Club for Morgan Park residents, all of whom worked for U.S. Steel when the community was first built. Cost was $153,000. Constructed of concrete like most other Morgan Park buildings, the Club was faced in stucco and measured 158 by 258 feet with four wings grouped around a central core. The building featured an auditorium with seating for 480 people, a gymnasium, a running track, a cafeteria, bowling lanes, shower facilities, a youth section, and a swimming pool. There were outdoor courts for volleyball, basketball, tennis, lawn bowling, and croquet. It was the center of social life in Morgan Park, and members paid $1.50 per month in dues.

By 1968 membership had declined, perhaps because in the 1940s Morgan Park was opened to all Duluth citizens and the city took control of the club. The building closed in 1980. When the city decided to demolish the club, the Minnesota Historical Society resisted: the building was considered part of a historic district. The *Duluth News Tribune* called it "an albatross." In October 1981 the Minnesota Historical Society relented and the building was demolished; later many residents of Morgan Park regretted the loss. A smaller clubhouse was built on the same location.

1869 St. Paul's Episcopal

209 North Lake Avenue
Architect: UNKNOWN
Built: 1869 | Lost: 1925

Completed in the fall of 1869, St. Paul's Episcopal stood as Duluth's first dedicated church building and held its first service on Christmas Day of that year. George Sargent, one of the Episcopalian elders who started the church, came to Duluth to act as Jay Cooke's representative. Sargent named the Church St. Paul's in recognition of the Cheltenham, Pennsylvania, church Cooke considered his home parish. And so St. Paul's in Duluth became known as "Jay Cooke's Church." The Pennsylvania church even paid for the Duluth church's baptismal font, made of brownstone cut from a Fond du Lac quarry in 1872. St. Paul's (right, date unknown) was a wooden building, probably designed by the carpenters who built it, with Gothic-style windows on the first story, round windows above, and a small belfry over the roof near the back. In 1869 it stood alone atop the hillside, overlooking the growing village of Duluth. The 1869 St. Paul's served Duluth's Episcopalians until 1913, when the congregation had grown so large a new building was necessary. Lots were purchased on East Superior Street and Seventeenth Avenue, and the new church (designed by renowned architect Bertram Goodhue) opened in 1913. The 1869 building was vacated in 1912 and demolished in June 1925 for a parking lot.

1870 First Presbyterian

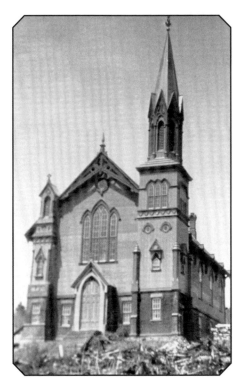

231 East 2nd Street
Architect: UNKNOWN
Built: 1870 | Lost: 1971

Although theirs was not the first church building in Duluth, the First Presbyterian congregation—established June 1, 1869—was Duluth Township's earliest organized church. Pioneers Luke Marvin and John Hunter served as the church's first two elders, and their families and descendants led the church for generations. Until the church was finished in 1870, parishioners took turns hosting services in their homes. Duluth's second church building served the Presbyterians until 1891. The picturesque wooden building (left, date unknown), designed in the Gothic style, featured a tall corner tower, Gothic windows and doors, and bargeboards in the gable. Photos indicate it was likely painted in several colors. Three of the tower's windows appear to make a face looking out over Duluth.

After the Presbyterians moved into their new church (designed by Traphagen and Fitzpatrick) diagonally across Second Street in 1891, the 1870 building served as home for other congregations. From 1891 to 1923 it was home to the German Roman Catholic Church of St. Anthony of Padua. It next became the Finnish Evangelical Lutheran Church (which later changed its name to Messiah Lutheran Church) from 1923 to 1970. It was demolished in 1971; the lot is now used by the Rainbow Community Center's parking lot.

1888 Pilgrim Congregational

2 East 2nd Street

Architect: UNKNOWN

Built: 1888 | Lost: 1915

Reverend Charles C. Salter came to Duluth from Minneapolis to organize and serve as minister of Duluth's Pilgrim Congregational Church, which he established on January 18, 1871 (see page 62). A wood-frame church was built on the corner of Second Street and First Avenue East that same year and served until 1888 when this Gothic structure was built at Lake Avenue and Second Street at a cost of $55,828 (about $1.3 million today). The sandstone church—its body was gray and its trim pink—could seat 750 parishioners on the main floor and 250 more in the balcony. The church (right, ca. 1891) featured a tall corner tower, a large rose window on the Second Street façade, and many Gothic-style windows. By 1914 most of its wealthy congregation had moved farther east in the city. In 1916 the church's building committee purchased lots at 2310 East Fourth Street where they built a new church designed by Frederick German and Leif Jennsen. The 1888 church was demolished in 1915 and some of its slate and stone was used in the new church. Ward Ames and Julius Barnes, who financed the city's early Y.M.C.A. and Y.W.C.A. buildings, built the Ames-Barnes Building on the site of the 1888 church. That building was used as the Boys Department of the YMCA; today it is home to Minnesota Teen Challenge, which helps young adults struggling with drug and alcohol addiction.

1892 Merritt Memorial Methodist
(aka Central Avenue Methodist)

4600 West Superior Street

Architect: UNKNOWN

Built: 1892 | Lost: 1993

Reverend James Peet, Oneota's first Methodist minister, lived in Superior, Wisconsin, and canoed across the bay to conduct services in Oneota from 1856 until he moved there in 1859. He first held services in homes and then at Oneota School. In 1870 Oneota built a small one-room wooden church at Forty-Sixth Avenue West and Superior Street. That building served until 1892, when the congregation built a new church on the same site, a Romanesque Revival structure with a square tower and arched windows (left, date unknown). Its first pastor, Lucien F. Merritt, served from 1890 to 1895. After he died in Ohio in 1900, the church was renamed the L. F. Merritt Memorial Methodist Episcopal Church in his honor. In 1921 Merritt Memorial merged with Asbury Methodist. The newly joined congregation had the building moved to 728 Central Avenue North and rechristened it Central Avenue Methodist Church. April 1992 saw the final service at the 1892 church; it was razed a year later (the new Laura MacArthur Elementary was built over part of its lot). The congregation built a new church at 6682 Grand Avenue and changed its name again, this time to Asbury United Methodist Church. One of the 1892 church's stained-glass windows now graces Asbury United.

1871 & 1893 First Methodist

301 West 2nd Street
Architect: UNKNOWN
Built: 1871 | Lost: CA. 1893

215 North 3rd Avenue West
Architects: McMILLEN & RADCLIFFE
Built: 1893 | Lost: 1968

The Reverend Harvey Webb arrived in Duluth in October 1869 and began conducting Methodist church services at Portland Township's school house on Superior Street at Third Avenue East. In 1870 his congregation (including trustees Luther Mendenhall, George C. Stone, and Clinton Markell) took a loan from Jay Cooke's Western Land Association and built their first church building, a wood-frame structure with Gothic details, at the northwest corner of Third Avenue West and Second Street (top left, date unknown). The Panic of 1873, which had bankrupted Cooke, took its toll on the church as well: many of its members ran businesses financed by Cooke. By 1882, First Methodist had just eighty-six active members.

But Duluth boomed back in the mid 1880s, and so did the Methodist congregation. They purchased lots directly behind their church in 1886, and in 1893 the congregation moved straight up from the old church to a new and very large Gothic church of red brownstone (shown in the undated photos below). The imposing structure (built for $120,000 or nearly $3 million today) had a tall square corner tower with belfry and a shorter tower along the avenue. A Gothic window faced Third Avenue and a stained-glass rose window graced the Third Street façade. It sat 1,600 people. In 1925 the congregation built a community building called "The Meth" on the site of the first church, which had been dismantled, moved to Virginia, Minnesota, and reassembled as Virginia's First Methodist Church.

Chimes were gifted to the Methodist Church in 1921 by Thomas and George Martin in memory of their mother, Sara Jane Martin. Forged of Lake Superior copper, the chimes' ten bells weighed from 200 to 1,800 pounds each. They could be heard a mile away and rang every Sunday for services, each day at noon, and on national holidays—but never at funerals, as the Martins had stipulated. The chimes fell silent in 1966 when the congregation moved to First United Methodist Church (the "Coppertop Church," designed by world-renowned church architect Pietro Bellushi) on seven acres along Skyline Parkway at Central Entrance. The parish then sold the chimes and the 1893 church. In 1969 the building was demolished to make room for a Duluth Clinic parking lot, now an Essentia Health parking lot.

1895 First Evangelical Lutheran

31 East 3rd Street

Architect: UNKNOWN

Built: 1895 | Lost: 1972

Fifty Duluthians organized the First Norwegian Danish Evangelical Lutheran Church congregation in October 1871. For a short time they held services at St. Paul's Episcopal Church before building their own facility at Fourth Avenue East and Tenth Street in 1871. Unfortunately, it was literally torn apart by the legendary "gales of November"—a windstorm in November 1874 destroyed the building. The parish then purchased the former Swedish Methodist Church at Fourth Avenue West and Fourth Street, but didn't stay long. In 1887 they built another at Third Street and First Avenue East, but that one went down in an 1895 blaze.

That same year the undaunted Evangelicals built a clapboard-sided two-and-a-half-story church with a gothic steeple on the 1887 church's foundation (right, date unknown). This time the building lasted seventy-seven years, serving its congregation until 1950 when the parish built a church at 1100 East Superior Street and changed its name to First Lutheran. Christ Temple Church moved into the 1895 church and held its services there until 1970; the church was razed in 1972. The lot it sat on is now the southwest corner of Central Hillside Park.

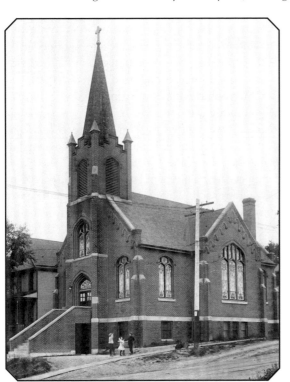

1902 Bethesda Norwegian Lutheran

531 East 5th Street

Architect: UNKNOWN

Built: 1902 | Lost: 1977

Between fifteen or nineteen members of the First Evangelical Lutheran Church broke away in 1892 to form Bethesda Norwegian Lutheran Church. It took the congregation twelve years to build its first church building, a brick Gothic Revival church that went up on the corner of Sixth Avenue East and Fifth Street (left, date unknown). In 1945 Bethesda Norwegian merged with the very church its founders walked away from in 1892, and in 1950 its congregation moved to the new Superior Street First Lutheran Church. St. Matthew's American Lutheran Church called the 1902 church home from 1950 to 1967, after which The Church of God of Prophecy moved in. That congregation left in 1974 and the building stood empty until its 1977 demolition, which made way for a Seven-Eleven store; that building is currently AutoMedics, an auto repair shop.

1870 Sacred Heart Roman Catholic

Prior to 1870 Catholics in Duluth attended masses at various locations led by Slovenian missionary priest John Chebul. In 1870 land was donated for a Catholic church on the corner of Fourth Street and Second Avenue West, and Father Chebul began an effort to raise funds for a

> 201 West 4th Street
> Architect: UNKNOWN
> Built: 1870 | Lost: 1892

building. Chebul himself gave $1,700 (over $28,000 today) and others contributed enough to build the wooden church and rectory shown at right (date unknown). The church opened in February 1871, the same year Father George Keller of Lacrosse, Wisconsin, became Duluth's first permanent pastor. Chebul continued opening other Catholic churches in the region. Painted white, Sacred Heart measured seventy by thirty-five feet and featured Gothic windows and a small squat steeple which could be seen from far out on Lake Superior. The steeple held no bell until 1877. The church primarily served Duluth's Polish and Irish Catholics. A kerosene lamp used to illuminate the building accidentally set it on fire the evening of July 2, 1892. Flames quickly spread to the steeple, and the church burned to the ground; the next door rectory was damaged. A nearby church hall held masses until a new brick-and-brownstone Sacred Heart Cathedral, designed by Gearhard Tenbusch, opened in 1896.

1894 St. Stephen's Lutheran (and Good Shepherd Catholic)

Organized in 1890, St. Stephen's Lutheran German Evangelical congregation built its church in 1894 on the southwest corner of Sixty-Seventh Avenue West and Raleigh Street in

> 109 South 59th Avenue West
> Architect: UNKNOWN
> Built: 1894 | Lost: 1959

West Duluth. The small, white clapboard building had a short tower but no steeple.

In 1916 the congregation of St. Stephen's moved on, selling their church for $200 to the Good Shepherd Roman Catholic parish, organized in 1914. Good Shepherd purchased lots at 5905 Raleigh Street and moved the church building to the new site by rolling it down Raleigh Street on logs. By 1919 the building (shown here in 1921) had been enlarged and remodeled with the addition of a steeple, a new entrance, and a stained-glass window. The church served until 1959 when the congregation had it demolished to make room for a new church. The Duluth Diocese closed the newer Good Shepherd in 1997 due to "a shortage of priests." That church has been home to the Raleigh-Edison Charter School since 1999.

1885 & 1904 St. Jean-Baptiste Catholic

1100 East Superior Street (1885)
Architect: UNKNOWN
Built: 1885 | Lost: CA. 1925

2432 West 3rd Street (1904)
Architects: GERMAN & LIGNELL
Built: 1904 | Lost: 1996

The French left their mark on Duluth as early as 1679, when namesake Daniel Greysolon Sieur du Lhut portaged across Minnesota Point at *Onigamiinsing* ("Little Portage"), the spot where Duluthians later dug a ship canal. Soon after came the voyageurs. When the fur trade died, French-Canadians worked in mines and lumber camps.

Prior to the 1880s, Duluth's Catholic French-Canadian population attended Mass at Sacred Heart. By 1884 the French-Canadians made up the largest Catholic population in Duluth and they organized their own French national parish, St. Jean-Baptiste. A year later they built a modest wooden structure in the heart of The Glenn beneath Point of Rocks at Eleventh Avenue West and Superior Street (below, left). The French-Canadian population, employed for the most part as laborers and building tradesmen, continued to grow. In 1888 two hundred French Canadians called Duluth home; by 1902, that number had grown to five hundred. In 1904 the parish decided it was time for a bigger church.

At this same time Duluth's growing population of Italian immigrants (many of whom already lived in the Glenn) had no church of its own, one with a priest who could give sermons in both Italian and English. So they bought the 1885 St. Jean-Baptiste and renamed it St. Peter's. It stood until 1926 when a new St. Peter's was built atop Point of Rocks (see next page).

The French moved deeper into Duluth's West End in 1905, building a new church and school at Third Street and Twenty-Fifth Avenue West (below, right). The two-story red brick church employed an unusual design, with its school on the first floor and the church on the second. The front gable's tall triple-arched windows stood over a stone arched entrance; the gables were adorned with decorative brick work.

St. Jean-Baptiste absorbed St. Clement's congregation in 1975 when the German church was sold (see next page) and joined with Sts. Peter and Paul's, originally built to serve Duluth's Poles. The congregation celebrated Mass at both churches until 1996, when St. Jean-Baptiste was razed and replaced by the Holy Family Catholic Church, where both former parishioners of and artifacts from all three churches found a new home.

1926 St. Peter's Catholic Church

In 1925, outgrowing the former St. Jean-Baptiste Church they had purchased from the French in 1905, St. Peter's congregation built a Romanesque-Gothic church—designed by parishioner Peter Summers, son of Duluth's first Italian immigrants—at 818 West Third Street. Its position atop Point of Rocks was wonderfully appropriate for a church named after the disciple Simon, who Christ renamed Peter, the "rock" upon which he would build his church.

Although most of St. Peter's parishioners were southern Italian, a few were highly-skilled stone masons from northern Italy. They constructed much of the brick and stone work that still graces Duluth, including the Sellwood building, Old Central and Denfeld High Schools, St. Scholastica's Tower Hall, the Lakeside Pumping Station, countless bluestone foundations and retaining walls, Enger Tower, and the bridges of Seven Bridges Road. These artisans volunteered to build the church out of blue, yellow, and gray native stone harvested from Duluth's hillside near Twin Ponds.

The Catholic Diocese closed St. Peter's in 2010. At the time of this writing former parishioners are attempting to save the building and convert it into a community center. The Diocese plans to demolish the church and sell the lot.

1911 St. Clement's Catholic

I n 1887 Catholic German immigrants in the West End built a wooden church along West Third Street. That building lasted to 1910, when fire destroyed it.

> 2032 West 3rd Street
> Architect: ERHARD BRIELMAIER
> Built: 1911 | Lost: 1992

St. Clement's looked to German-born Milwaukee architect Erhard Brielmaier, who had designed Milwaukee's Basilica of St. Josephat, which he modeled after Rome's St. Peter's Basilica. The two-story brick St. Clement's featured both Gothic and Romanesque styling and sported arched windows, turrets, and two towers, one a 134-foot square bell tower with an open belfry which held the bell from the first St. Clement's. A triple-arched stone entrance was surmounted by a large rose window in the front gable.

As Duluth's neighborhoods became less ethnically divided, so did its churches. Mass attendance also started to decline. Soon the West End had more Catholic churches than it needed. St. Clement's closed in 1972, its congregation absorbed by St. Jean-Baptiste's.

In 1975 St. Clement's Church was purchased by the Twin Ports Ministry to Seafarers, an ecumenical organization that ministers to "those who visit our ports by ship." The Seafarers converted the rectory into their facilities and demolished the church in 1992. The former church lot now provides parking for the Seafarer's facility.

1922 Tifereth Israel

302 East 4th Street
Architect: UNKNOWN
Built: 1922 | Lost: CA. 1995

Duluth's first residents of Jewish descent were brothers Asa and Henry Leopold and newlyweds Bernard and Nettie Silberstein. The Silbersteins were immigrants from Hungary who arrived in the United States in the 1860s, married in Detroit, and came to Duluth in 1870. Bernard set up a dry goods store. The Leopold brothers opened the first mercantile store in Duluth in 1869. Together with other western European Jews, the Silbersteins and Leopolds founded Duluth's first synagogue, Temple Emanuel, in 1891. There was no building and services were performed by "pious local elders" and occasionally a visiting rabbi. Most of Duluth's Jewish population was Russian or Eastern European. They began arriving in Duluth in the 1880s. By 1900 Duluth had four synagogues—Tifereth Israel, Temple Emanuel, Adas Israel, and B'nai Israel—serving about 1,500 members. At one point six separate synagogues served Duluth, but the Zenith City's Jewish population would grow no higher than its peak of 4,000 in the 1930s.

Russian Jewish immigrants organized the Orthodox Kofereth Israel Congregation in 1893, later changing the name to Tifereth Israel. They purchased a small house at Third Avenue East and Fifth Street and converted it into a synagogue. With no formal rabbi, the congregants conducted services themselves. Cantors served at the High Holidays, and from time to time the rabbi from another Duluth synagogue, Adas Israel, helped out as well.

In 1922 the congregation spent $50,000 to build a two-story brick synagogue on the southeast corner of Third Avenue East and Fourth Street,

with a round Star of David window centered in the front gable. The synagogue (shown here, date unknown) remained Orthodox until 1945 when its members voted to become Conservative. Tifereth Israel was often referred to as the Fourth Street Synagogue.

In November 1969, after Duluth's Jewish population dropped below 1,200, Conservative congregation, Tifereth Israel, joined with Reform congregation, Temple Emanuel, to form a new congregation, Temple Israel. The Tifereth Israel congregation left their synagogue to attend services at the Temple Emanuel building at 1902 East Fourth Street. That building was later purchased by the Glad Tidings Assembly of God Church; Glad Tidings has since changed its name to The River Church. Temple Israel is now housed at 1602 East Second Street, the former Jewish Educational Center.

Messiah Lutheran Church purchased the Tifereth Israel building and held services there until 1994. The building was demolished in about 1995; a parking ramp for St. Mary's Medical Center now occupies the lot.

Duluth's only other remaining synagogue is Orthodox Adas Israel Congregation at 302 East Third Street, also known as the Third Street Synagogue. The congregation, originally Lithuanian Orthodox Jews, was organized in the 1880s in today's Canal Park Business District south of Buchanan Street. In 1930, the West End's B'nai Israel Synagogue disbanded, as many of its members had moved to the Central Hillside. Adas Israel, Tifereth Israel, Shaara Tzedak, and Talmud Torah Congregation absorbed its members.

PART THREE

LOST COMMERCIAL BUILDINGS

The Spalding Hotel (1889 – 1963)

Lost Commercial Buildings

Until 1870, buildings in Duluth were made entirely of wood, and many constructed for commercial use either burned or were knocked down to make room for more modern buildings. Little record remains of individual buildings such as these. Duluth's first commercial building—the 1856 Jefferson House—was Duluth's first home, its first hotel, St. Louis County's first seat of government, and the home of Duluth's first newspaper. It wasn't until William Branch built Branch's Hall in 1870 that Duluth began using bricks (and soon, locally quarried sandstone) to construct its buildings.

With little housing in place during its first two boom periods, hotels played an important role in Duluth's development, not only as housing for travelers, but as places to conduct business and, for some young men of means, to live until they married and built homes for their families. Most of Duluth's historic downtown hotels—some grand, some pedestrian—are long gone or have ben adapted for other use. The Cascade Hotel at 101 West Third Street has been turned into an apartment house, and the Arrowhead Hotel at 225 North First Avenue West now serves recovering addicts. The last historic hotel to be built in downtown Duluth—the Hotel Duluth at 227 East Superior Street—is used primarily as a senior living facility.

Duluth first became a theater town in 1869, and over the years it enjoyed a host of facilities—some quite extravagant—that were often described as the largest or most beautiful "in the Midwest." Each one is gone. The only standing reminder of Duluth's heydays as a theater town is the NorShor Theatre, built as an Art Deco movie house in 1940 out of the gutted interiors of the Orpheum Theatre and Orpheum Garage. The city of Duluth purchased the NorShor in 2010, and it remains closed while architects develop plans for renovation that put the building in compliance with the Americans with Disabilities Act.

When Duluth started building business blocks—buildings that serve multiple purposes, usually with retail storefronts on the first floor and offices and/or apartments above—there seems to have been a race to see who could build the most architecturally interesting building. Many featured brownstone trim and carved stonework that could not be replaced today. Those not featured among these pages include the Brown Brothers Block at 10 East Superior, the Fowler Building at 2 West Superior Street (home

to Fremuith's Department store), and the Fidelity Building next to it. The Fowler and Fidelity were razed in 1968 to make way for Minnesota Power Plaza. Many others still stand, but their original architectural features have been removed or hidden by changes to their exterior that are not always historically sensitive. These include the Commercial Club/Athletic Club, the Temple Opera Block, the 1902 Masonic Temple, the Hayes Block, the Weiland Block, and the Silberstein-Bondy Building. Many of these are featured in this book's "Missing Pieces" section.

Fortunately, Duluth has retained a large portion of its historic building stock, many found in downtown Duluth: the 1895 Board of Trade Building (that's the original 1885 Board of Trade pictured in flames in the photo above), the Torrey Building, the Lonsdale Building, the Wolvin (now Missabe) Building, the Medical Arts Building, the Alworth Building, the Sellwood Building, the Wirth Block, the Kitchi Gammi Club, the DeWitt-Seitz Building, and the Canal Block. Other historic commercial buildings can still be found in the business districts of Gary/New Duluth, West Duluth, the West End, Lakeside, and Woodland.

The Clark House

West 100 Block of Superior Street

Architect: UNKNOWN

Built: 1870 | Lost: 1881

As Duluth's first building boom began in 1869 in anticipation of Jay Cooke's Great Northern Railroad, George Sargent—Cooke's agent in Duluth—directed the construction of the Clark House, a large, three-story hotel with a mansard roof, cupola, and a 150-foot veranda across the front. The building faced Superior Street but had a large wing protruding from the rear of the building that stretched toward First Street; its central core measured 50 by 100 feet, the wing 40 by 110 feet. When it opened in July, 1870, the Clark House was Duluth's second hotel: the much more simply designed Bay View House had sprung up in 1869. (While the 1856 Jefferson House did serve as a hotel and boarding house, it was built as a family home.) The Clark House's name referenced the E. W. Clark brokerage firm in Philadelphia, where Cooke began his career.

Under the direction of its first proprietor, Dr. Quincy Adams Scott of Pittsburgh, the Clark House became the site of Duluth's important social events, as it was the only building in town with facilities to handle large gatherings. An annual ball given by the Duluth firemen of the volunteer department was held at the Clark House beginning in 1872. Soon after the Lake Superior and Mississippi Railway reached Duluth in August of 1870, members of the Minnesota State Legislature took the train to Duluth to conduct a meeting in the Clark House and to take part in a huge celebration thrown by Duluthians.

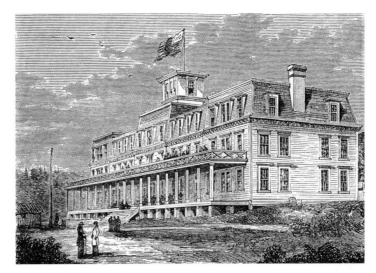

When Eastern and European capitalists came to Duluth to do business, they stayed at the Clark House. (Some historians have reported that Jay Cooke himself once stayed at the Clark House, and have offered a photograph of several bearded men at the Clark House as proof; but Cooke visited Duluth just once, in 1866.)

Scott had left the Clark House by 1880, and Thomas Cullyford took over the Hotel's management. On November 16, 1881, a fire began in the boiler room of the Clark House and quickly spread to all parts of the wooden structure. The hotel was completely destroyed in what was at that time the biggest fire the town had ever witnessed. The loss was estimated at $50,000, over $1 million today.

While the volunteer fire department (then made up of the town's businessman and other professionals) fought valiantly, the best they could do was to keep the fire from spreading to other buildings. They also managed to retrieve a great deal of furniture (much of it already damaged beyond repair) before the building was consumed, and the *Duluth Daily News* reported that "the large stock of liquors was saved and is stored at different places about town." The Clark House was replaced a year later when the Metropolitan Block was built on the site; that building still stands, although it has seen several renovations.

Bay View House

401 West Superior Street

Architect: UNKNOWN

Built: 1869 | Lost: 1888

The first building in Duluth constructed specifically as a hotel, the Bay View House offered sanctuary to those lucky enough to get a room during the winter of 1869–'70, when the town was booming and there was no other public house for the waves of people arriving daily. It was full almost year-round, but business declined when the Clark House opened in the summer of 1870. Bay View House was forced to drop its rates from $4.50 a day to $2.50 a day to compete with the more opulent hotel three blocks east. Located on the western edge of downtown Duluth in the middle of mud streets and plank sidewalks, the Bay View was a three-story wood frame structure; its original entrance faced Fourth Avenue West. The building was later enlarged, and the entrance relocated along Superior Street. The Bay View was demolished in 1888 to make room for the original Palladio Building, lost in 1937.

Merchant's Hotel

202 – 204 West Superior Street

Architect: GEORGE WIRTH

Built: 1882 | Lost: 1907

When first constructed, the Merchant's Hotel was a three-story wood frame building with a corner entrance. It burned on February 28, 1884 (shown in the photo below right), but was immediately rebuilt with a brick façade, entrances on both Superior Street and Second Avenue West, and an addition off the back. Oliver Traphagen, who at that time worked as a carpenter in Duluth for St. Paul architect George Wirth, oversaw the building's reconstruction. When it was complete, he promptly moved in, staying in the hotel until his 1891 marriage.

Merchant's was operated by German immigrant William Meinhardt and specifically catered to "commercial travelers," who were charged between $2 and $4 a day, depending on which of the fifty-eight "strictly first class" rooms were available. The hotel was outfitted with electric light and steam heat. It closed in 1907 and was demolished to make room for the Sellwood Building, which still stands.

First & Second St. Louis Hotels

318 – 330 West Superior St
Architects: George Wirth, Oliver Traphagen
Built: 1882, 1888 | Lost: 1893

Architects: Traphagen & Fitzpatrick
Built: 1894 | Lost: 1932

After his beloved Clark House burned in 1881, proprietor Thomas Cullyford hired St. Paul's George Wirth to design the St. Louis Hotel on the southeast corner of Fourth Avenue West and Superior Street. A typical Victorian design of four stories with red and white brick, the St. Louis—named for the river that creates the Duluth-Superior harbor—featured two square roof towers, columns, balconies, and decorative window hoods all capped with an elaborate cornice. The hotel resembled the Metropolitan block, another Wirth creation.

Like the Clark House before it, Cullyford's new hotel would serve as a gathering place for financiers and politicians, though in a few years it would have competition from the Spalding Hotel and the Kitchi Gammi Club for that distinction. It was also "famous for its food and hospitality."

In 1888—as the grand Spalding Hotel was being built one block west—Cullyford hired Wirth's former protégé, Oliver Traphagen, to design an eastern wing for the building that would nearly double the hotel's size. The new wing, called the Brighton Hotel, repeated the architectural features of the original. Cullyford managed it himself while he hired James Butchart and Alexander Michaud to manage the St. Louis, which had become a favored temporary home for touring performers booked at the nearby Lyceum Theatre—and the unofficial home of the Duluth Snowshoe and Toboggan Association.

Tragedy struck the St. Louis on January 13, 1893, when two people perished in a fire that ultimately destroyed the original hotel building. Smoke and water damaged the Brighton, but not enough to keep it from reopening that March.

The following year Traphagen and his partner, Francis Fitzpatrick, designed a new St Louis Hotel, which was located east of and atop the Brighton lot. The new St. Louis stood six stories tall with a patterned brick cornice and carved stone ornamentation. Under the direction of Butchart and Michaud and their partner Louis Rouchleau, the new St. Louis regained its previous popularity with visitors. But by the late 1920s it was in decline, described in a 1948 WEBC radio program as "a rat's nest and fire trap" at the end of its life. It was razed in 1932 to make room for the Medical Arts Building, an Art Deco masterpiece which still stands today.

The Spalding Hotel

424 West Superior Street
Architect: JAMES J. EGAN
Built: 1889 | Lost: 1963

It took two years after ground was broken in June of 1887 for tradesmen to complete the massive, two-hundred room Spalding Hotel, built to rival the St. Louis Hotel one block east. Although the hotel's investors included such prominent Duluthians as R. S. Munger, G. G. Hartley, Owen Fargusson, Luther Mendenhall, and George Spencer, it was named for the group's president, William W. Spalding (pictured; Mr. Spalding's residence is featured on page 25), a Pennsylvania native who first came to Duluth in 1869 with his brother I. C. Together the Spalding brothers built a general store on the southeast corner of Superior Street and Fifth Avenue West, the same spot on which the Spalding would rise twenty years later.

Standing seven stories high over Superior Street and eight stories over Michigan Street, the Spalding dominated downtown Duluth when it was first constructed. Built of brown sandstone, red brick, and terra cotta, the Spalding's top floor was capped with a mansard roof covered with tile shingles and featured many dormers and round corner towers. Its architect, Chicago's James J. Egan, was nationally known for his church and hotel designs. When it opened, the Spalding was described as an "artistic blending of Gothic, Corinthian, and Egyptian styles." The interior walls were paneled and trimmed with quarter-sawn oak.

The Spalding opened on June 10, 1889, with a grand ball to show off its finery. Besides guests rooms, facilities included a Ladies Writing Room (below) and Ladies Waiting Room (page 81, bottom left; the Spalding also had a separate entrance for women on Fifth Avenue), a grand lobby outfitted with overstuffed furniture (page 81, top left), a Sun Room (page 81, top right), a billiard room, and the "largest and handsomest"

barroom in the city. It also featured a rooftop pavilion and several dining rooms, including the Palm Room (pictured, bottom right) and a separate dining room for children. Its sixth-floor main dining room, said to offer the finest views of the harbor, measured forty by eighty-two feet and had a twenty-five-foot-tall vaulted ceiling; its walls were adorned with "delicate and beautiful" frescoes. To keep diners happy, the Spalding's 2,550-square foot kitchen turned out fine cuisine, its planked whitefish a house speciality. (Legend has it that in its early days the Spalding served the freshest duck in town: the land behind the Spalding was still quite marshy, a perfect waterfowl habitat; when someone ordered the roast duck, a waiter was sent out back with a shotgun to procure the meat.)

When it first opened, the Spalding was the only hotel in Minnesota

with an "indicator dial" in each room with which the occupant could give up to twenty-seven different orders to the hotel office. Its investors spared no expense outfitting the hotel with the best furniture, carpeting, linens, table wear, and other finery available at the time. Not every sleeping room had its own bathroom, but even the common facilities were elegantly appointed.

Like the St. Louis, the Spalding became a popular temporary home for unmarried professional men newly arrived in Duluth as well as traveling investors and land agents. During Duluth's expansion in the 1890s, many of the real-estate transactions that shaped the city took place within its walls.

Throughout its seventy-four years of operation the Spalding hosted many prominent guests, including boxer Jack Dempsey, Presidents Theodore Roosevelt and Harry S. Truman, and Polish Prime Minister (and celebrated pianist) Ignace Paderewski. As the neighboring Bowery—which stretched from Fourth Avenue west to Mesaba Avenue along Michigan Street and Superior Street west of Fifth Avenue—grew around it, the Spalding's popularity declined and, like many other buildings around it, fell into disrepair. By the time it was set to be demolished in September 1963 as part of Duluth's Gateway Urban Renewal Project, it had become a residential hotel. Prior to demolition one of the Spalding's grand wooden doorway arches was salvaged and is now installed in O'Gara's restaurant in St. Paul. The Ordean Building now stands on the Spalding site.

Hotel Phillips / Cody Hotel

332 North Central Avenue
Architect: UNKNOWN
Built: 1888 | Lost: 1973

I n 1888, the same year the Village of West Duluth was established, J. W. Phillips built a hotel—financed by Union Blast Furnace—and named it for himself. The three-story frame building featured a second-floor porch that stretched across the building along Central Avenue. Guests were offered twenty-two rooms on the second and third floors while the first was reserved for retail businesses, including (over the years) the City Drug Store, the National Tea Company, the Cody Liquor Store, and the Pekin Chinese Restaurant.

Daniel Fitzpatrick purchased the hotel in 1910 and changed the name to Cody Hotel to honor Buffalo Bill Cody. Cody's sister, Helen Cody Wetmore, lived in West Duluth where she ran a publishing company. Her grand home was called "Codyview," and West Duluth's Cody Street and Cody neighborhood are named for her and her brother. She encouraged her brother to invest in Duluth, and he built the People's Press building in the West End. Helen Cody once described Buffalo Bill's first visit to Duluth: "My brother had not yet seen the Zenith City. So in January of 1894 he arranged to make a short visit to Duluth. We issued invitations for a general reception, and the response was of the genuine Western kind—eighteen hundred guests assembling in the new Duluth Press Building to bid welcome and do honor to the world-famed Buffalo Bill." In 1973 the vacant structure was demolished to make room for a parking lot.

Hotel Grand

I n 1910 West Duluth realtor J. J. Frey opened the Hotel Grand (often referred to as the Grand Hotel; it is labeled with both names in the photo at right). The Grand offered

5219 Ramsey Street
Architect: UNKNOWN
Built: 1911 | Lost: CA. 1968

forty guest rooms in what was then the largest commercial structure in West Duluth: three stories tall. It was called the Hoyt Block briefly, from 1915 to 1916, and in 1950 its name changed to the Ramsey Hotel. The Ramsey closed its doors just four years later; the building stood empty until it was razed in the late 1960s; its lot is currently vacant.

Lester Park Hotel

In 1888 Duluth's Lakeside Land Company, which developed Lakeside and Lester Park, advertised that it planned to build a "mammoth hotel" outfitted with "all the latest improvements." Despite this announcement and architect Oliver Traphagen's grand original design (top right), the hotel was a rather plain, two-and-a-half story wood-frame building with a two-story veranda facing Lake Superior (below). Originally called The Lakeside House, the hotel could be reached by the Duluth and Iron Range Railway and, later, the Duluth Streetcar Rail Line, both of which ran within a block of the hotel.

6003 London Road
Architect: OLIVER TRAPHAGEN
Built: 1889 | Lost: 1887

The hotel opened under the direction of W. B. Dow; by 1895, when Fred Pinkman took the reins, the hotel had three other proprietors. Pinkman advertised the hotel as a vacation retreat for those who enjoyed "boating, bathing, and fishing," where "the invalid or pleasure seeker will find this the pleasantest summer resort in the Northwest, with all the comforts and conveniences of home." Pinkman opened a restaurant in the hotel and converted it into a boarding house.

In 1897 the hotel hosted teamsters hired by the city to transport steel pipe for construction of the nearby Lakewood Pumping Station. Those very teamsters may have led to the hotel's destruction. On March 30, 1897, fire consumed the hotel. The fire started in a shed east of the building, where lamp oil was stored; it was a habit for the teamsters to fill their lanterns with oil after breakfast, and they began work well before sunrise. Pinkman speculated a dropped match or a spark from a lit pipe may have set off some spilled lamp oil that had soaked into the wood floor; a brisk east wind carried the flames to the hotel.

Declared a total loss, the hotel was not rebuilt. In 1902 a house was built on the site by Dr. Joseph D. Titcomb. The then-rural location and access to a trout stream must have been very alluring to Dr. Titcomb. An avid outdoorsman and member of the League of American Sportsman, he once reported the Spalding Hotel for violating state law by serving quail out of season at a St. Louis County Medical Society banquet. Dr. Titcomb's house still stands.

Holland Hotel

501 West Superior Street
Architects: BRAY & NYSTROM
Built: 1910 | Lost: CA. 1965

The six-story Holland Hotel had its grand opening on June 17, 1910, timed with the opening of the Soo Line Passenger Depot one block east of the hotel, which essentially brought out-of-town visitors to the hotel's front door. The hotel was such a success that just a year later its owners added four more stories to the building. Built of red brick, the Holland offered 250 rooms by the time the top four floors were added.

When it opened, the Holland advertised itself as "the first fireproof hotel in Duluth." As with most other hotels at the time, not each room was furnished with its own bathroom; guests using rooms without a bathroom had access to communal bathrooms on each floor (150 of the Holland's rooms had their own baths). And like others of its time, it offered rates on both the "European Plan" and the "American Plan." On the European Plan, the guest was charged for

just the room, while the American Plan included meals. Travelers preferred the European plan.

The Holland also followed the lead of the nearby St. Louis and Spalding Hotels, offering upscale amenities such as an extravagant lobby (top right), a large dining room whose walls featured wood-paneled wainscoting below fresco murals depicting Lake Superior scenes (bottom right), and of course a cocktail lounge, which appears to have been remodeled in an Art Deco motif sometime before 1926 (bottom left).

And sadly, like almost every other hotel in the neighborhood, by the 1950s the Holland House saw a dramatic decline in popularity; it closed in 1961. It was then demolished as part of the Gateway Urban Renewal Project. Duluth's Radisson Hotel was built on the Holland House lot in 1970.

Hotel McKay

430 West 1st Street

Architect: UNKNOWN

Built: 1901 | Lost: CA. 1965

The hotel W. A. McKay built on First Street was a rather simple affair: a three-story brick building—four stories along the avenue—with brownstone entryways on the street and avenue and brownstone trim on the second-floor windows. The McKay's lodge-like lobby (left), filled with pillars and wooden rocking chairs, was dominated by a grand brick fireplace and decorated for sportsmen, with mounted trophies of north woods game adorning the walls. A few years after the McKay opened, historian Dwight Woodbridge called it "a most comfortable and attractive lounging place at any season of the year."

The hotel offered a Turkish bath, something the NFL's Duluth Eskimos took advantage of in preparation for their notorious 1926 season. The Eskimos practiced at a gas-lit field across the street from the hotel (where City Hall stands today), and the McKay served as the team's clubhouse, training quarters, and dressing room. The McKay became apartments in 1957, but was vacant by 1964 and demolished as part of the Gateway Urban Renewal Project. The Duluth News-Tribune Building now occupies the lot.

Lenox Hotel

601 West Superior Street

Architect: JOHN J. WANGENSTEIN

Built: 1904 | Lost: CA. 1965

Built by Edward Ribenack and his brothers, Henry and Albert, the yellow brick Lenox Hotel originally stood four stories tall and offered 110 rooms. Within two years the Ribenacks added two more stories, increasing capacity to 205 rooms. Like the Spalding, it had a separate "Ladies Entrance" along the avenue. In the 1930s a remodeling effort created the popular Lenox Bar and Grill, which included a cocktail lounge that could hold 190 customers. Edward, who ran the hotel until 1947, also enjoyed a long career in the Minnesota State Legislature, serving in both the House and Senate.

Despite the big new lounge, the Lenox struggled. It changed hands several times, finally becoming part of the Midwestern Hotels chain. By 1958 the management struggled financially; at one point its electricity was cut and workers' salaries withheld. The Lenox managed to stay open until 1961 when its sixty-five tenants vacated prior to its demolition as part of the Gateway Urban Renewal Project. The Incline Station Bowling Center stands in its place.

Duluth's Gateway Urban Renewal Project

When Duluth's Union Depot was constructed in 1892, it helped cement Fifth Avenue West's status as an "entrance" to the Zenith City. The grand Lyceum Theatre and luxury hotels like the St. Louis and the Spalding already stood nearby, as did many other, lower-rent hotels and saloons, many of which catered to lumberjacks, miners, and sailors between seasons with time on their hands. By 1894 Reverend C. C. Salter–whose Bethel on South Lake Avenue (see page 62) ministered to those suffering from alcoholism– decided to open another Bethel along the 500 block of Michigan Street.

The surrounding area–essentially Fourth Avenue West to Mesaba Avenue along Michigan and Superior Streets–became known as The Bowery. (Like many communities across the U.S., Duluth's Bowery was named for a section of Manhattan notorious for similar social problems.) Prohibition didn't end the Bowery's ills, and the city's clearing of saloons and brothels on Minnesota Point between South Lake Avenue and St. Croix Avenue in the 1930s only increased the Bowery's marginalized population. After World War II, the area became populated by retired laborers with no pensions and troubled young men returning from service overseas. Many had alcohol problems.

In the 1950s urban renewal projects swept the nation, trying to eliminate perceived blighted areas to increase urban business opportunities while populations moved out of cities and into suburbs. Duluth targeted the Bowery with its Gateway Urban Renewal Project. The city began purchasing and condemning almost every building in the Bowery and many on First Street west of Fifth Avenue. By 1970, nearly all had fallen.

Minnesota Woolen Company, Dove Clothing Company, Al's Grill, and the St. Paul Restaurant. The Union Gospel Mission, which was there to help the Bowery's residents, also came down, as did two houses.

The 1894 fire station on First Street and a gas station on Superior Street were supposed to remain, as were the Holland House and Fifth Avenue Hotel, but in the end all were demolished. The Soo Line Depot was to be saved and turned into the Saint Louis County Heritage and Arts Center but its basement filled with water, damaging the foundation beyond repair. The Union Depot, slated for demolition, became the Center. (The photo at lower left shows men standing in the Depot's entry, watching Michigan Street buildings under demolition.)

In the 1960 s and 1970s new buildings rose in the former Bowery, including the Ordean Building, Duluth Public Library, KDLH TV studios, the Duluth News Tribune Building, the Radisson Hotel, the Incline Station, and the Gateway and Lenox Towers senior high-rises; none are considered great architectural achievements. The entire "gateway" concept was compromised in the 1980s when expansion of I-35 allowed drivers to bypass downtown.

Many of the razed buildings had once been significant architectural and cultural landmarks, including the McKay Hotel, Holland Hotel, Spalding Hotel, and Lyceum Theatre (that's its stage seen during demolition in the photo above right). Most, however, were not, and many contributed to the Bowery's social ills. They included the Cleft Hotel, Grace Hotel, Saratoga Hotel, Perovich Hotel, Hill Hotel, Hotel Liberty, Royal Hotel, Park Hotel, First Street Hotel, Sixth Avenue Hotel, Fifth Avenue Hotel and Lamplighter Lounge, Rex Hotel and Eagle Tavern, Salena Hotel and Tavern, The Classy Lumberjack (below right), Green's Crystal Terrace, Pal's Corner Tavern, Soder's Bar, the original Club Saratoga, and the Union Liquor Depot. Other businesses fell as well: The Moose Lodge Hall, Chief Motors auto storage, M & M Supply Company, Mork Food Supply,

Lincoln Hotel

309 – 317 West 2nd Street

Architects: STARIN & MELANDER

Built: 1926 | Lost: 2004

Designed by Harold Starin and A. Reinhold Melander, the Lincoln Hotel was called a "model of elegance" and "the last word in comfort" by the *Duluth Herald* when it opened in 1926. The hotel was four stories of red brick, with a first-floor Bedford limestone façade and a decorative marquee along Second Street. Patterned brick adorned the building above the fourth floor. Jacobsen Brothers, a contracting outfit, was hired to build the Lincoln. They had become well-respected in the region, building several churches, the McDougal terminal, Hibbing High School, and the Hotel Duluth.

M. E. Scott acted as the building's proprietor (records shows the owners as "Messrs. Nelson and Hafner") overseeing operation not only of the hotel, but of its café and restaurant, which were also open to the general public. Its large lobby (top left) was roughly forty square feet and luxuriously appointed, with a separate writing room in the rear and a ladies parlor outfitted with a grand piano. The Lincoln had 105 rooms described as "cheery and sunny": a center courtyard allowed light into rooms on both sides of the hotel. While not all the guest rooms had bathroom facilities, a number of rooms were set up as suites and contained their own kitchenettes.

Scott put on what the *Duluth Herald* described as an "elaborate musical program" on the hotel's opening night, July 14, 1926. It featured an orchestra and "vocal selections" by Miss Francis Mundigel, a graduate of Minneapolis's McPhail School of Music, which still operates today. (A year later, in 1927, polka legend Lawrence Welk would graduate McPhail.)

By 1973 the hotel was no longer a popular place for visitors and underwent conversion to low-income housing. In 1981 it became a residence for senior citizens. In 1987, owner Don Henderson couldn't afford the $75,000 worth of improvements needed to bring the facility up to modern building codes. The Lincoln closed in 1988, displacing fifty-four residents. It stood vacant, deteriorating from neglect, until 2003 when the city purchased the hotel and demolished it to make a parking lot.

Clarendon & New Clarendon Hotel

1538 West Superior Street
Architect: UNKNOWN
Built: 1887 | Lost: 1942

In 1883 Dr. Samuel S. Walbank constructed the Walbank Building on the southeast corner of Superior Street and Garfield Avenue. But Dr. Walbank didn't really want a building block; he wanted a hotel. Records indicate that no businesses operated at the Walbank's address until 1887, when the building opened as the Clarendon Hotel. Manager W. G. Knowles advertised the brick-veneered building as the only hotel on Rice's Point. What now seems like an illogical location for a hotel made a lot of sense back in its day, especially after the Interstate Bridge to Superior opened in 1897. The bridge could only be accessed via Garfield Avenue, and soon the intersection of Superior Street, Garfield Avenue, and Piedmont Avenue just outside the Clarendon's doors became the busiest in Duluth. Still, the hotel closed about 1900. In 1903 Louis Loeb purchased the building, had it remodeled and refurnished, and reopened it as the New Clarendon. By 1932 the hotel stood vacant; it was condemned in 1938 and demolished in 1942. A much wider Garfield Avenue now covers the hotel's lot.

The First Garfield News Building

James W. Monaghan began operating a confectionery at 1602 West Superior Street in 1908, in the little building pictured here in front of the New Clarendon Hotel. It operated as The Garfield News Stand and sold newspapers, magazines, candy, cigars, and cigarettes. Joseph B. Archambault took over in 1909, and four years later Bernard Pierce replaced him and stayed on until 1930 when Louis Szoztak took over the property.

In 1938 Szoztak hired Abraham Holstead to design the yellow brick Art Deco Garfield News Building, which stands on the corner today. The new building also contained a small counter and stools and served breakfast and lunch. Its location at what was then the city's busiest

intersection made it a popular stop for those waiting for the bus to Superior (or entering Duluth from Superior) to stop and grab a cup of coffee, some cigarettes, or a newspaper.

The Szostak women—Louis's daughter Alyce and daughter-in-law Leona—ran the place until 1978 when Leona died. (Louis worked at Duluth's Zenith Broom Co. for seventy years, since he was thirteen years old.) Louis's son Ted, a postal carrier for thirty years, took over after that. He kept the Garfield open despite very limited stock until 1990, when he moved into an assisted care facility; he died in 1993. Despite an award-winning interior renovation by owner Alessandro Giulianni, the 1938 Garfield News Building currently stands unoccupied.

Metropole Hotel

101 ~ 105 South Lake Avenue

Architect: J. J. WANGENSTEIN

Built: 1903 | Lost: 1973

Located on the southwest corner of Lake Avenue and West Michigan Street, the Metropole Hotel served as a de facto "gateway" to what is known today as the Canal Park Business District. The brick building, built by Louis Loeb, stood three stories high with two round-corner towers facing Lake Avenue. When it first opened under the direction of John Cargill and Joseph Kenny, the Metropole offered seventy-five guest rooms and a restaurant, barbershop, and tavern on the first floor, but its most popular tenant would be Joe Huie's Café. The Metropole attracted a certain type of clientele, and some of its early residents (and owners) had faced civil and criminal charges for gambling, the illegal sale of alcohol, theft, assaults, and even attempted murder. When the Metropole was closed as a hotel in 1972, it had more than fifty full-time residents. Then-owner Melvin Gallop said of his tenants, "None of the people that left here went with relatives and none left with friends; all their friends were right here at the Metropole." It was demolished the next year. Lake Avenue was realigned and widened over the hotel's former site.

Joe Huie's Café

Many residents of the Metropole took their meals at Joe Huie's Café, adjacent to the hotel. Huie's served classic Chinese and American food, and was a favorite of Duluthians. The restaurant was famous for its jumbo butterfly shrimp and remained open twenty-four hours a day; a sign on the door read "lost key, we never close."

According to June Drenning Holmquist's *They Chose Minnesota*, Joe Huie (pictured) came to Duluth from China's Guangdong Province in 1925 to work for a relative who owned Duluth's St. Paul restaurant. Over the next twenty-five years he would return to his native land many times for different reasons: to retrieve his wife and son, to remarry after his first wife's death, and to "help the people" of China, who were struggling first with Japan and later with emerging Communism. He moved to

Duluth for the last time in 1951 with his two older sons; he opened his café, and two years later the rest of his family followed him to Duluth.

In the early 1970s former Vice President Hubert Humphrey visited Duluth; while driving out of town Humphrey saw Joe Huie on the street. He stopped the motorcade, jumped out, gave Huie a hug, and stood talking to him while his aides tried to get the politician back in the car and off to the airport.

When the café was lost in the Metropole demolition, the "we never close" sign reportedly later became part of Grandma's Saloon & Deli's memorabilia collection. Legend has it that when the restaurant closed Huie placed an ad in the *Duluth News-Tribune* that read: "Lost key found—will now close."

In 1964, Joe's elder son Wing Ying Huie opened the Chinese Lantern in the Palladio Building on Superior Street. In 1976, at employee Rose Chida's suggestion, he moved the Chinese Lantern into the former Duluth Athletic Club at 402 West First Street (originally the Duluth Commercial Club) and also opened the Brass Phoenix Night Club. The many who dined there included vice President Walter Mondale, Pearl Bailey, and Elvis Presley. A fire in 1994 gutted the restaurant, and it never reopened. Today a Huie family relative runs Duluth's Chopsticks Inn. Joe's youngest son, Wing Young Huie, is a noted Minneapolis photographer.

The Flame Restaurant

1400 London Road
Architect: UNKNOWN
Built: 1930 | Lost: 1942

363 South 5th Avenue West
Architects: FREDERICK GERMAN
& HAROLD ST. CLAIR STARIN
Built: 1912/1946 | Lost: 1998

Duluth's Flame restaurant—a fixture of the town for over fifty years, started as a humble one-room barbecue stand on London Road, opened by Jimmy Oreck and Alex Zurovsky during the heart of the Great Depression. A year later Zurovsky dropped his end of the bargain, leaving Oreck and his wife Ruth to run the stand, which they turned into what would be called "the Northwest's finest supper club." The Art Deco-inspired Flame Building on London Road boasted large picture windows that looked out over a garden of "trees and shrubs, a waterfall, trout pool, and stuffed wild animals." It also had the town's first custom-made semi-circular booths, strolling musicians, a cigarette girl, and a dwarf doorman decked out in a red uniform.

Charlie Kassmit managed the Flame, and he and Oreck did their best to make the experience unique. Coffee was served by "The Sultan of the Second Cup," a man wearing a turban and curl-toed shoes. Meat cooked slowly over a rotisserie that was enclosed with glass (shown in the photo below) and the Flame was famous for its pop-overs made fresh by Ruth every day. At first it could seat just thirty patrons, but Oreck added wings and—after Prohibition was repealed—a variety of bars and lounges, including the Rooster Room, named for the Flame's logo, a flame red cockerel.

When fire claimed the Flame in 1942, Oreck moved the restaurant to 110 West Superior Street. Meanwhile he purchased a grocery warehouse along the harbor. The three-story fire-proof building originally housed the Duluth Marine Supply Company, a grocery retail firm specializing in selling foods to Lake Superior vessels. By 1936 Duluth Marine Supply had moved; the building remained a grocery warehouse until Oreck bought it and hired architect Harold St. Clair Starin to convert it into The Flame. The new Flame (pictured below) sat four hundred diners. Its semicircular terrazzo dance floor was framed with "inverted Roman-like columns flooded with multicolored lights." The Flame included a glass stair tower and many windows that looked out over the harbor, including five twelve-foot windows in the dining room that created a "wall of glass."

But Oreck wasn't happy with the building because of compromises made due to war-related shortages. In 1955 Oreck moved the business to Superior Street, reworked the old Flame, and by 1956 was back at the Fifth Avenue building along the "seaway," as Oreck called the waterfront. Oreck sold the Flame to a Memphis developer in 1971, and the restaurant closed in 1973. The Anchor Inn rented the building until 1982. In 1983 Micky Paulucci of Grandma's Restaurants reopened the Flame in its Fifth Avenue location, but it closed just eighteen months later. The vacant building was demolished in 1998 to make room for the Great Lakes Aquarium.

Other Duluth Restaurants that Have Passed into Memory

The Flame (page 90) certainly isn't the only old restaurant that Duluthians remember fondly; Joe Huie's Café and his Chinese Lantern (page 89) quickly jump to the top of that list. Hundreds—perhaps thousands—of restaurants have come and gone in Duluth. We'd be remiss without mentioning at least a few.

Old postcards remind us of Duluth's many eateries from the 1920s and 30s: the Atlas Tea Room at 124 East First, Lake View Tea and Dining Room at 728 East Superior Street (now Coppola Artistica), Jack's Café at 220 East Superior Street (top; now the Zeitgeist Arts Café and once the Red Lion Lounge) was originally built in 1910 as the Albert Salter Saloon. Known as "a popular place for women, especially, to have lunch and see and be seen," the Greysolon Tea Room originally graced the Glass Block, but closed at that location in 1940 to create more retail space for the department store. It later opened in the Plaza Shopping Center and became the Dinner Belle.

Some in town may still remember Vivian Lee's, housed in a barge on Connie's Landing in Riverside, or Diamond's Pool Hall and Luncheonette above Woolworths on Superior Street. A big favorite for many years was the Captain's Table Café in the Medical Arts Building, a buffet-style eatery with a nautical theme (including a parrot named "Amigo") that closed in 1972. It was the Miller Café (center) until 1959, a direct descendant of the Miller Cafeteria A. W. Miller founded back in 1883 and run by his family until 1953, when Jack and Shirley Garber purchased it. A 1959 remodeling inspired the name change.

London Road in the 1960s and '70s offered a line of locally-owned eateries along its "Motel Row": Sandy's at 1515 London Road, (there was also a Sandy's in the Denfeld neighborhood), Henry's Hamburgers at Twenty-Sixth Avenue East (and in the West End at Twenty-Third Avenue West) sold fifteen-cent burger in 1961, and the London Inn on the northeast corner at Seventeenth

MILLER'S CAFETERIA and Fountain Service
Fine Food at Low Cost — Coast to Coast Patronage

Avenue East was famous for its onion rings. London Road also included two franchise exceptions: a Dairy Queen and a beloved A & W franchise. The Lemon Drop on a hill at 2631 London Road lasted until 1988. Its name lives on through Duluth's Grandma's Marathon, as "Lemon Drop Hill" is the race's toughest portion. More recently London Road lost Louie's Café, which specialized in Greek cuisine and pancakes in the former Orchard Pie Shop location.

The Kenwood community was served by Duffy's Drive-In on Cleveland Street, popular for its broasted chicken (bottom). And before the Canal Park Business District filled with upscale restaurants and luxury hotels it was home to King Leo's, another hamburger stand famous for its onion rings. King Leo's later became the Canal Park Inn, where tourists bought French fries and then fed them to seagulls, annoying the locals. It later became a Burger King, which was demolished for a hotel.

Since 1980 Duluth has seen the demise of many long-standing restaurants, including downtown's Jolly Fisher, which specialized in seafood, and Natchio's, which served up Greek cuisine (and, on Saturday nights, belly dancers). West Duluth lost two great Grand Avenue diners with the closings of Ketola's Kafé and Joyce's Kitchen (both joining Morrie's at 5434 Grand, which had closed many years before they had). The Hillside's Fourth Street lost Jim's Hamburgers (another Jim's in the West End closed in 2012) and the House of Donuts, once popular not only with locals during the day but also with college students very late at night—and very early in the morning. On top of the hill the Buena Vista, with its Sunday brunch and the best view in town, came down for a condominium development.

The last historic restaurant standing is The Pickwick, which began life as the Fitger's Brewery Saloon in 1915 and takes its name from a non-alcoholic beverage Fitger's sold during Prohibition (customers would supply their own alcohol and mix it with a Pickwick). The Wisocki family, owners since 1916, sold the restaurant in 2010.

Grand Opera House

333 West Superior Street
Architect: GEORGE WIRTH
Built: 1883 | Lost: 1889

In the early 1880s, after the developing grain trade helped Duluth recover from the financial panic of 1873, pioneers and civic leaders Roger Munger and Clinton Markell felt the city's growing population could support a major theater to attract musical, dramatic, and literary productions. They hired St. Paul architect George Wirth to design the Grand Opera House, which stood on the northeast corner of Fourth Avenue West and Superior Street.

Perhaps the most architecturally adorned building that ever graced Duluth, the Grand Opera House stood four stories tall and was capped with a Mansard roof executed in several different shades of purple and crowned with iron cresting. Its exterior walls were brick with terra cotta and brownstone trim. Its central pavilion along Superior Street featured the grand entrance over which sat an arched balcony and a dome with dormers, columns, and

finials. A round tower topped the building's corner, and the entire building was adorned with a profusion of carved ornamentation. The building was fitted for steam, water, and gas and included a hydraulic elevator.

The auditorium held 1,000 seats at a time when only 13,000 people lived in Duluth; it could house 8 percent of the entire population. At thirty-three feet deep, fifty-two feet wide, and thirty-five feet high, its stage was unusually large for its day. It was built by master stage carpenter G. H. Carter of Chicago. The *Duluth Weekly Tribune* announced that, "There is no modern improvement or convenience that he has not adopted." The stage was outfitted with a "dozen sets and fifty or more wing pieces" and two drop curtains. One curtain showed a view of Venice, Italy, and the other was "of satin of old gold color, with heavy trimming at the bottom

of crimson and gold." At $1,100—nearly $41,000 today—the curtain was described as "the most costly in America."

The theater held six private boxes holding a total of thirty-two seats. The *Duluth Weekly Tribune* described their lavishness: "over the upper box a very handsome 'hood' in ornamental and gilded iron work reaches to the ceiling. The boxes are enclosed by nickel-plated rails, and draped with maroon silk and blue Turkish satin curtains."

Duluth's social elite, including Luther Mendenhall and Judge J. D. Ensign, scrambled for the best private box in the house but were outbid by A. J. Whiteman. They were all in attendance opening night, September 20, 1883, when the Emma Abbott Opera Company presented the popular opera *Martha* to a full house, which included architect George Wirth and his wife, who traveled from St. Paul for the event (Wirth's sketch of the grand opera House is shown at right).

Duluthians relished their elegant show place—the *Duluth Daily News* referred to it as "Duluth's pride and joy." In addition to the auditorium, which brought world-class

Duluth Grand Opera House.

entertainment to Duluth, the Grand Opera House served Duluth in many other ways. It was home to the Chamber of Commerce, the Ladies Literary Library (which would evolve into the Duluth Public Library), a few sleeping rooms, Gasser's Grocery, several offices (including those of the West Duluth Land Company and Munger and Markell's Lake Superior Elevator Company) and the Kitchi Gammi Club, which occupied most of the top floor.

Only six years after the Grand Opera House opened, a disastrous fire of unknown origin began in Grasser's Grocery on the bitterly cold night of January 28, 1889. The *Duluth Daily News* cited fire fighting delays and blunders for allowing it to grow out of control. Fire spread rapidly, leaving the building in ruins. Twelve people were asleep inside, including the janitor and his family. The last one out was A. J. Whitemen, who later became notorious as a forger known as "Jim the Penman." (Then a "handsome" senator, Whiteman had to be rescued by ladder; years later he would be captured by Pinkerton detectives attempting to escape them from his family home in New York by crawling down a ladder. See page 28.) The next day the last standing brick wall collapsed, killing Elmer Chamberlain, who was working next door at the book and stationery store he owned with William. S. Albertson. The theater was not rebuilt; the following year the original Phoenix Building was constructed on the site.

Temple Opera House

8 – 12 2nd Avenue East
Architects: McMillen & Stebbins; Oscar Cobb
Built: 1889 | Lost: 1896

After fire destroyed Duluth's Grand Opera House, Duluth's Masons ordered the construction of a new Masonic Temple. The new facility, called the Temple Opera Block, would include an adjacent opera house to take the place of the Grand Opera House.

The Temple Opera House was attached to the back of the Temple Opera Block and matched that building's Richardsonian Romanesque architecture, enhanced by Moorish details. Its Second Avenue East façade (shown at left and below, in a photo of Duluth's Swedish Immigrants celebrating their homeland) featured ornate wrought-iron lettering.

Theater architect Oscar Cobb consulted on the Opera House's design, including its extravagant Second Avenue entrance. On opening night, October 23, 1889, Duluth's elite gathered to watch Rose Coghlan perform the play *Jocelyn*. The next day the *Duluth Daily News* described the building as: "Grand, imposing, beautiful! The Temple is indeed the ideal of the artist's dream and the actor's cherished hope. Beautiful in design, nothing of the practical has been sacrificed for effect, but rather has been made to lend to the beauty of the whole. From the avenue the massive pile, illuminated by nearly one thousand incandescent lights, presented a picture most beautiful. But inside the beautiful Temple! Its gorgeous colors and brilliant lights; its beautiful scenery, the sweet strains of orchestral music—indeed it was an event in the dramatic history of the Northwest that will not soon be forgotten."

The newspaper also gushed over Cobb's work on the auditorium (next page, bottom left): "The proscenium boxes are marvels of beauty and comfort…. There are eighteen boxes, nine on each side, in three tiers of three boxes each. Each box has a railing of brass highly polished, which adds to the rich

effects. The parquet and dress circles are seated in solid blue, with Wilton carpet in terra cotta in the aisles. The foyer is richly dressed. The windows are curtained in gorgeous Vallours [sic] in old gold. Two of its fine doors are in Vallours [sic] in solid Spanish red portieres and valances, and the other three are in Spanish red portieres and old gold valances, all hung on brass poles."

It wasn't always highbrow music and theatre on

the Temple Opera House stage, as the photo of a "strong man" performance (below right) suggests. And besides the public theater, the Temple Opera House also held the Mason's Scottish Rite (pictured top right), a theater-like facility wherein members earned different levels of Masonic degrees. Kitchens and dining rooms used by the Masons were found in the Opera House, which also contained an art gallery, whose entrance can be seen in the photo at right on page 94.

On October 12, 1895, fire claimed the Temple Opera House, also destroying the Scottish Rite. Newspapers reported that the entire building was lost within thirty minutes and describe the fire dramatically: "The interior of the building was like a hell. The flames were a perfect cyclone. They shot nearly 200 feet into the air." A firewall prevented the fire from damaging the Temple Opera Block. The Temple Opera House was not rebuilt, and the building's ruins sat empty for ten years.

In 1905 the Temple Opera House ruins were converted into the Temple Rink, a roller skating facility designed by J. J. Wangenstein boasting a skating surface 140 feet long and 70 feet wide. In 1910, Guilford Hartley purchased the property, demolished the rink, and built the Orpheum Theatre on the lot.

Lyceum Theatre

423 – 431 West Superior Street
Architects: TRAPHAGEN & FITZPATRICK
Built: 1891 | Lost: 1966

The Lyceum's auditorium, which could seat 1,368 patrons under crystal chandeliers and an ornamental ceiling, opened August 3, 1891, with Emma Abbott starring in Alexander Bisson's three-act comedy *Mrs. Wilkenson's Widows*. The room was seventy feet high, seventy-six feet wide, and sixty-three feet deep and boasted three horse-shoe-shaped balconies. About 1,400 light bulbs illuminated the room, and its bronze-and-stained-glass doors closed silently to avoid distracting performances. The emphasis lay on comfort: the seats offered ample room and padded arm rests and had perforated leather bottoms to keep them cool. In the balconies, the chairs were spaced three feet apart.

In the 1890s only Chicago's famed Auditorium had a stage that rivaled the Lyceum's, which measured fifty-six feet wide and forty-five feet deep; the opening of its proscenium was forty feet wide and forty feet high. The Chicago firm of Sosman and Landis hand-painted thirty backdrops for a

When wealthy timber and mining magnate Andreas M. Miller noted the success of the newly-opened Temple Opera House in 1889, he hired Traphagen and Fitzpatrick to design the Lyceum, essentially an office building wrapped around a grand theater. The *Duluth News Tribune* would describe the building as the "Handsomest and Costliest Building in the Northwest."

The massive Romanesque building—it stood six stories high, with short towers rising on each of the four corners—was faced with buff-colored brick and sandstone with terra cotta trim and stretched 125 feet along Superior Street and 140 feet up Fifth Avenue West. The street-level storefront windows utilized a new innovation: double thick plate glass. Its triple arched Superior Street entrance was twenty-two feet wide and featured ornately carved decorations by George Thrana, including the theatrical masks of Tragedy and Comedy; two sandstone lions guarded the granite entrance stairway, its steps were hewn from gray granite and white marble. The main door was outfitted with hardware made of brass, copper, and nickel.

variety of sets, from pastoral scenes to palaces and prisons. Its drop curtain, decorated with "an oriental scene," was made of fireproof asbestos. Some of the productions were extravagant. In 1903 *Ben Hur* played at the theater, with a cast of 350 and a chariot race featuring eight horses racing on stage. The Lyceum's was also the first stage in the United States on which Charlie Chaplin performed.

After the Temple Opera House burned in 1896, the Lyceum became Duluth's only grand theatre. Miller sold his interest in the building a year later. By 1915 the five-year-old Orpheum Theatre was drawing patrons away from the Lyceum, as were other forms of entertainment. By the 1920s the Lyceum began showing movies in order to keep the auditorium financially afloat. The building's spectacular entrance arches were removed and replaced with store fronts and a marquee. By 1960 the Lyceum was in such disrepair it was referred to as the "Rat's Palladium." In February, 1966, it was razed as part of Duluth's Gateway Urban Renewal Project. The stone lions were given to the Duluth Zoo and the theatrical masks to the Duluth Playhouse at the St Louis County Heritage and Arts Center. The Lyceum was replaced by a building for KDHL-TV and a parking lot. KDLH abandoned the building in 2005 when it merged with KBJR-TV.

Orpheum Theatre

8 – 12 2nd Avenue East

Architect: J. E. O. PRIDEMORE

Built: 1910 | Lost: 1939 (FAÇADE EXTANT)

In 1912 Duluth businessman Guilford Hartley purchased the Temple Opera Block and the site of the Temple Opera House. He also purchased the block of property east of the Temple Opera Block, from 207 to 213 East Superior Street.

On the site of the old Temple Opera House Hartley built the Orpheum Theatre. On the outside the building's only architectural interest was its Neoclassical façade along Second Avenue East, with its awning of ornamental iron covering the entrance. Inside it was opulent. Patrons entered upon a marble-tiled floor, and marble staircases with ornamental iron railings led them to their auditorium seats. The auditorium itself held two balconies and ten private boxes. The seats were built of mahogany and upholstered with silk velour. It was one of the first theaters to utilize cantilever construction, allowing the auditorium to stand free of visible support columns, ensuring every seat in the house had a clear view of the stage.

On his Superior Street property Hartley built the Orpheum Garage. The Garage adjoined the theater; it operated as a parking garage and included offices for the Orpheum. Like the Opera House, the Orpheum included a small art gallery, whose entrance can be seen at the lower left corner of the building in the photo at left. The sign above the entrance advertises the Orpheum Garage's services: welding, washing, and greasing.

The *Duluth Herald* reported that on opening night, August 22, 1912, "the audience filled every seat from boxes to gallery. It came with a rush,

flooding the street for a block on either side lined with autos. All of social Duluth was there.... The spirit of freedom was infectious, all were there for enjoyment of the splendor of the theater in every detail and the completeness of its appointment brought a feeling of satisfaction that let loose the floodlights of appreciation." The theater's manager claimed Duluth's audience "is more metropolitan than any I have seen outside of New York, Philadelphia, and Boston."

Mayor Marcus Cullum addressed the audience, told them they were "looking swell," and gave a short speech that included the following remark:

"It takes confidence as well as money to build such a house as this and it does Mr. Hartley credit and shows his confidence in the future of Duluth. High class vaudeville is as essential in metropolitan life as street cars and automobiles. No city can pretend to verge upon the metropolitan until it can claim such a line of amusement features as the Orpheum provides."

The Orpheum was, until about 1925, Duluth's premier vaudeville stage, competing only with the Lyceum Theatre for quality acts. As a member of

the nationwide Orpheum Theatre circuit, Duluth's Orpheum was all but guaranteed to book the nation's finest talent. Mary Pickford, W. C. Fields, Charlie Chaplin, Jack Benny, the Marx Brothers, and a young Jackie "Uncle Fester" Coogan all graced the Orpheum's stage; Al Jolson played there as well, in blackface.

But in the 1920s the popularity of talking motion pictures began killing vaudeville. When Guilford Hartley died in 1922 the buildings became the possession of the Hartley Company and later the Hartley Family Trust. In 1929 The Orpheum added movie equipment (note the projector booth in the balcony in the photo below left, taken in 1929). That same year its main entry was moved to 207 East Superior Street, the first bay of the Orpheum Garage. The Second Avenue awning was also relocated to Superior Street at that time and a large vertical sign for the Orpheum was attached to the Temple Opera Block (see photo, above). It was managed by the same company that ran Duluth's Garrick Theatre.

But those changes weren't enough to keep the grand vaudeville theater lucrative, especially since many movie houses had popped up in downtown Duluth by then. From 1934 to 1939, the theater was closed except for a few sporadic attempts to make it work once again as a venue for live theater and movies. In 1939 the building was gutted and, along with portions of the Orpheum Garage, transformed into the NorShor Theatre and the NorShor Annex.

The Grand, Lyric, and New Lyric Theatre

213 West Superior Street
Architects: WANGENTEIN & GILIUSON
Built: 1914 | Lost: 1976

Mose and Barney Cook's Grand Theatre opened on August 20, 1914, to praise from the *Duluth Herald*, which called the theater "one of the finest in the state in point of arrangement, architecture, and interior decorations." The architects called the brick and terra cotta building's design "Modern French Renaissance," but details included classical columns. Its steel-and-glass canopy covered arched mahogany doors with glass panels bound in brass. Its entrance vestibule featured high curved ceilings and carved marble paneling (page 101, top center).

The auditorium (page 101, bottom) sat 1,200 patrons and its owners boasted that the seats were "of unusual comfort" and perfectly arranged to ensure there was not a bad view in the house. Its stage—forty feet wide and thirty-five deep—was equipped with seven sets of scenery. The stage's heavy, fireproof asbestos curtain was adorned with a reproduction of Jean-Baptiste Corot's "Dance of the Nymphs;" the proscenium arch was decorated with a painting of Apollo riding Pegasus. Fifteen private boxes ringed the theater above the house seats and below the balcony. Since children under four were not permitted to attend performances, the facility included a nursery and playroom; parents could drop off their children and enjoy the show.

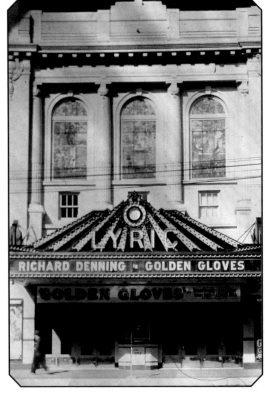

Although it was built as a vaudeville house, it couldn't compete with the Lyceum and Orpheum at drawing top-notch national acts (Babe Ruth was its most famous "act"). And like those two theatres, when vaudeville began dying in the 1920s, the Grand converted to a movie house to stay competitive. In 1922 the Grand merged with the Lyric Theatre, which had been housed at 116 West Superior Street since 1917; the theater's name changed to the Lyric at that time. According to long-time *Duluth News-Tribune* columnist Jim Heffernan, by the 1950s the theater—now the New Lyric—was showing "second- or third-run double features" that cost adults a quarter; kids under twelve paid twelve cents. Popcorn cost a dime.

The theatre closed its doors in 1959, when it was under the ownership of the Minnesota Amusement Company. In 1965 the *Duluth News-Tribune* called the theater's marquee "an eyesore [serving] no purpose other than a roosting place for pigeons;" it was hauled to a landfill in 1965. The building was allowed to fall further into disrepair. Although demolition was approved in 1972, Mayor Ben Boo allowed a delay requested by citizen groups who hoped to save the building. They developed no feasible plan, and the building came down in March of 1976, along with eight others. They were replaced by the Normandy Mall, Hotel, and parking ramp (the buildings are now the Holiday Center and Holiday Inn).

Other Lost Theaters

According to the *Minnesotian*, performance art (of questionable quality) first arrived in Duluth on June 4, 1869, via the sailing vessel *Meteor*, which brought "some kind of 'fat woman' stage show." That same year George P. "Big Red" Hanson built Duluth's first theater, the Theatre Shed (aka, the Pine-Clad Shed, the Pine Shed, the Opera House, and the Political Wigwam), on the northeast corner of Superior Street and Second Avenue West. It was a simple affair: the stage had no curtain, and patrons sat on plank benches. It changed hands after Big Red's wife shot him dead in Iowa (a jury acquitted her and commended her self-defense skills). In 1871 the Shed hosted the first Shakespeare production in Duluth; some have suggested it also hosted prostitutes and their patrons.

William Branch purchased the Shed in 1872, tore it down, and planned to build a three-story brownstone opera house on the same location. But when the Panic of 1873 struck Duluth, construction stopped when the building was still only two stories tall. Community members then provided entertainment performing at Branch's other building on Superior at Fourth Avenue East (see page 104).

The panic didn't stop the 1873 construction of the Dramatic Temple on the southwest corner of Superior Street and Second Avenue West, a two-story theater with a five-hundred-seat auditorium on the second floor and a restaurant on the first. It became the Duluth stop for traveling theater troupes.

As Duluth began to thrive in the 1880s, investors saw the need to entertain the growing population. In 1882 the Duluth Theatre went up on the west side Second Avenue West, just off the Superior Street Alley. It was out of business by 1884 but reopened as The Parlour by new owner Ole Olson, who had run a theater/saloon of the same name just south of the Duluth Theatre. His establishment was more of a gathering place that also offered entertainment than a dedicated theater. Duluth's more "refined" citizens frequented the Grand Opera House (see page 92), the Temple Opera House (see page 94) and the Lyceum Theatre (see page 96) beginning in the 1880s. After 1910 the Orpheum (see page 98) and

Grand (later Lyric, see page 100) theaters provided Duluth with the nation's best vaudeville acts.

Smaller theaters came and went along the way, some in their own buildings, others in buildings originally designed for other purposes. (While the theaters are gone, some of the buildings remain). The Metropolitan Opera House (pictured bottom left) opened in the heart of the Bowery on Christmas Day, 1902. Despite booking top acts, it didn't fare well: Duluth's well-heeled theater patrons avoided the Bowery, whose residents couldn't afford the Metropolitan's prices. By 1907 it had ceased to book legitimate theater and became a burlesque house; it was gone by 1910, replaced by the Soo Line Passenger Depot.

The lower side of the 100 block of East Superior Street hosted several theaters over the years. The Bijou Theatre stood at 12 East Superior Street and operated as part of the Sullivan and Considine vaudeville circuit from 1903 until 1911, when it became the Empress Theatre (above right). The Empress burned in May of 1915, and the building was converted for retail sales; it is now home to the Electric Fetus. The Strand, at 16 East Superior Street, was built in 1906 as a meat market, but by 1915 it was showing movies and did so until 1951. The building stood vacant until 1971, when it reopened as an adult theater. It closed again in 1986, remaining vacant until its 1998 demolition; the lot is now part of a condominium complex and medical offices. Various theaters moved in and out of the Weiland and Hayes buildings at the eastern end of the block over the years, including the Star in the Weiland and the Savoy at the Hayes during the first decades of the century. The Lake Theatre occupied the Savoy location from 1935 to 1950 and operated as the World Theatre from 195 to 1956.

The Sunbeam (page 103, center), a dedicated movie house, opened at 109 West Superior in 1920, but in 1922 it moved to 103 West Superior Street and the New Astor Theatre took over its previous location. The Sunbeam was gone by 1930, and the New Astor ten years

later, replaced with Snyder's Drug. The Rex Theatre at 18–20 Second Avenue West was built in 1913. Over 1,000 patrons could be seated in its auditorium and balcony. In 1925 its name was changed to the New Garrick (top left), and in 1940 it was modernized by the Minnesota Amusement Company. The building was razed in 1956, replaced with a parking ramp; the building next door is still called the Garrick Center. The Zelda Theatre (top right) was housed at 311 West Superior from 1920 until 1929, when it was replaced by the Zelda Inn and later Boyce Drug Store. The building became Peterson-Anderson Florists in 1985. Other lost downtown Duluth theaters include the Happy Hour at 129 West Superior, the Diamond (originally at 124 East Superior and later at Superior Street and Fourth Avenue West), the Kozy at 419 East Fourth Street (not to be confused with the Kozy Bar and Apartments in the former Pastoret Terrace at 129–131 East First Street), the Granada at 109 East Superior Street, as well as the Colonial, the United States, and the Astor.

Downtown Duluth wasn't the only place to take in a play or movie. West Duluth had at least three theaters. The Alhambra showed films at 321 Central Avenue from 1913 to 1926; it opened for a year as the State Theater, then closed again in 1928. The Doric at 5715 Grand Avenue opened in 1925 with seating for 800. In 1955 the theater closed and the building was remodeled as an office complex. The West, built in 1937 at 317 North Central Avenue, was primarily as second-run movie house. After a 1966 remodeling it was renamed The Duluth and showed popular movies that stayed in theaters for months, such as *The Sound of Music* and *Doctor Zhivago*; later it showed a variety of films, including some considered pornographic. In newspaper ads it was sometimes referred to as the "Duluth Spirit Valley Theatre;" the building is currently vacant. In the West End, the Majestic Theatre at 2021 West Superior Street operated for less than two years, from 1907 to 1909. The West End Star Theatre opened at 2110 West Superior Street in 1908, moved across the street to 2110 West

Superior, and operated until the early 1950s; the building then became a furniture store. In the east, the Lakeside Theatre (sometimes referred to as the Lakeside Art Theater) stood at 4619 East Superior Street from 1934 until 1970 when it was converted into a medical clinic; it became Lakeside Medical Center by 1978 and Duluth Clinic in 1982. In 2008 it was razed to make room for a new medical clinic.

In the early 1950s Duluth was served by twelve movie houses; by 1959, when the Lyric closed, it was down to just four: the NorShor, the West, the Granada, and the Lyceum. In the 1960s and 1970s movie houses sprung up in new retail developments and drew heavily from downtown audiences, and a few of the dedicated theater buildings that still stood were converted into adult movie houses. The Lyceum was destroyed in 1966, and the Granada became an adult bookstore until it was demolished in 1987. Various attempts to keep the Nor Shor operating after its initial 1982 closing have included showing movies.

Today the Marcus Duluth Multiplex Theatre next to the Duluth Entertainment and Convention Center shows first-run movies and downtown's Zinema 2 shows current and art house films.

Branch's Hall

416 East Superior Street

Architect: UNKNOWN

Built: 1870 | Lost: 1986

Duluth's first building made with bricks, Branch's Hall was constructed in 1870 by William H. Branch with the financial help of pioneers Sidney Luce and J. D. Ray. The two-story red-brick structure had arched windows on the second floor, stone quoins on the corners, and a bracketed cornice (pictured below between Elevator A and the first Portland School, shown photographed under construction in the 1870s).

Branch, a native of Ohio, moved to St. Paul in 1852 and served on its city council and in the state legislature. In the late 1860s he moved to Duluth as a director of the Lake Superior and Mississippi Railway. The railroad produced Duluth's first boom, and Branch bought up land and built his hall. He died only two years later and his family moved back to St Paul.

In its early days, Branch's Hall served many functions: Duluth's first public hall, a school, and home of the Grand Army of the Republic (the Union's Civil War veterans' association). It served as meat packing plant in the late 1880s, a feed store in the early 1900s. In 1915 the buildings' second floor was converted into the club room and dance hall for the Duluth People's Society. At one point it was painted white, covering most of its architectural details. From 1919 until it the 1980s it was an auto dealership and, finally, the General Trading Company, which sold auto parts. Branch's Hall was razed in 1986 for the Interstate 35 eastern expansion.

Interstate 35 Eastern Expansion

The expansion of Interstate 35 through Duluth was planned as early as 1958, although the project wasn't completed until the 1990s. The plans changed many times over the years, and portions of it were highly controversial, none more than the section that would cut through downtown Duluth and stretch to Twenty-Sixth Avenue East.

Because of public outcry—including lawsuits—the demolition of historic buildings between The Pickwick and the Hartley Building (including Fitger's Brewery) was prevented by changing the plans to include a tunnel. The final look included four tunnels and spared much of Leif Erikson Park. The 1912 Duluth Curling Club was saved, only to be lost to a suspicious fire (see page 174).

Still, many buildings were lost, including all those along the lower side of Michigan Street from First Avenue West to First Avenue East, which included old wholesale food warehouses, the Metropole Hotel, a plumbing supply company, the former home of Arco Coffee, a sheet metal works, an old feed barn, other storage facilities, and Zalk-Josephs Wholesale Hardware. Every building between Fourth and Fifth Avenues East along lower Superior Street and from Fifth Avenue East to Eighth Avenue East on Superior Street's upper side also came down. This included Branch's Hall (left) and a collection of buildings referred to as Automobile Row, as most were car dealerships, repair shops, auto parts stores, and filling stations.

Thirteen houses and several buildings were also lost along the lower side of South Street between Tenth and Twenty-Sixth Avenues East. On London Road, the Lemon Drop Restaurant, Flamette Motel, a gas station, and a liquor store were razed. The 1899 DM&IR Endion Passenger Depot, which sat at Fifteenth Avenue East and South Street, was saved. It was moved (shown below) to its present location below Lake Place Park in the Canal Park Business District.

The 1883 & 1886 Fargusson Blocks

406 ~ 408 West Superior Street
Architect: GEORGE WIRTH
Built: 1883 | Lost: 1892

402 ~ 404 West Superior Street
Architect: OLIVER TRAPHAGEN
Built: 1886 | Lost: 1892

As one of the 1881 incorporators of the Duluth Board of Trade, Owen Fargusson made a fortune as a grain commissioner and served as the board's president from 1888 to 1889. In 1883, with grain money lining his pockets, Fargusson commissioned George Wirth to design a business block that deserved attention.

The Fargusson block was four stories of white Lamont marble topped with an elaborate iron cornice, squat towers above the cornice, and classical detailing on the façade—and the Fargusson name carved in stone. In 1886 he added a second building next door. The second Fargusson Building looked very different from its neighbor: at three stories high it was shorter, and its brick-and-brownstone facing contrasted with the white marble of the 1883 building. It featured elaborate details as well: a rounded corner and twelve decorative pillars at the roof line, a patterned-brick cornice, and stone lintels. Fire gutted both buildings on December 27, 1892. While the 1886 building was heavily damaged, the 1883 Fargusson was completely destroyed. In March of 1893 the older marble building was razed. The 1886 building was rebuilt, but without any of its original design features. It was later extended west over the footprint of the first Fargusson block and converted into Duluth's Greyhound Bus Station, operating as such until 1983. Today it is home to National Title and other businesses.

H. F. Williamson Block

125 ~ 127 W Superior St.
Architect: GEORGE WIRTH
Built: 1883 | Lost: 1953

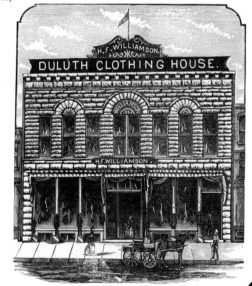

Harvey Williamson Sr. also hired George Wirth in 1883 to design a building, this one to house his clothing company. The two-story building was faced in brownstone and featured three arched windows on the second story. Like Fargusson's first building, Williamson displayed his name prominently across the bottom of the middle window. In 1887 Edward Mendenhall became a partner in the business with Williamson's son, H. Frank Williamson, and the store operated until 1943 when the Livingston family bought the business. They moved the store to another location in 1948 and other businesses occupied the building, including Allen's Shoe Store, the Patty Cake Shop, Leed's Women's Clothing, and Dworshak's photo studio. On December 31, 1953, fire of unknown origin quickly spread to all businesses and caused the roof to collapse. The building was demolished and in 1954 two one-story shops replaced the Williamson Block; those two building were later combined as one, currently the home of North Shore Mortgage.

Costello Block

22 & 24 East Superiior Street
Architect: GEORGE WIRTH
Built: 1884 | Lost: 2007

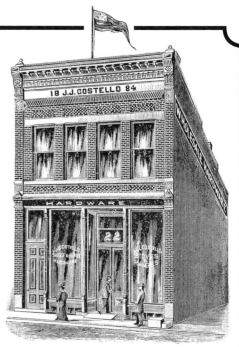

As early as 1873 John J. Costello had established a hardware store in Duluth, and in 1884 he hired George Wirth (who else?) to design a new store specializing in general hardware, stoves, heaters, and works of art for the home. The two-story red brick building was adorned with patterned brick work, carved Fond du Lac brownstone, and a metal cornice that featured brackets and dentils. The store doubled in size in 1891 when (who else?) Oliver Traphagen and Francis Fitzpatrick duplicated the original style on the lot next door.

Costello, a Duluth alderman and sometimes acting mayor, conducted his business here until his death in 1892. By 1896 it was home to Kelley Hardware, which would later sponsor a professional football team, the Duluth Kelleys, the team that later became the NFL's legendary Duluth Eskimos. After 1900 the Costello Block served several different businesses, including a paint store, an appliance store, an interior decorator, and Abalan's Pianos. In April, 2007 both sections of the still structurally sound Costello Block were demolished for a condominium development. After most of the housing units failed to sell, much of the brand new condo space was converted into the offices of P. S. Rudie and Associates, a medical practice.

Miles Block

19 West Superior
Architect: GEORGE WIRTH
Built: 1884 | Lost: CA. 1910

Alexander Miles' 1884 business block was another George Wirth design, three stories of brick and brownstone with stone carvings of faces, floral designs, columns, and the building's name decorating the second and third floors. The first floor was used as retail space.

Miles, an African American native of Ohio, moved to Duluth about 1880 and opened a barbershop in the St. Louis Hotel; his wife Candace, described as "a white woman from New York," found work in the hotel as a dressmaker. He invested in real estate, building six rental houses and this business block. Miles was Duluth's first Black member of the Duluth Chamber of Commerce and designed and patented a mechanism for automatically opening and closing elevator doors (Miles' invention would eventually put him in the National Inventors' Hall of Fame). In 1900 Miles and his family moved to Chicago and sold the building a year later. That same year the *Duluth News-Tribune* called him the "wealthiest colored man in the Northwest." In Chicago he began an insurance agency designed to eliminate the discrimination of Blacks within the industry. The Miles Block was demolished about 1910 and Kelly Furniture was built on the site in 1912 in a design that duplicated the 1905 Stack Company Dry Goods building at 21 West Superior Street. In 1993 both of those buildings were joined visually with a new brick façade. Another Wirth Building, the 1883 Haug Brothers Block at 15 West Superior Street (between the Miles Block and the Wirth Block) was demolished in 1995; its lot is now empty.

1885 Board of Trade

302 – 304 West Superior Street
Architects: WIRTH & TRAPHAGEN
Built: 1885 | Lost: 1894

Constructed of pressed brick with Fond du Lac sandstone and terra cotta trim, the four-story, Romanesque Revival Board of Trade Building was the first design from the newly formed architectural partnership of George Wirth and Oliver Traphagen. It included both arched and flat-headed windows, grand arched entrances on both Third Avenue West and Superior Street, and square corner columns and towers. Atop the building along its Superior Street façade a triangular carved-sandstone pediment showed a freighter under full sail with the 1885 date and the words "Board of Trade."

Clinton Markell, George C. Stone, Owen Fargusson, and others organized the Duluth Board of Trade in 1881 to deal with the growing volume of wheat reaching Duluth for marketing and shipping. Members of the board met in other downtown buildings until January, 1886, when they all moved into the Board of Trade, which held thirty-two offices for the use of grain commissioners.

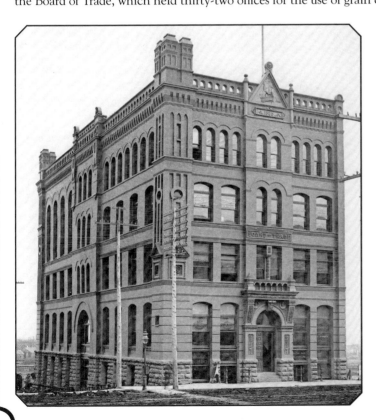

The Board of Trade was the pride of Duluth until February 11, 1894, when fire broke out. An attempt by commissioners to extinguish the flames failed due to lack of water. When firefighters arrived they found the closest hydrants frozen and had to thaw them out before they could fight the fire. The delay was disastrous and the fire spread so fast, aided by a cold wind off the lake, that the Board of Trade Building could not be saved. Large crowds gathered to watch and had to be chased out of harm's way when the east wall fell photo page 76). The building was completely destroyed. Grain commissioners moved to other buildings until the new Board of Trade Building at 301 West Superior was completed in 1895. That same year the Lonsdale Building replaced the original Board of Trade.

George Wirth: 1880s Architect

George Wirth (1861–1935), a native of Bavaria, Germany, first came to the U.S. in 1869 to study architecture at Cornell College. In 1879 he opened a practice in St. Paul, where he designed many significant homes and commercial buildings. He hired Oliver Traphagen as a carpenter and sent him north to oversee the construction of his designs in Duluth, launching Traphagen's career in the Zenith City. Wirth never lived in Duluth; In 1886 he returned to Germany.

Wirth designed Duluth's Grand Opera House, the 1883 Fargusson Block, the Williamson Block, the Costello Block, the Miles Block, the 1885 Board of Trade (left), and many others. Only two Wirth buildings remain in Duluth: the 1883 Bell & Eyster Bank at 3 West Superior Street (currently vacant) and the Wirth Building at 13 West Superior Street (home to Lizzard's Gallery), which he built for his brother Max, a pharmacist. Wirth also did the 1884 Silberstein-Bondy building at 9–11 West Superior Street, and the 1882 Metropolitan Block, 113–119 West Superior Street, but most of his work has been lost to remodeling.

American Exchange Bank

230 West Superior Street
Architect: OLIVER TRAPHAGEN
Built: 1887 | Lost: 1955

Hamilton M. Peyton helped create the American Exchange Bank in 1879 by reorganizing the failing Duluth Savings Bank. The Exchange started with a capital stock of $25,000, less than $600,000 today. But under the direction of Peyton, who served as the bank's only president, it thrived until his death in 1928. The bank—whose name had changed to American Exchange National—merged with First National Bank in 1929, just months before the stock market crashed; the two became the First American National Bank.

Another Traphagen Romanesque design, the four-story, brick-faced American Exchange Bank stood on a foundation of Fond du Lac brownstone, which also trimmed its windows and doors. Its corner tower, which does not fit the building's overall design, is thought to be a last-minute addition to please George Spencer, the driving force behind the bank's construction. After the merger with First National, the building continued to serve downtown Duluth as the Exchange Building, which housed a number of businesses. After the Exchange Building's demolition in September, 1955, a brand new First American National Bank went up on the same lot; it later became home to Norwest Bank, today's Wells Fargo.

Duluth National Bank

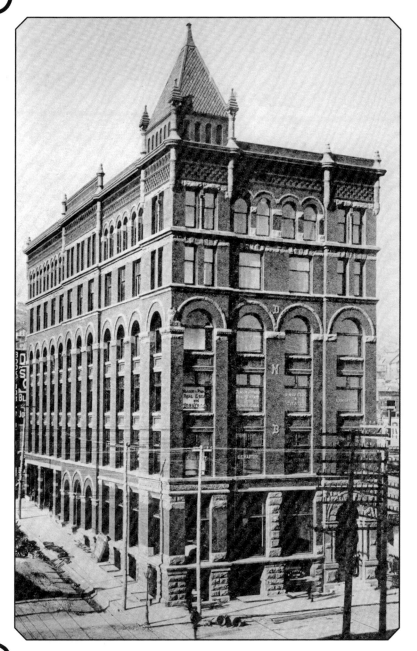

Built right across Superior street from the American Exchange Bank building, the massive brick six-story Duluth National Bank building was another fine example of the Romanesque Revival style, but it featured more decorative details than the Exchange. Its first floor featured an arched entrance with carved columns of Fond du Lac sandstone and a splendid square corner tower with turrets. The letters "DNB" were placed vertically on the front façade of the second through fourth stories.

229 – 231 West Superior Street
Architect: OLIVER G. TRAPHAGEN
Built: 1887 | Lost: 1958

The bank had been organized in 1882 with Luther Mendenhall (shown in sketch) as president and a financial stake of $150,000, unusually high for its day. Albert L. Ordean took the helm when the bank moved into this building. In February, 1888, Duluth National merged with Union National Bank less than a year after opening the building, becoming the Duluth Union National Bank (and rendering the letters on the building obsolete). A year later the Duluth Union National merged with the Merchants National to become the First National Bank of Duluth.

In 1929, a short time before the stock market crashed, First National merged with American Exchange Bank to become First American National Bank. The new bank conducted business in this building until 1957 when it moved to a new building on the site of the Exchange Bank. The Duluth Bank was demolished in 1958 for a parking lot. In 1977 the Normandy Mall, later renamed the Holiday Center, was built over the former footprint of the Duluth National Bank and other buildings.

Pastoret-Stenson Block (aka Lowell Block)

Along with his partner Oliver Stenson, Michael Pastoret (shown in sketch) built the Pastoret-Stenson Block, yet another Traphagen-designed Richardsonian Romanesque building faced with brownstone quarried in Fond du Lac. The six-story building featured a rounded corner with a carved entrance where Superior Street meets First Avenue East. Plaques carved with "O. Stenson" and "M. Pastoret" sat above columns on either side of the entrance. Arched windows on the top floor along with carved stone bands of scrolls and leaves between floors added to the building's visual appeal.

29 ~ 33 East Superior Street
Architect: OLIVER G. TRAPHAGEN
Built: 1888 | Lost: 1999

First used to house Michael Pastoret and Owen Stenson's dry goods store, the building was later rented to a number of businesses over the years: an undertaker, Singer Sewing Machines, Gotkins Greater Markets, the B & Y Cap Company, King Korn Stamps, the Duluth Sewing Center, and even a Radio Shack. The third through sixth floors were converted into apartments, and the building's name was changed to the Lowell Block.

In 1930 a fire that started in the B & Y Cap Company spread to the top floors where two adults and two children were trapped—and died. America was still under Prohibition, and rumors circulated that the fire was caused by a still operating in the cap factory. Only the bottom three floors were saved. The building's last residents were John's Used Furniture and the Last Place on Earth. In 1999 the building was demolished and replaced with another whose first three floors replicate those of the original.

The East 100 Block of Upper Superior Street

In 1999 A & L Development built what was referred to as the "Soft Center" or "Technology Center," a building complex its developers promised would help Duluth become a major center for technology-related jobs. That idea never came to fruition. Before construction started, however, nearly an entire block of historic buildings came down. From the 1881 Hosmer Building at 13–15 East Superior to the 1893 Wright/Jones Block next to it east to the Lowell Block (the former Pastoret-Stenson Block, see above), all were demolished in 1999 despite a lawsuit aimed at preventing their destruction. The Benz Block at 1 East Superior and the Long's Block at 3–9 East Superior (pictured) had been demolished years before, replaced with a parking lot.

The unsuccessful lawsuit, brought by Dr. Eric Ringsred and others, did result in one positive outcome for Duluth's historic buildings: The presiding judge allowed the demolition, but also decreed that all future permit applications for demolition of buildings in downtown Duluth must include an independently prepared Environmental Impact Statement. That won't necessarily prevent demolition, but it may cause potential developers to pause and assess whether a historic building could be successfully adapted for reuse.

Manhattan Building

410 – 416 West Superior Street
Architect: HENRY RAEDER
Built: 1889 | Lost: 1941

When Chicago architects Raeder, Coffin and Crocker were selected by Duluth's Chamber of Commerce to build a grand office building, Henry Raeder created this high Victorian design: two almost identical six-story wings separated by an open court but joined by a first-story arched entrance of elaborately carved rock-faced stone. The ornate structure was topped near the back with a 140-foot Gothic tower complete with turrets and a balcony. Façades featured brick, red tile, sandstone, polished granite, terra cotta, and copper. Columns with carved capitals standing three stories tall decorated both wings.

Because of its owners—who occupied the top three floors from 1889 to 1903—the Manhattan Building was commonly called the Chamber of Commerce building. The Chamber merged with the Duluth Commercial Club in 1902 and moved to the Torrey Building. In 1909 the organization would build the Commercial Club at 402 West First Street, which was renovated into the Duluth Athletic Club in the 1940s. After the Chamber left the Manhattan, attorneys, real estate firms, mining companies, and forest product businesses occupied the building's many offices.

By the 1930s its popularity dropped and many of its offices sat vacant. The building was razed in 1941. In 1942 the Northland Building was built on the site of the Manhattan; it remains there today.

Manufacturer's Bank
(aka Woodward Building)

302 – 304 Central Avenue North
Architect: OLIVER G. TRAPHAGEN
Built: 1888 | Lost: 1977

Manufacturer's bank (left) was the first banking house established in the new Village of West Duluth in 1888. Unfortunately, unlike other Duluth banks, it did not successfully ride out the financial panic of 1893 and it failed in 1896. The three-story brick building had a stone entrance, decorative brick trim, arched windows on the second floor, and a brick cornice. After the bank failed, the building was renamed the Woodward Building and the second and third floors were converted into apartments. The first floor at various times housed a real estate office, department store, grocery, and a pharmacy. By 1976 the building sat vacant; a year later it was condemned and demolished to make room for a parking lot.

1889 Palladio Building

401 – 403 West Superior Street

Architect: HENRY RAEDER

Built: 1889 | Lost: 1937

The Bay View House, Duluth's first hotel, stood on the northwest corner of Superior Street and Fourth Avenue West from 1869 to 1888 when it was demolished to make room for the Palladio Building. Designed by Chicago architect Henry Raeder, the brick and stone office building stood eight stories tall. The first two stories were constructed of sandstone outfitted with decorative entrances on both Superior Street and Fourth Avenue West. Arched windows and a patterned brick frieze beneath the cornice further decorated the building. The Superior Street entry (pictured, top right) was particularly impressive.

Columns on either side of the entry featured carved stone figures whose torsos appear to sprout from the stone. The muscled-and-bearded figures have their arms crossed above their heads, as if holding up the columns—and the building—themselves. Merchants Bank occupied the first floor for less than a year until it merged with First National Bank; professional offices filled the upper floors.

In 1937 the Palladio was razed to its foundation and replaced with the three-story WEBC Radio Building, headquarters for the oldest radio station in the region, which first broadcast in June of 1924 with 50 watts of power. In 1928, when then-President Calvin Coolidge was visiting Duluth and Superior (he spent that summer on Wisconsin's Brule River, fishing for trout) the station temporarily boosted its signal to 500 watts and joined the NBC radio network as a convenience to the president and his staff, who wanted to listen to coverage of the national political conventions. Because of this, the *New York Times* nicknamed WEBC "The President's Station." In 1968 the building was rededicated as the Palladio Building. Today its main tenant is the Beacon Bank.

C. H. Oppel Block

115 ~ 117 E. Superior

Architect: OLIVER G. TRAPHAGEN

Built: 1889 | Lost: 1987

German immigrant Christian H. Oppel and his wife Christina arrived in Duluth in 1870, opening one of the city's first grocery and dry goods stores By the 1880s the firm had changed its name to Oppel and Sons with Frank, Herman, and Charles Oppel partnering with their father. The firm was the first to ship goods into Duluth using the Duluth & Iron Range Railway and they also ran a store in Tower, Minnesota, that dealt in furs and birch bark canoes.

The three-story Oppel building was faced in brick and featured carved stone trim and the name C. H. Oppel carved on the cornice pediment. The main floor store offered men's and boys' clothing on one side and groceries on the other. The Oppel family lived on the upper two floors, and they needed them both: the Oppels had eleven children—you can see many of them in the windows and outside the building in the photo at right. The Oppel stores closed in 1907 when Christian was eighty years old. (The family later changed the spelling of its last name to "Opal.") Other businesses occupied the building until its demolition in 1987; its last occupant was the Granada Center adult bookstore. Next door, the Granada Theatre at 109 East Superior Street was also demolished. The site of both buildings now hosts the Fond du Lac Casino parking ramp.

1889 Phoenix Block

325 ~ 335 West Superior Street

Architect: OLIVER G. TRAPHAGEN

Built: 1889 | Lost: 1994

Like the Palladio Block, the Phoenix Block that stands in Duluth today is not the original. Built over the lot on which the Grand Opera House stood before it was consumed by fire, the Phoenix was so-named because it "rose from the ashes" of what was then Duluth's grandest architectural achievement. Like the opera house, The Phoenix's main arched entrance was in the center of its Superior Street façade, and it also featured a diagonally cut corner entry to the Boyce Drug Store, which operated out of the Phoenix for many years.

The Phoenix was a two-story red-brick office building with arched windows on the second floor. Sometime in the 1930s metal paneling was applied over the brick façade. It was a popular location for professional offices until it was destroyed in a fire, believed to be arson, in December, 1994. Officials told the *Duluth News Tribune* that the building could have been saved it if had been equipped with a sprinkler system. Its successor, also named the Phoenix Block, was built in 1995. Today the building's chief tenants are a Starbucks coffee shop and the offices of the Duluth Superior Symphony Orchestra.

Howe Building (a.k.a. Glencoe Building)

228 East 1st Street

Architects: McMillen & Radcliffe

Built: 1891 | Lost: 1946

Colonel George C. Howe, a pioneer in Duluth real estate, built the three-story Howe Block in 1891. The Kitchi Gammi Club, which had been burned out of its home at the Grand Opera House after a fire in 1889 destroyed its facilities, leased rooms within the Howe that same year. The Howe Block's first floor was reserved for retail space, and the Club occupied the second and third floors , staying there until its own building was constructed in 1912. The brick-and-stone Romanesque Revival building featured a round corner tower and a second-floor balcony overlooking First Street. Howe sold the building when he moved to Minneapolis in 1912. It then became the Glencoe Building, a name it carried until its demolition in 1945 to make room for a bowling alley and a commercial building.

Glass Block

128 West Superior Street

Architects: McMillen & Radcliffe

Built: 1892 | Lost: 1981

In March of 1887 John Panton and Joseph Watson opened a small, one-room dry goods store on Superior Street near First Avenue West. In November of that year they moved to a larger store at 118 West Superior Street. Their store's continued success encouraged them to build their own two-story building of red Tiffany brick and sandstone trim in 1892. In 1896 William White took over Watson's share of the business and the name became Panton and White, but it was called "The Glass Block," a term used in Minneapolis at the time for dry goods and department stores (Panton learned his trade working for the forerunner of Minneapolis's Donaldson's Department store). By 1902 another expansion added three more stories and a classical cornice to what was now called the Panton & White Glass Block Store. When the F. A. Patrick Company purchased the store in 1911, the name officially changed to The Glass Block Store. The new owners installed the Greysolon Tea Rooms with elegant, oak-paneled rooms featuring views of Lake Superior. It was a cornerstone of the Glass Block until 1940, when it relocated.

Glass Block opened a second store in the new Miller Hill Mall in 1973, but continued operation of the downtown facility until 1981 when it closed, much to the dismay of downtown shoppers. The building was demolished to make room for First Bank Duluth; that building is now home to US Bank.

Bradley Building

2 – 10 East Superior Street
Architects: GERMAN & JENSSEN
Built: 1909, 1924 | Lost: 1979

In 1909 Richard M. Bradley, owner of Boston's Bradley Real Estate Company, built this two-story office building and hired Duluth's William M. Prindle Company to manage it. The original architect is not recorded; Frederick German and Leif Jenssen designed a 1924 addition that increased the building by two floors and added a new façade of brick, tile, and terra cotta. The four-story, Commercial-style building had a flattened corner and few decorative elements except for classical detailing along the cornice.

During its lifetime the Bradley's first floor was home to Kelley Hardware, (sponsor of Duluth's NFL franchise, later known as the Duluth Eskimos), White Swan Drug Store, Smith Shoe Company, the Duluth Fur Company, and Floan-Liveroos-Ahlen Company, a clothing store for men. The upper floors had professional offices and from 1937 to 1966 housed the KDAL radio and television studios. WDSE-TV occupied the KDAL space from 1966 until 1978.

In 1979 the Bradley Building was demolished in order to widen Lake Avenue and turn its viaduct into a highway overpass for the expanding I-35. Today what remains of the lot is occupied by an entrance to Lake Place Park and the Lakewalk and features the Lake Superior Fountain by local artist Ben Effinger.

McMillen, Stebbins, & Radcliffe

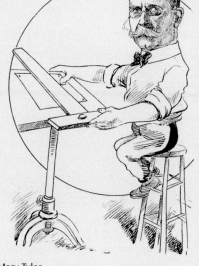

Born in Ireland, Charles M. McMillen (1860–1907) came to Duluth in about 1884. While in Duluth he partnered with Minneapolis architect Edward Stebbins (1854–1934), a native of Boston educated at M.I.T. Stebbins designed many Minneapolis schools and the Kenwood Parkway house made famous in the opening credits of the "Mary Tyler Moore Show" (Tyler Moore's character, Mary Richards, lived in the house). Five of the Minnesota buildings McMillen designed are on the National Register of Historic Places. Together McMillen and Stebbins designed many homes and buildings in Duluth, including the Ensign House (page 19), both Ray Houses (page 21), Jackson School (page 54), Adams School (page 52), and the Temple Opera House (page 94). McMillen also designed Duluth's first Boat Club (page 172). He moved to North Carolina in 1899 and to Oklahoma in 1907, where he died.

Elmira, New York, native Edwin S. Radcliffe (1861–1935, shown in sketch) moved to St. Paul in 1858 and practiced at his father Abraham's firm until moving to Duluth in 1889, where he practiced with McMillen until 1892. Together they designed the Spalding House (page 25), the Burrows Block, Whittier School (page 59), the 1893 First Methodist Church (page 69) and the Howe/Glencoe Building and Glass Block (previous page). After splitting from McMillen, Radcliffe partnered with Charles E. Willoughby until 1900. He practiced alone until 1907, when he formed a new partnership with Vernon J. Price. Several of Radcliffe's designs still grace Duluth: the 1893 Jefferson School (916 East 3rd Street, now apartments), the 1910 George and Irene Fay House at 2032 East Superior Street), and the 1886 Duluth Armory at 201-207 East First Street, which became the Shrine Auditorium in 1917 (it is now a youth center).

French & Bassett Block

302 West First Street

Architects: LONG & KEES

Built: 1905 | Lost: 1948

Duluth's Weiland brothers built a business block at 24 East Superior Street in 1882 to house their furniture store. While the building remains, Weiland Brothers Furniture was bought out by the George A. French Company (originally Rainey & French), which in 1892 changed its name to French & Bassett. The firm specialized in furniture for homes, businesses, and schools. In 1905 French & Bassett commissioned Minneapolis architects Long & Kees—designers of Minneapolis's City Hall—to design a new furniture store. The three-story Romanesque Revival structure, built of brick and stone, featured prominent square towers on each corner, three entrances on First Street, and an elaborate curved main entrance on Third Avenue (pictured above). A 1907 addition added a fourth floor with a Mansard roof and other ornamentation to the building's exterior. By 1936 the firm was operating as French, Bassett & Scott, and in 1947 it moved into a new building at 2–6 East Superior Street along with A. F. Butchart & Sons, a dinnerware company, and Martha Strassburger's women's apparel shop. Maurice A. Rudolph opened a furniture store in the former French & Bassett location, but just a year later the building was destroyed by an enormous fire. Many surrounding buildings were damaged, and the collapsing building buried several cars.

Columbus Block

28–30 West Superior Street

Architects: PEABODY & STEARNS

Built: 1894 | Altered: 1908, 1955

When the three-story brick Columbus Block opened in 1894, glass and crockery sales firm F. A. Parker & Company moved in as its first tenant. William Pattison purchased the building in 1908 and added two floors that same year. Minnesota Power & Light leased the building in 1924. The firm first organized as the Great Northern Power Company, which in 1906 harnessed the St. Louis River by building the Thompson Dam at the old logging town of Thomson. At the time it powered up, the Thomson Dam was the third largest waterpower plant in the world. In 1955, MP&L purchased the buildings next door to the Columbus at 24 and 26 West Superior Street, razed them, and made a significant addition to the Columbus. The Columbus Block isn't lost; it is hidden from view: the only visible remnants of the old façade are the building's rear windows. The firm later dropped the "& Light" from its name. Today Minnesota Power is owned by the Allete Corporation and provides power to 144,000 customers in Northwestern Minnesota and Northern Wisconsin.

Burrows Block (a.k.a. Columbia Building)

301–303 West Superior Street

Architects: McMillen & Radcliffe

Built: 1891 | Altered: 1958, 2010

Built as a five-story Romanesque Revival style retail and office complex of brick with brownstone trim, the Burrows Block was built to house Matthew S. Burrow's Great Eastern Clothing Store, which first opened in 1886 in another location. Burrows sold men's and children's clothing on the first two floors and leased the upper floors as office space. Burrows loved using giveaways to increase sales. Customers shopping close to Thanksgiving often went home with a free turkey and children received skates when their parent purchased winter clothes for them. In 1900, Burrows announced that his employees would throw suits of clothes out the upper floors to patrons in the street; the crowd blocked streetcars on Superior Street. In 1905 Burrows sold his business to Columbia Clothing and moved to Michigan, and the block became known as the Columbia Building. The Burrows Block/ Columbia Building is not lost, but none of its original exterior is visible. In 1958 the building was remodeled and renamed the Beal Building. A year earlier the *Duluth Herald* described the remodel, announcing that the "drab brownstone and red brick building will be sheathed with enameled steel paneling in two tones of blue and a pattern of silver-aluminum stripping." The alteration, designed by Ellingsen Associates of Duluth, also removed the entire top floor. Another façade change took place in 2010 when Duluth's LHB Architects covered the porcelain-coated steel with blue and gray composite fiber-cement panels.

Metropolitan Block

113–119 West Superior Street

Architect: George Wirth

Built: 1882 | Altered: 1911, 1960, 1989

When first built, the Metropolitan Block's Queen Anne façade was highly adorned and faced with patterned brick, Ohio sandstone, and terra cotta trim. The building still serves Duluth, but its architect, George Wirth, wouldn't recognize it if he were alive to see it: its façade has been altered repeatedly over the years. Commissioned by Duluth George Spencer and Melvin Forbes, the Metropolitan was built to house the American Exchange Bank and offices for the newly formed Board of Trade—but it is known best as a dry goods store. First Metropolitan Dry Goods (1882–1884), then Friemuth's Dry Goods (1884–1900), the Gray-Tallent Store, George A. Gray & Company, and finally Wahl's Department Store (1936–1960). In 1911 Gray remodeled the building inside and out, covering the exterior with a more restrained look featuring neo-classical elements. Fifty years later, Wahl's gave it another new exterior. When Wahl's closed in 1989, Maurices purchased the building and connected it to its office building next-door, again altering the façade, this time to tie in seamlessly with its neighboring building.

Odd Fellows Hall

20 North Lake Avenue
Architect: OLIVER G. TRAPHAGEN
Built: 1888 | Lost: 1975

The Independent Order of Odd Fellows was a secret fraternal society founded in England during the eighteenth century. The first lodge in the United States was organized in 1819 as a benevolent club to aid widows and orphans. Duluthians established an Odd Fellows lodge in 1870, and by the time their headquarters was constructed their rolls had grown to 155 members. Twelve years after the building was constructed, enrolment was said to be over 1,000.

Duluth's brick-and-stone Odd fellow's Hall was designed by architect Oliver Traphagen, himself a member of the Odd Fellows (when he moved to Honolulu in 1896 he joined a local chapter and in 1904 designed that city's Odd Fellow's Hall). The red brick Romanesque Revival building had a square tower with a balcony and pyramidal cap, arched windows, a granite entrance arch, and a profusion of carved stone symbols on the Lake Avenue façade.

The Odd Fellows meeting rooms were on the third floor; the Duluth, Missabe and Iron Range Railway offices occupied the second, and retail stores were located on the first. The Odd Fellows left the building about 1917, after which it became home to furniture stores, including Whelan-Linck in the 1920s and '30s and Rudolph's in the 1950s. By the 1970s the Odd Fellows building sat vacant; it was demolished in 1975. The lot now contains a portion of a parking ramp.

Modern Woodmen's Hall

2031 West 1st Street
Architect: ABRAHAM HOLSTEAD
Built: 1912 | Lost: 2004

The Modern Woodmen of America was a fraternal life insurance society founded in Iowa about 1890; they called their lodges camps. During the late 1800s the Woodmen popularized "tree stump" grave markers, which symbolize a life cut short. Today there are over 750,000 members in 2,300 camps and 700 youth groups across America.

Duluth had several camps in West Duluth as early as 1897. In 1912 they joined together to build Modern Woodmen Hall, a two-story brick building containing meeting halls and an auditorium which was rented out for meetings and parties. The Modern Woodmen camps moved out of the building in 1990, after which the building was occupied by a printer and a carpet store before being razed in 2004. The lot remains empty.

PART FOUR

LOST INDUSTRIES

Iron Bay Works / National Iron Company (1889 – 1993)

The Fur Trade (1816–1839)

As the first industry introduced to the New World by Europeans, the fur trade predated Duluth—in fact, it was essentially gone by the time Duluth Township was first established in 1856. From roughly 1550 to the 1850, European gentlemen distinguished themselves by donning felt hats made from beaver underfur. Trappers had driven the beaver to extinction throughout western Europe and nearly wiped them out in Russia and Scandinavia by the end of the sixteenth century. So Europeans, particularly the French, set out for the New World in search of more fur.

Explorers such as Robert de La Salle, Jean Nicollet, Jacques Marquette, Louis Joliet, Pierre Esprit Radisson, and Sieur des Groseilliers—along with Jesuit missionaries including Jacque Marquette, Claude Jean Allouez, and Louis Hennepin—traveled with French soldiers and native guides throughout the Great Lakes area, mapping the region (which they claimed as New France) and opening trade with the various tribes they encountered. Well established at Saulte Ste. Marie and La Pointe on Madeline Island among the Apostle Islands, the Ojibwe became natural trading partners with the French, who called Lake Superior Lac Tracey after the Marquis Prouville de Tracy, governor of New France.

Wars between the Dakota and Ojibwe complicated trade. That's how Duluth's namesake, Daniel Greysolon Sieur du Luht, first entered the picture. Born in Saint-Germain-Laval, France, du Luht was stationed in Montreal in 1678 when he set out to the head of the lakes in part to establish peace among the tribes who lived on the shores of Lake Superior. In 1679 his party landed at *Onigamiinsing* ("Little Portage") on Minnesota Point—an Ojibwe portage later platted as Duluth's Portage Street and since 1871 the site of Duluth's ship canal. While du Luht successfully established peace among the Ojibwe, Dakota, Cree, and Assiniboin peoples, it was short lived.

Beside the Ojibwe, independent French agents licensed by France called *Coureur des bois* ("wood runners") were also trapping fur-bearing animals. Those *Coureur des bois* who traveled by canoe became known as *Voyaguers*. These independent agents would later go to work for France's North West Company. Grand Portage, on the Lake Superior shore near today's U.S.-Canada border, became a major trading center.

The British, who still controled the American colonies at the time, also entered the fur trade. The competition between the two nations came to a head when Europe's Seven Years War spilled over to North America as the French and Indian War, which lasted from 1754 to 1763.

Trade was complicated by the war, and the French and British continued to clash after the war ended, with voyageurs of the French-controled

North West Company competing with the British-run Hudson's Bay Company to see who could send home the most hat-making material.

The War of Independence established the United States of America and changed the fur trade. In the 1780s the North West Company established Fort St. Louis at the mouth of the St. Louis River at what is now Superior, Wisconsin; the post became the region's center of trade and remained so until it burned in 1800. In 1809 German immigrant John Jacob Astor—said to be the world's first millionaire—formed the **American Fur Company** and set up a post at Fond du Lac, where the Ojibwe had established themselves by 1770. While the Ojibwe preferred to trade with the French and British, the War of 1812 put an end to all that: the post-war American Congress barred foreigners from trading in American territory. And so in 1816 Astor took over the North West Company's interests and a year later built a new fort at Fond du Lac, managed by William Morrison.

Astor's facility included a two-story log building, a granary, an ice house, a stable, a dormitory for traders, and the post commander's house. The fort was surrounded by a cedar-post fence. It faced the St. Louis River near today's 133rd Avenue West. (Its ruins are pictured above, around 1900). An Ojibwe village stood on an island directly across from the post.

The outpost became a center of trade and a natural spot for gatherings. In 1826 Michigan territorial governor William Cass and Colonel Thomas L. McKenney, the head of the newly formed United States Indian Department, gathered native leaders from throughout the region at Fond du Lac to ratify a treaty designed to both stop fighting among the Ojibwe, Dakota, and other tribes as well as to establish U.S. dominance in the region. Artist James Otto Lewis traveled with McKinney to Fond du Lac and painted watercolors of both the treaty signing and Astor's fur post, shown on the previous page depicting both the front (left) and back (right) of the post.

Unfortunately for Astor, the fur trade declined steeply just five years later. The 1830s saw the fur post turn to commercial fishing to bolster its profits. Astor's charter expired in 1833, leaving trader Ramsay Crooks in charge of the post. At this same time Protestant missionaries like Edmund Ely came to the region. Ely helped establish a mission and taught grammar and arithmetic to the native and mixed-race children who lived near the fort. Ely also worked on converting locals to Christianity and set to work on a Chippewa language dictionary. But economic realities continued to hinder population growth: A financial panic in 1837 coincided with the increased popularity of silk hats in Europe, and the European fur trade came to a screeching halt. The fisheries operated by the fur company saw bountiful harvests, but had few customers (see next page). The company failed in 1842, the fur post ceased operating by 1847, and the mission closed its doors in 1849.

The post was abandoned and soon fell into decay. The photograph at left shows part of the post's ruins shortly before they were destroyed in about 1900. In the 1930s a replica of the trading post (pictured below) was built in nearby Chamber's Grove Park. Created as a tourist attraction, it was much smaller than the original post and its popularity was short lived. The long-neglected reconstruction was demolished in 1968. The actual fur post site was set aside as Astor Park, recently renamed Historical Park.

Commercial Fishing (1834–1960s)

Commercial fishing along Lake Superior's North Shore first began in 1834, when the American Fur Company set up fisheries on Encampment Island, Grand Portage, and Isle Royale. In 1839 they caught five thousand barrels of fish, but had no market for sales. The operation closed in 1842. Ojibwe continued to harvest fish at Fond du Lac, hauling in record numbers of walleyes from the St. Louis River rapids for three weeks each spring. Reports stated that in 1853 two fishermen with one net filled a two-fathom canoe in less than an hour. In 1860, Reverend James Peet of Oneota wrote that he had helped pull in a seine holding 523 walleye. He also reported that a commercial fisherman named Harrington had caught over fifteen thousand fish and that "Mr. Barlow's party have caught over thirty barrels" at roughly ninety fish per barrel. Up the lake's north shore, H. H. McCullough sold fish caught by Ojibwe at Grand Portage. No one found great success: there was still relatively no local market nor an efficient way to bring fish to customers.

The industry remained nearly dormant in Duluth until the 1870 arrival of the Lake Superior & Mississippi Railroad: fisheries could now ship their product to distant markets. Scandinavian immigrants who had previously made their living fishing homeland waters also began arriving in the 1870s.

Fisheries popped up in settlements along the western Lake Superior shores at Isle Royale, and the Apostle Islands, harvesting chubs, yellow perch, sturgeon, lake trout, and herring and whitefish by the ton.

In 1871 Duluth pioneers Jerome Cooley and George Lavaque established the **Cooley-Lavaque Fishery** at 437 Lake Avenue and 14 Morse Street in today's Canal Park Business District. **A. Booth and Sons Packing Company** of Chicago, wholesale dealers in fish, purchased Cooley-Lavaque in 1886. A. Booth and other fisheries found markets for their yield in Minneapolis, St. Paul, Chicago, Kansas City, and St. Louis. A. Booth also recruited fisherman from Norway and Sweden to immigrate to the United States and establish fishing villages along western Lake Superior's north and south shores and at Isle Royale. Booth quickly became western Lake Superior's dominant fishery. In 1909, 1912, and 1915 the company enlarged or built new cold storage buildings for its fishery. The building shown at left was at the Morse Street location in the early 1900s (the site of the once-adjacent buildings is now a parking lot).

Herring fishing reached its peak in the early 1890s, providing 78 percent of herring caught in the United States. In 1897 Sam Johnson, a Swedish immigrant who learned to fish on the Baltic Sea, founded **Sam Johnson & Sons Fisheries Inc.** directly across the street from Booth Fisheries (pictured above). Other Duluth fisheries active at the time included **H. Christianson & Sons, Hogstad Fisheries, Scandia Fish Company, Bray Fish Company, Goldish Fisheries, A. Kemp Fisheries**, and **Sivertson Brothers**.

In 1892 Severin Sivertson and his two brothers emigrated from Norway and settled along the North Shore. He soon joined the fishing communities on Isle Royale. Sivertson Brothers Fisheries was established in Duluth in 1921 to "extend the markets for the catch of the Isle Royale and North Shore fishermen." Fishing villages such as the one pictured above were also established on the south shore at Port Wing, Cornucopia, and other Wisconsin communities. The industry continued to thrive. Outfits like A. Booth supported their fisherman by sending steamers, including the *America* (see sidebar at right), to supply the villages, allowing mostly Norwegian (with some Finnish and Swedish) fishermen to spend more time working the waters.

The industry reached its peak in 1915 with a record catch of 20 million pounds in Duluth alone. In the 1920s, more than two hundred fishermen operated between Beaver Bay and the Pigeon River. But the 1930s were a different story. The lake's catch dwindled to below 8 million pounds. The industry never quite recovered. Predatory lamprey eels and over-harvesting nearly wiped out the trout in the 1950s. Today the Lake Superior fishing industry is all but a memory; the annual harvest is less than two thousand pounds.

In 1940 the Sivertsons purchased the Hogstad Fisheries, which had purchased A. Booth in 1928. In the 1960s it began operating as the **Lake Superior Fish Company**, which it had acquired with its purchase of Goldish Fisheries. The company still operates today, and two of Sivertson's grandchildren and their families remain involved. **A. Kemp Fisheries**, established in Duluth in 1930 by Aron and Abe Kemp, still operates. In the 1970s the company became **Louis Kemp's**, named for its owner (a childhood friend of Bob Dylan, who also managed Dylan's 1976 "Rolling Thunder" tour), who developed a process for making *surimi*, artificial crab meat made of pollock and whitefish. Today, Louis Kemp's is a subsidiary of Trident Seafoods Corporation of Seattle, selling its Crab Delight throughout the world.

The Steamer America

The *America*, owned by the A. Booth Company, was a beloved ship on Lake Superior, serving for most of its life as a transportation link between Duluth, Port Arthur (now Thunder Bay, Ontario), Isle Royale, and settlements along the North Shore. It brought people and goods to remote outposts and fishing villages along the shore and at Isle Royale, supplying A. Booth's contracted fishermen. She also supplied the Split Rock Lighthouse and its keeper and family. This made the *America* an important communication tool, as shipments often included mail and other messages.

The excursion boat *America* first hit the water in 1898, when it was built by the Detroit Dry Dock Company in Wyandotte, Michigan. Designed to make daily trips between Michigan City and Chicago, she could hold 277 passengers and 40 crew. The Booth Steamship Line purchased her in 1902. In 1908 a forest fire threatened the very North Shore townships the *America* served, and Minnesota governor John Johnson called on the vessel to evacuate Beaver Bay. She rescued about three hundred villagers.

On June 6, 1928, the *America* left Grand Marais for Isle Royale to drop off passengers before heading to Port Arthur. In the early morning hours of June 7, she struck a reef near Isle Royale's Washington Harbor, skidding over the rocks four times and ripping a hole in her hull just below the engine room on the starboard side. The ship's pumps couldn't keep up with the water pouring in. The captain ordered the ship to steer for the north gap of Washington Harbor in an attempt to beach her, but it struck more rocks and stopped ninety feet from shore. All thirty-one passengers and crew managed to get off the *America* before she slid off into deep water.

The Lumber Industry (1880s–1970s)

In 1856 Henry W. Wheeler famously walked from St. Paul to Oneota and, with machinery shipped from Detroit, built the first sawmill in what would become the city of Duluth along the bay at about Forty-Fourth Avenue West. Pioneers J. B. Culver and William Nettleton started the first sawmill in Duluth Township. The Wheeler mill burned in 1870, two years after it halted operation. By then mills had popped up on western Lake Superior's shores wherever log rafts, and later trains, could reach them—on the north shore from Duluth to Beaver Bay and along the south shore from Superior to Ashland. Historian Dwight Woodbridge reported that in 1894 the following firms were operating sawmills in Duluth: **Mitchell & McClure**; **Merrill & Ring Lumber Company**; **Duncan, Brewer & Co.**; **J. B. Stevens**; **Peycott, Kimball & Barber**; **C. B. Murray and Co.**; **B. B. Richards Lumber Company**; **Hubbard & Vincent**; **W. P. Heimbach**; **Scott-Holsten Lumber Company**; **Howard Lumber Company**; **M. Carrol**; and **Herman Becklinger**. In northern Wisconsin, nine mills operated out of Washburn, Bayfield, and Ashland alone; it was said that the sawdust generated by the mills covered all of Chequamegon Bay.

In the 1880s area mills produced an average of 10 million board feet a year; in 1890 they produced 150 million feet. By 1894 thirty-two mills employed 7,700 in Duluth and Superior—and more mills operated along the western Lake Superior shores. Twin Ports milling peaked in 1902, when 443 million board feet were produced. During the first ten years of the twentieth century over 3 billion board feet of lumber came out of Duluth's mills, but just over 1 billion feet was cut from 1910 to 1921, the year many declared the industry played out. Indeed, the sawmilling industry had been in decline since at least 1910, when operations in Duluth dropped to just six major sawmills. Lumber mills operated as close as they could to lumber camps, and by then most of the old growth forests in the area had been cleared; it no longer made sense to operate a mill in the Zenith City. In 1922 only one mill operated out of Duluth; by 1927 it was gone.

Logs reached the mills either by rail or water, and the mills converted the raw material into lumber. The logs were placed into a barker, a machine which stripped off the bark. Once the logs were stripped, sawyers ran them through a variety of saws, starting with the double gang, a large set of parallel blades powered by water that sawed the logs into boards. Gate saws (sometimes called sash or frame saws), which sat in a frame and moved up and down by power generated from the mill's waterwheel, were also used. (A gang saw was a set of gate saws working in unison.) Ripsaws cut the boards to narrower widths. The edgerman trimmed the boards' edges, which afterward were cut to length with a cutoff saw. In the industry's early days, lumber was cut manually using whipsaws or pit saws, which were operated by two men, one of which literally stood in a pit while sawing; each board was cut individually. All the saws were maintained by the filer, highly skilled at sharpening saw blades. Finally the boards were placed in a large shed called a drying kiln where steam heat dried them out. After the lumber had dried, off-bearers carried the finished product away to the lumberyard, where it awaited transport by train or ship.

Newly married and graduated from the University of Michigan, young Zar D. Scott brought his bride to Duluth in the 1870s, where he used "a wheelbarrow and a rowboat to haul materials from the wilds of Park Point to his shop." In 1879 he and David Holsten began operating a sawmill on Lake Avenue South, forming **Scott-Holsten Lumber**. In 1890 the firm acquired the Graff Little Company, closed its mill, and moved into a new Scott-Holsten mill near Twenty-Fourth Avenue West and Michigan Street (pictured on page 124). There the firm built a drying kiln, sash and door plant, office building, and warehouse. Besides those who worked the mill the firm employed five hundred men in lumber camps. At its peak the mill cut 6 million board feet per year. The company changed its name to **Scott-Graff** in 1900 and, like other area mills, gradually withdrew from logging and sawmill activities. Working with the University of Minnesota in 1908, Scott-Graf became a pioneer in reforestation when it seeded and hand-

planted 142,250 white pines, 3,100 white ash, 41,750 Norway spruce, and tens of thousands of other species on lands its logging operations had cleared of old-growth timber. By 1927 the sawmill had shut down and Scott-Graff turned its focus to millwork. As World War II began, Scott-Graff concentrated on government defense contracts to build wooden invasion barges and ammunitions boxes. The company's support of the war effort earned it an "M Pennant" from the U. S. Maritime commission. Pacific Mutual Door Company purchased Scott-Graff in 1967 and the Duluth plant became a distribution warehouse. In 1978 Pacific Mutual closed the plant and sold the

property to the Duluth Transit Authority which demolished the Scott-Graff buildings and built a bus maintenance facility.

In 1890 Jethro Mitchell of Cincinnati, Ohio, and William C. McClure of Saginaw, Michigan, invested in a sawmill in Duluth to cut lumber being harvested in northern Minnesota. Mitchell remained in Cincinnati, but McClure moved to Duluth, setting up housekeeping in the Spalding Hotel and later established an office in the Lyceum Theatre building across the street. When the **Mitchell & McClure Sawmill** opened in 1891 at Fifty-First Avenue West along the bay (pictured above), its owners claimed it was the

build garages in West Duluth. A paper plant was built on the site in 1988.

The **Duncan Brewer Sawmill** was established in Duluth in 1887 and in 1892 built a sawmill at Thirty-Ninth Avenue West. In 1902, having run out of lumber to cut, the mill was purchased by the **Red Cliff Lumber Company**. Red Cliff operated the mill until it closed in 1913.

Huntress & Brown (pictured below) set up shop on Grassy Point in 1890, but only lasted sixteen years.

Grassy Point was also the site of **Merrill & Ring** (pictured at left) another former Michigan outfit that moved to Duluth after running out of lumber in Michigan. Like many other operations, Merrill & Ring invested in more than just their sawmill. In 1899 the firm established the Split Rock

The Lumber Industry, continued...

largest in the world, with a 2,400-foot dock to serve cargo ships. While the impressive facility was outfitted with the latest machinery, the mill was second in capacity in the United States at the time, just shy of that of the Young Mill in Clinton, Iowa. Still, it could produce over 3 million board feet of lumber in one week. In 1894, at the peak of the Minnesota logging industry, Mitchell and McClure employed 200 workers in the West Duluth mill and 450 loggers in the woods. The company built sixty houses and a boarding house near the sawmill for employees.

In 1903 the **Alger Smith Company** purchased and took over the mill's operation. In September 1920, with the clearing of most of the white pine and the decline in the lumber industry in northern Minnesota, the sawmill was dismantled. According to a newspaper story about the mill's demolition, much of the lumber from the sawmill was sold to individuals who used it to

Lumber Company to hire lumberjacks to harvest an estimated 200 million board feet of timber on land it had recently purchased. It then built a logging railroad to bring the logs to the mill on St. Louis Bay.

Logging in Northern Minnesota

Much of the logging in the western Lake Superior region took place in the Arrowhead along the lake's north shore (northern Wisconsin was also logged thoroughly, as were Isle Royale and the Apostle Islands). Minnesota lumberjacks felled enough timber between 1891 and 1924 to produce nearly eight billion board feet of lumber. The work was hard and the conditions cold; the logging season stretched from November to April as the frozen ground prevented oxen and draft horses from bogging down under their loads. A timber cruiser was sent ahead by lumber companies to scout which trees to harvest. At the work site, the foreman oversaw everything, from building the camp to tree selection—even where the trees should fall.

A logging crew typically consisted of two sawyers, a swamper, a chainer, a teamster, a sled tender, a decker, and a groundhog. The sawyers notched trees with an axe then worked in pairs with a cross-cut saw to take the trees down; on a good day a team could cut up to one hundred white pines. Swampers trimmed limbs off felled trees, cleared brush, kept roadways clear, and removed manure. Teamsters (also called skidders) used horses to pull felled trees from where they were cut to landing areas where they were later loaded and sent to lumber mills. If the tree was less than a mile from the loading area, it was dragged out with chains (attached by the chainer to a go-devil, a wishbone-shaped tree crotch); when trees were felled further away, the groundhogs stacked logs on sleighs pulled by teams of oxen or draft horses using cant hooks. (Horses were later replaced by steam-powered tractors called log-haulers.) The road monkey was in charge of building and maintaining logging roads, often made of ice so the sleighs could move more easily. Along downhill grades, a worker called the hayman-on-the-hill threw hay on the ice to slow the sleighs so they would not overcome the horses pulling them.

Once at the landing area, deckers made parallel stacks of logs so they could more easily be rolled into the river for transport to the mills. In the water men tied the logs into giant rafts which they floated or towed downstream to Lake Superior and the mills. The men who worked these rafts—called rivermen, river drivers, and riverhogs—used cant hooks to maneuver logs. Their task was called cordelling: walking along the river bank keeping the logs moving wherever boats could not help navigate the rafts. Occasionally they had to walk out on the logs to keep a raft moving. This job was the task of the birler, a highly skilled riverhog who wore calked (spiked) boots and used small, quick steps to spin logs into place as he moved about a log raft. Occasionally logs would pile up during a drive, creating a literal logjam. In extreme cases, dynamite was used to clear the jams.

Once a raft was brought to Lake Superior's shores, logging outfits leased tugs, steam barges, and scows to tow them to mills in Duluth and other mill towns. Later trains were used to transport the logs; flat cars were loaded at first by a loading gang of groundhogs using jammers, crane-like devices powered by horse (later replaced with steam loaders). Lumber companies laid hundreds of miles of track to harvest trees on the North Shore.

Much of life in a lumber camp revolved around the cook and his crew, which included a helper called a cookie and a chore boy known as the bull cook. The camp woke at 5 A.M.; breakfast came an hour later. The jacks had twelve minutes to eat, and the cooks allowed no talking (most likely to thwart criticism that could escalate into mutiny; if the crew was dissatisfied with the chow, their recourse was to stop work in protest, an action called "walking the cook"). They then went straight to work until 11:30 A.M., when the bull cook brought them flaggins, hot lunches packed in large cans. At noon they were back to work and toiled until the sun set. After a leisurely twenty-minute dinner, the loggers occupied themselves by relaxing on long pew-like seats called deacon's benches, repairing clothes and equipment or playing a few hands of cards. Lights went out at 9 P.M. Besides the jacks and the cooking crew, the camp was populated by the camp's clerk, called an inkslinger. Most camps were small; a camp of forty to fifty men was considered large.

On Sundays the men were allowed to bathe and boil up their clothes (washing them by placing them in boiling water), write letters home, and pack their beds with fresh straw. On days off they would travel to Duluth to spend their money. The Schroeder Company actually built two saloons and a brothel in order to keep men in camp on their days off—too often a trip to Duluth was extended by a stay in the local jail, and missing jacks slowed production. When a camp needed workers, they relied on recruiters to fill the roles; these men were known as man-catchers.

The success of the logging industry rose and fell with the economy—when Duluth boomed, so did timber production. Major logging outfits included the Schroeder Company, which logged along the Cross and Temperance rivers, and the Alger-Smith Company, the largest operation to log the Arrowhead. Logging reached its peak during the first decade of the twentieth century and was thought all but dead in Duluth by 1920. Still, it hung on through the twenties, but was hit particularly hard by the Great Depression and the creation of the Superior National Forest, and never quite recovered. In 1941 the last logging railroad was dismantled. Some logging still takes place in northern Minnesota, but most of it is done outside the Arrowhead region. Today's loggers use heavy machinery rather than hand tools, and transport logs on flatbed semis.

Beer Brewing (1850s–1970s)

As a financial panic gripped the nation in 1857, H. S. Burke, Gilbert Falconer, Harry Fargo, and J. Gottlieb Busch found themselves unemployed in Duluth Township. Gottlieb had brewing skills, so he and his companions set up shop on land lent to them by Sidney Luce at First Street and Washington Avenue in what was then Portland Township. They named an adjacent creek, from which they drew water for brewing, "Brewery Creek." The **Luce/Busch Brewery** was the first in the Zenith City, but more would follow. Breweries that came and went included **Klein & Kiichli** (1859–1861), **Gustave Kiene** (1869–1876), **Kreimer Brothers** (1871–1872), **Camahl & Busse** (1874–1875), **Benjamin Decker Brewery** (1882–1884), **W. Franke & Co.** (1884–1885), **C. J. Johnson / Scandia Bottling** (1901–1906), **West End Malt Ale Co.** (1910–1914), and **E. F. Burg** (1907). The most successful of all these were **Fitger's Brewery**, **Duluth Brewing & Malting Company**, and **People's Brewery**.

Although it produced a wide range of beers (including a cream ale, a stock ale, and a wheat ale) the Luce/Busch Brewery itself barely survived Duluth's tough economy of the 1860s. In 1865, Luce sold the brewery to Nicholas Decker. Decker died in 1875, and two years later his family leased the brewery to Michael Fink. In 1882 Fink hired August Fitger to run his brewery; less than half a year later Fitger and his partner Percy Anneke bought the Brewery from Fink and changed the name of the Decker Brewery to **A. Fitger & Co. Lake Superior Brewery**.

Fitger and Anneke had much greater success than their predecessors. The company grew throughout the late nineteenth and early twentieth centuries, adding buildings and employees to their facility at 600 East Superior Street as the years progressed. In 1890 the brewery installed Minnesota's first ice machine. Sales continued to grow.

That growth stopped abruptly in 1918, when Prohibition shut down beer manufacturing and sales. Fitger and Anneke scrabbled to keep the brewery operational and Duluthians employed. They sold their Brewery Saloon to bartender Joseph Wisocki. Wisocki would later rename the saloon The Pickwick after a non-alcoholic beverage made by Fitger's that mixed well with the bootleg liquor many patrons brought to the saloon themselves. During Prohibition, Fitger's made candy, distributed cigars, and manufactured non-alcoholic beverages. Their most popular brand was Silver Spray, and they turned part of the brewery into the Silver Spray Boxing Gym.

Fitger's survived Prohibition to become a major regional brewery, but they couldn't survive the post-war consolidation and expansion of breweries such as Miller and Budweiser. On September 19, 1972, the final shift reported to the bottling house.

The image at left shows the masthead of Fitger's Brewery corporate stationery, circa 1905. Some of the buildings, like the stables at left, were never built.

Plans for the rooftop of the main office building included lavish gardens and a large statue of Gambrenius, the mythical Flemish King of Beers. The brewery closed in 1972 and is now a hotel and retail complex with many fine shops and restaurants.

Fitger's had no serious competition in Duluth until 1895, when brewmaster Reiner Hoch established the **Duluth Brewing & Malting Company**. (Hoch would later be joined in Duluth by his business partner Charles Meeske after their brewery in Marquette, Michigan, failed). In 1896 Hoch hired Duluth architect John J. Wangenstein (see next page) to design a six-story brick building at Twenty-Ninth Avenue West and Helm Street (right). The massive building featured arched windows and at least three towers and was trimmed with stone quarried at Fond du Lac.

Duluth Brewing & Malting was one of the few breweries in the country which had its own malting plant (the only other one in Minnesota was at St. Paul's Hamm's Brewery). Most other breweries purchased malt for their beers and lagers. Some of the more well-known beers Duluth Brewing & Malting produced included Moose Lager (and its low-alcohol cousin, Our Tame Moose), Castlebrew, Gold Shield, Royal Bohemian, and Karlsbrau. It also manufactured Lovit brand soft drinks. (In the 1920s Fitger's purchased the Lovit brand along with the rights to all the Duluth Brewing & Malting's beer labels; of these, Fitger's produced the Moose and Rex brands, and Rex later became one of Fitger's most popular beers.)

During Prohibition, Duluth Brewing & Malting changed its

name to **The Sobriety Company** and turned solely to making soft drinks. But times were tough, and after the stock market crash of 1929 the facility suspended production. As Prohibition ended, Meeske's son Carl retooled the brewery and hired brewmaster Henry Schmidt. Schmidt would introduce Karlsbrau (or "Karl's brew," named for Carl Meeske) which became the brewery's flagship brand. After World War II the brewery expanded its market throughout the midwest and to Alaska and enlarged the plant on Helm Street. The Royal name was revived in 1951 and applied to a new beer with 5.7 percent alcohol, and Royal 57 was born. Because of the Heinz 57 brand, Royal 57 became known as "the ketchup beer." They quickly changed the name to Royal 58 and advertised it with the slogan "Make a date with 58."

Despite the popularity of its beers, competition from larger breweries caused the company to cease production in 1966. The Minnesota Highway

John J. Wangenstein

The Duluth Brewing & Malting Company facilities were designed by architect John J. Wangenstein (1858–1942; his sketch of the brewery is pictured below). Wangenstein was born in Valdres, Norway, in 1858 and studied in Trondheim before coming to Duluth in 1883 where he established a private architectural firm six years later. He partnered with William E. Baillie from 1892 to 1895, but for the most part worked independently. During his prolific career Wangenstein designed numerous commercial, residential, and religious buildings throughout Duluth and St. Louis County. Buildings in Duluth designed by Wangenstein include the Loeb House (1900), the Wolvin Building (1901, now the Missabe Building), the second Boat Club (1903), the second Masonic Temple (1904), the Bridgeman-Russell Building (1907), and the DeWitt Seitz Building (1911). Wangenstein also designed a number of Duluth's East End residences, including the Gorham and Gertrude Taylor House (2325 East Second Street, 1896), the John and Hildegarde Hunt House (2132 East First Street, 1902), the Marcus and Sarah Fay House (2105 East Superior Street,1902), the James and Selina Pearce House (2109–11 East Superior Street, 1903), the Daniel and Alice Waite House (2510 East Superior Street, 1904), the William and Helen Eklund House (224 North Twenty-Fourth Avenue East, 1908), and the Morris and Bessie Cook House (211 NorthTwenty-Fourth Avenue East, 1924).

Wangenstein stopped practicing in about 1935, retiring to his home at 121 West Marie Street. He died in a Duluth hospital in 1942 at age eighty-three. His obituary pointed out that Wangenstein was "a life member of the Duluth Boat Club, charter member of the Kitchi Gammi club, and belonged to the old Duluth Commercial club, American Association of Architects and Engineers, and Glen Avon Presbyterian church."

Beer Brewing, continued…

Department purchased all of the original buildings a year later for the expansion of Interstate 35. The only building still standing is the 1915 bottling works which had been built across Helm Street from the brew and malt houses.

Bolstered by socialist ideas brought to the region by eastern European immigrants, West Duluth tavern owners Martin Smith, F. G. Sandstedt, and Michael J. Gleeson came together in 1907 to form **People's Brewery** to avoid having to buy beer from Fitger's and large national breweries and so they could, according to brewery historian Doug Hoverson, "resist the evils of capitalism."

People's was the smallest brewery in Duluth, establishing an office in the Burrows Building. It first produced beer at 4230 West Second Street in 1908 under president Frank G. Sandstadt and brewmaster Ernest A. Koenig. Sections of the new brewery stood five stories high and were faced with brick and Bedford stone trim. At first it sold its beer only to "member saloons."

People's Brewery operated from 1908 until 1920 when Prohibition stopped production of beer. It produced soft drinks, including 7UP, during the 1920s and resumed beer production in 1933 when Prohibition ended. Carl O. Hanson reorganized the brewery and began touting its beer as being made with "Crystal Clear-Chemically Pure Lake Superior Water." Some of People's better-known brands included Stag, Olde English 600 (a malt liquor originally labeled Ruff's Stout, Olde English 600 found successful sales as far away as the Pacific Northwest and Puerto Rico), and Regal Supreme, the brewery's most popular beer. The Regal Supreme label featured a likeness of Duluth's namesake, Daniel Greysolon Sieur du Luht, and was advertised with a print campaign describing du Luht's exploits in the Western Lake Superior region, including the time he had two Ojibwe executed for the murder of two of his French compatriots.

In the 1950s, Duluth was the only city in Minnesota operating three breweries—until People's closed in 1956. Most of the building was razed in about 1975 with the exception of a two-story section which was occupied first by Standard

Brick and today by the Brock White Company, which supplies brick, stone, and landscape supplies.

Commercial brewing in Duluth was revived in 1994 with the opening of the Lake Superior Brewery, which was first located in the repurposed Fitger's Brewery Complex before moving to Duluth's West End. The brewery now makes Special Ale, Kayak Kolsch, Mesabi Red Ale, Sir Duluth Oatmeal Stout, and a variety of seasonal and specialty beers. In September 1995 Fitger's Brewhouse opened in the Fitger's complex as Duluth's first brewpub and is now the highest-producing brewpub in Minnesota. Its first brewer was Mike Hoops, who turned over the reigns to his brother Dave when he went to work for Minneapolis's Town Hall Brewery. Both Hoops brothers have won many brewing awards for their work with the Brewhouse. Since the Brewhouse found success, other Duluth drinking establishments have begun brewing their own beer, including Carmody Irish Pub & Brewing (Carmody is owned in part by Eddie Gleeson, grandson of People's Brewery founder M. J. Gleeson). A new brewpub, the Canal Park Brewing Company, is slated to open in Duluth's Canal Park Business District in 2012.

Brownstone Quarrying (1870–1910)

Credited with setting up Duluth's first sawmill in Oneota in 1856, Henry Wheeler (see page 124) also quarried the first brownstone from Fond du Lac, using the stone as the foundation of his sawmill's boiler/engine house, and some Fond du Lac brownstone was used in Minnesota Point Lighthouse in 1858. But as an industry, brownstone quarrying would not take off until the 1870s, when the rest of Duluth did. It reached its peak in the late 1880s and by the time the industry had played out in 1910, Fond du Lac brownstone was in use in buildings from New York to Omaha, but primarily in Chicago.

Lumberman Edmund Ingalls first came to the region in 1861 to establish a sawmill and set up a logging operation. By 1870 his attention had turned to brownstone, naturally formed sandstone found in a variety of colors from reds to yellows that came to popularity in the latter half of the nineteenth century with the rise of Richardsonian Romanesque architecture.

In 1869 Ingall purchased Durfee's Farm, a sixty-three acre lot on the Wisconsin side of the St. Louis River at Fond du Lac. A year later the site was known as **Ingalls Quarry** and featured a bluff fifty feet high and up to four hundred feet deep. It would become the region's most productive quarry, but not under Ingalls' watch. Described by one historian as an intelligent businessman (but one who "did not regard an obligation or his word as of any value"), Ingalls left Duluth after the Financial Panic of 1873 and in 1879 leased operation to Nils Nelson. By 1885 Ingalls had returned to the Zenith City and traded his property with that of A. M. Miller, who turned quarry

management over to John H. Crowley. Ingalls remained active in Duluth business until his death in 1895.

The summer of 1879 saw a surge in business for the Ingalls Quarry. it won a fifteen-year contract to build St. Paul's Union Depot; the agreement demanded twenty thousand tons of brownstone per year. Local buildings constructed with stone from the Ingalls Quarry (sometimes called the "Crowley Quarry") included the Clark Block, the H. F. Williamson Block, the Costello Building, the Ingalls Block, the C. H. Oppel Block, the Pastoret-Stenson Block, the American Exchange Building, Duluth National Bank, the Guilford Hartley House, and the John Erickson House, all of which have been destroyed. The only buildings featuring Ingalls/Crowley brownstone that remain standing in Duluth are the Hunters Block and Wirth Block.

Fond du Lac's second great quarryman was Charles Adolph Krause, who moved to the township as a child and stayed his entire life, even serving as the community's postmaster in the 1870s. He learned the brownstone business quarrying along Fond du Lac's Mission Creek, where Nehemiah Hulett had established a quarry back in 1872. In 1882 Krause and Martin Boyle leased the quarry together, but their relationship has been described by historians as "turbulent." It seems Boyle was the turbulent one, and in 1883 was accused by the local press of skipping town on his creditors—the headline in the *Duluth Tribune* read "Where is Martin Boyle?"

The press also lauded the news that Krause would take over sole operation of the quarry, describing him as "a substantial and reliable man." The **Krause Quarry** quickly gained a reputation as producing the area's best stone, and the quarry operated steadily until the industry's demise. While most of it was shipped for use outside the region, Krause Quarry stone was incorporated in Duluth's first Board of Trade Building and Marinette Iron Works, both of which have been destroyed. Krause and his wife lived out their lives as celebrated citizens of Fond du Lac, where he died in 1937.

Duluth's last quarryman was hardly a quarryman at all, but an Irish auctioneer transplanted from St. Paul (see sidebar). In 1869 Michael Chambers purchased property in Fond du Lac known as Colonel Carlton's farm, which included a plum orchard and, conveniently, a brownstone quarry. **Chambers Quarry** (pictured twice on previous page, also known as the **Fond du Lac Quarry**) would utilize the coming Lake Superior & Mississippi Railroad to help transport its stone, described as "dark chocolate" in color.

Along with the rest of the country, Chambers panicked with the financial crisis of 1873. He posted an ad to sell his quarry but received no offers. Four years later he threatened to tear down his home rather than pay property taxes, and he skipped town in 1879. The cantankerous Martin Boyle took charge of the operation in Chambers' absence. Chambers was essentially out of the brownstone game until his death in 1895.

Duluth landmarks constructed with Fond du Lac brownstone included the Banning & Branch Block, the Grand Opera House, the Spalding Hotel, Franklin School, and Duluth Brewing & Malting. The 1891 City Hall and the Jail next door, Fire Hall Number 1, and portions of Fitger's Brewery Complex are the only examples of the stone's use in buildings still standing in Duluth. By 1910, all Duluth quarries had ceased production.

From 1868 to 1910, more quarries operated in the Apostle Islands and along the Wisconsin south shore of western Lake Superior. According to historian Kathryn Bishop Eckert, "Twenty-four companies extracted sandstone from fifteen quarries in the [region]. Nine quarries were clustered in the vicinity of Bayfield and Washburn and on three of the Apostle Islands...; six were scattered along the south shore of Lake Superior...on the Cranberry, Flag, Iron, and Amnicon Rivers."

Michael & Emily Chambers House

Michael and Emily Chambers began building their home near his Fond du Lac quarry in 1870 and finished in 1872. The two-story mansion was constructed with brownstone from his own quarry. It included more than twenty rooms with deep stone walls and tall, narrow arched windows. The house stood on high ground overlooking the St. Louis River and attracted sightseers who traveled to Fond du Lac for a view of the mansion. Chambers and his wife often entertained in the house's large second-floor drawing room, which housed a grand piano. They covered the floors with Brussels carpeting, which they in turn covered with burlap for dances. (Newspaper reports indicate the house may have operated as a hotel in the mid 1870s.)

While Emily Chambers was quite refined (she was educated in a Quebec convent, spoke French fluidly, and was an accomplished pianist), Michael Chambers could be difficult to deal with. Born in County Cork, Ireland, Chambers first emigrated to Canada before arriving in St. Paul in the 1860s, where he became a successful auctioneer. Historian William Coventry describes Chambers' career as "punctuated by friction with partners, unstable financial situations, and scuffles with the law."

Chambers' absence from Duluth in 1879 was noted in the *Duluth Weekly Tribune*. His creditors assumed he had skipped town, but he returned claiming an attack of neuralgia had left him partially demented, and he had traveled from Duluth to Nova Scotia to California before he "came to." Over the years he accused James Hayes of a "murderous assault" (case dismissed), attempted to sue A. R. McFarlane for defamation of character (case dismissed), and in 1882 was himself accused of illegally selling liquor to an Ojibwe (case dismissed). That same year Martin Boyle of the Krause Quarry confronted Chambers on a train, grabbed Chambers "by the beard," and struck him repeatedly before pulling a revolver; fellow passengers intervened to halt the violence. In May 1891 Chambers was again assaulted, this time by Alphonse Guerard over a property dispute. That July an arson fire gutted the Chambers' mansion; Guerard was suspected of starting it. Months later, Mr. Guerard's home was also destroyed by an arson fire. No legal action was taken in either case.

The mansion was never rebuilt. Michael Chambers died in 1895, but the ruins of his home were not removed until 1912. Before Emily Chambers' death in 1926, the City of Duluth purchased 577 acres from her. Ten of those acres east of the quarry and the home site were developed into Duluth's Chambers Grove Park. Remnants of the home remain.

The Grain Trade (1870–1972)

In 1869 Jay Cooke financed Duluth's first grain elevator at the very corner of Lake Superior, where Third Avenue East once met the shore next to Sidney Luce's warehouse. Cooke's Union Improvement and Elevator Company purchased wood from Roger Munger's sawmill on Lake Avenue to build Elevator A (below), a grain terminal that could hold 350,000 bushels of grain and came equipped with a steam-powered conveyance system. Cooke's Lake Superior & Mississippi Railroad then brought rail to the elevator by building large docks. (Munger, along with Clinton Markell and C. H. Graves, also invested in the enterprise.) The railroad also added docks along a timber-and-stone breakwater that protected vessels from Lake Superior's often turbulent waters. On May 30, 1871, the steamer *St. Paul* took Elevator A's first load, 11,500 bushels of wheat, and became the first boat to carry a cargo of grain out of Duluth and down the lakes.

Only one other grain elevator, Elevator Q in 1878, was built on the lake itself. After the ship canal opened, allowing direct passage to the safety of the bay, all of Duluth's grain elevators were built on Rice's Point. The giant storage facilities first popped up on both Rice's Point and Conner's Point in Superior after 1878, but the grain trade wouldn't truly blossom in Duluth until the latter

half of the decade, when grain started flowing to Rice's Point from the farms of the Red River Valley in western Minnesota and eastern Dakota Territory.

By 1880 grain elevators had grown in capacity and could store 560,000 bushels each. In January 1881 local businessmen organized the **Duluth Board of Trade**, and that year over three million bushels of cereal grain (Duluth exclusively dealt in cereal crops) passed through the Zenith City. The Board established that its charter, based on its speculation of Duluth as a regional center of the grain trade, would last thirty years. Its essential function was to set and regulate grain prices to ensure fairness. Pioneer members included C. H. Graves, Roger Munger, George Spencer, Melvin Forbes, Walter Van Brunt, Owen Fargusson, and George G. Barnum. Barnum, cousin of P. T. Barnum and namesake of Barnum, Minnesota, was so admired for his leadership he was known as the "Grand old man of the Board of Trade." His Barnum Grain Company would later merge with others to form General Mills. Five years after the Board was formed, Duluth shipped more than 22 million bushels of grain. In 1886 the Board of Trade moved into its brand new headquarters on Superior Street (see page 107) and quickly found its offices fully leased. The Duluth Board of Trade had become the epicenter of the grain trade in the Upper Midwest. (It also ran the grain industry in Superior, except for the years 1894 and 1908, when Superior had its own Board of Trade.

Early grain elevators were made of wood, and grain dust is highly combustible; elevators often went up in flames. Elevators A and Q burned on November 27, 1886, taking with them about 500,000 bushels of grain and the lives of elevator foreman Edward Lee and fireman Charles Moore. The loss was so substantial it actually led to a rise in value of the Chicago grain market. The fire also consumed a saloon, a carriage factory, houses, and warehouses on the 400 block of East Superior Street. The following year wheat from both burned elevators remained on the site, rotting away. It was loaded onto barges and dumped into Lake Superior. In 1892, founders of the Duluth Curling Club used Elevator A's foundation to build the club's first rink, which was destroyed in a blizzard in March 1892.

Meanwhile, grain elevators continued to go up on Rice's Point, most between 1885 and 1902, including the Peavey Elevator in 1900, the first tubular concrete silo. Built by Frank H. Peavey and Charles H. Haglin, who perfected the design. Because of concrete's fireproof qualities, facilities like the Peavey elevator eventually replaced their wooden counterparts. By 1910 ten of the concrete storage facilities lined the eastern side of the point. (A sketch of Lake Superior Elevator's wooden Elevator D is shown at right; the photo below shows the storage facilities of Consolidated Elevator in the 1910s.)

By 1900 the Board had been trading for six years at the second Board of Trade Building, constructed on First Street in 1894 after fire destroyed the Board's first building. The new building's trading floor on the eighth floor featured the largest "free-standing, self-supporting skylight in the United States." The Board entered the durham wheat market in 1903 and were soon shipping 17 million bushels a year, mostly to Europe to be processed into macaroni. In 1906, the Board had outlived its pioneer members. In 1911 it reached its life expectancy and extended its charter.

By 1920, Duluth's grain elevators could hold over 36 million bushels of grain and loaded 62,723,563 bushels onto ships. Despite this, over the years Duluth's importance in the grain trade declined. In 1929, the nation's stock market crash and a change in grain inspection practices would reduce the amount of grain the Duluth Board of Trade sampled and graded. The grain trade through Duluth did not recover after the Great Depression came to an end, and in 1946 the Duluth Board of Trade made its last futures transaction. But grain continued to move through Duluth; in 1966 a record 252.6 million bushels of grain was shipped via the Port of Duluth. As historian Pat Lapinski wrote, the grain market "hadn't so much changed as had the methods of doing business." The Board of Trade held on until 1972, when the organization dissolved; a year later, the Board of Trade Building became the property of private investors.

While the Board of Trade is gone, its grand 1894 building remains (its trading floor is now the home of the Minnesota Ballet) and Duluth itself remains a center for grain shipping. Today three companies—General Mills, Cargill, and AGP Grain—still operate elevators on Rice's Point.

Flour Milling (1888–1957)

All the grain flowing from the Dakotas and Western Minnesota to Duluth's and Superior's mammoth grain elevators made the Twin Ports a natural spot for flour mills to flourish. The first, **Superior Roller Mills**, went up across the bay in west Superior in 1882, producing two hundred barrels a day. But shallow water hindered delivery of grain—and the mill's growth. In 1886 the **Duluth Roller Mill** arose along the bay at Sixth Avenue West about where Bayfront Festival Park sits today. It began as a small operation, producing about 250 barrels a day. It struggled financially and was sold through a Sheriff's auction in 1887. It reopened in 1888.

That same year pioneer Roger Munger partnered with Bradford C. Church and T. A. Olmstead and established **Imperial Mills** on the east side of Rice's Point at 600 Garfield Avenue (shown in an idealized sketch, below). While Duluthians had been milling flour for years at a modest capacity, the Imperial Mill—built with what was then considered an experimental design—was considered "the most complete ever built" and at six stories high was by far the largest in the Twin Ports. With crews working day and night, Imperial could pump out 1,500 barrels of flour each day in its new mill, which ran on the power supplied by a 600-horsepower Reynolds-Cross steam engine. By the end of 1889, the facility had increased production to 8,000 barrels a day, an earmark its owners claimed surpassed "previous records of

DULUTH IMPERIAL FLOUR

THE TEXT OF THE DULUTH IMPERIAL FLOUR AD ABOVE READS: "AS OUR AIRSHIP PROUDLY RAISES / ON HIGH WE HEAR THE PRAISES / AND OUR SONG THE WORLD AMAZES / BY ITS TRUTH, / FOR WE SING OF PRODUCT CEREAL / WHICH MAKES OUR BREAD ETHEREAL / AND IS KNOWN AS FLOUR 'IMPERIAL' / FROM DULUTH."

all other flour mills in the world." That year Imperial built wooden grain elevators #4 and #5. By 1892 Imperial was the largest flour mill in the world, producing 6,300 barrels a day. Red River wheat was delivered to the mill on railroad tracks, shoveled into the mill on one side and rolled out as flour in barrels on the other, where it was loaded straight into vessels docked there in slip # 1. At the end of the century, only Minneapolis's Pillsbury "A" mill could produce more flour than Duluth's Imperial.

By 1895 at least nine other flour mills operated in Duluth and Superior, but their capacities reached no where near that of Imperial's. In 1895 **Grand Republic Mills** produced 2,500 barrels; **Minkota**, 750; **Barclay Mills**, 600; and **Duluth Roller Mill**, whose capacity had been increased to 900, only 500. Across the bay in Superior, **Freeman** and **Superior Roller** turned out 800 and 500 barrels respectively, **Anchor** shipped 2,000 barrels, and Duluth-owned **Lake Superior Milling** produced 2,500 barrels at its **Listman Mill** and 3,000 at its **Lake Superior Mill** (by 1900, the mill doubled its capacity). To illustrate the promise of the Twin Ports as the flour milling center of the world, historians Dwight Woodward and John Pardee quoted an unnamed source from the period in their 1910 *History of St. Louis County, Past and Present:*

"It is only a question of a very few years when the great bulk of the wheat grown in northern Minnesota and the Dakotas will be ground into flour at the head of the lakes. The advantages possessed by Duluth over Minneapolis as a point for milling are too plain to require elaborate illustration. A look at the map is all that is needed. The geographical position of Duluth at the head of deep water navigation is supreme. She sits in the middle of a channel through which the No. 1 hard wheat of the Northwest must naturally find its way to the markets of the East and Europe. Whatever portion of this wheat is used by the Minneapolis mills is diverted from this channel at the expense of those mills and to the proportionate advantage of the Duluth mills, so it requires no lengthy argument to show that Duluth must soon pass Minneapolis as a milling center."

It never did. In fact, 1900 would prove to be the industry's apex in Duluth. That year **Duluth Universal Milling Company** (pictured at right) opened at the foot of South Twelfth Avenue West, with access to slip #7. W. A. Scott served as the firm's first president. More flour mills popped up throughout Duluth, including one built by Peavey on Rice's Point in the shadow of its grain elevators.

But the early part of the twentieth century also saw the beginning of a steady decline in flour production in the Twin Ports due to a number of changes that made the Head of the Lakes a less desirable place to mill flour. After the price of wheat dropped, farmers in the Red River Valley began to diversify their crops, forcing the Twin Ports mills to look further away for a grain source. At the same time railways began reducing shipping costs and made changes to tariffs which, according to historian Patrick Lapinski, caused "a shift away from Duluth-Superior and tipping the balance toward eastern cities like Buffalo."

Consolidation also played a role. Many millers combined their efforts into one organization, the United States Flour Milling Company. The conglomerate turned out to be a bad idea. A number of mills were closed, including Duluth's mighty Imperial Mill. After changing hands once or twice, it was sold to Duluth's **Capitol Elevator** in 1905 with one important clause:

the mill could never again be used for the "handling or production of flour." Capital operated the wooden elevators 4 and 5 and leased the mill, first to then-fledgling Minnesota Mining and Manufacturing—today's 3M—and later the F. A. Patrick Woolen Milling Company.

Universal, the last flour mill to operate in Duluth, held on until 1957; it was razed the next year. Peavey operated the former Standard Milling mill in Superior until 1970, when it moved operations to Hastings, Minnesota. By the 1970s International Multifoods owned the Capital elevators, once part of Imperial Mills. They razed Elevator 5 in 1977; the following January a spectacular fire destroyed Elevator 4 and badly damaged an iron ore steamer berthed next to the elevator in slip #1. It burned for more than seven hours, and thousand of people gathered along Skyline Parkway and other vantage points to watch the remnants of the Twin Ports flour industry go up in smoke.

Inside Duluth's Imperial Flour Mill

Once the largest flour mill in the world and second only in capacity to the Pillsbury "A" mill in Minneapolis, Duluth's Imperial Mill (pictured below) was built in 1889 of an experimental design. Its footprint measured 110 by 120 feet, and the building stood six stories tall. Chief Engineer Wilson Palmer oversaw all activity in the engine room, centered on a main engine, including the central pump for the fire extinguisher system, built in West Duluth by Marinette Iron Works. Three thousand sprinkler heads fed by rooftop tanks protected the mill in case of fire. A machine and blacksmith shop adjoined the engine room. Wheat was offloaded from trains onto an elevator and then a conveyor belt where it was cleaned and polished into a grain "berry." On the grinding floor the wheat was broken down to smaller and smaller particles through six separate sets of corrugated rollers before a final smooth set of rollers pulverized it through ten gradations into flour and a byproduct called middlings. The flour and middlings were separated in bolting machinery—essentially giant sifters—on the bolting floor. From there the flour was sent to the packing floor and packaged into sacks before awaiting shipment in the warehouse, which originally had a capacity of 25,000 barrels. Middlings were first purified and then packaged, often sold as feed grain for cattle. The unpackaged wheat, flour, and middling passed from floor to floor through a system of spouts. The third floor was known as the spouting floor and was filled with a maze of spouts which could be checked and tended to by workers known as "spout chasers" who ensured that everything flowed properly.

THE BOILER ROOM.

THE GRINDING FLOOR.

The Bolting Machinery.

The Packing Floor.

The Spouting Floor.

The Warehouse.

Metal Fabrication (1872–1985)

Duluth's earliest metal-fabricating shop was a modest affair that built rail cars for Jay Cooke's Great Northern Railway. In 1871 J. B. Culver, Luther Mendenhall, J. D. Ray, J. C. Hunter, and W. W. Spalding formed the **Duluth Blast Furnace Company** and built the city's first blast furnace—which allowed a foundry to make its own pig iron—on Rice's Point. They then lured Pittsburgh's John H. Schoenberger to operate the **Schoenberger and Bryant Car Company Foundry**. Before he entered the grain trade, George Barnum contracted with Duluth Blast Furnace to bring ore to Duluth from Marquette, Michigan (Minnesota's Iron Range had yet to open) using the steamships *Manistee* and *Metropolis*, the first two large steamers owned by Duluthians to operate on the Great Lakes. But, like most other Duluth businesses, Duluth Blast Furnace failed in 1873 in the national financial panic.

The **Duluth Iron & Steel Company** operated on the site from 1884 to 1888 before moving to West Duluth. The new facility sat along the St. Louis Bay between Fifty-Sixth and Fifty-Ninth Avenues West (shown in sketch, below). Designed by engineer John Berkenbine, the complex covered twenty-three acres and included a brick engine house and two deepwater docks. The company reformed as **West Duluth Blast Furnace** in 1892 but closed in 1895 as a result of the 1893 financial panic.

In 1902 Captain A. B. Wolvin and his associates incorporated **Zenith Furnace** and rebuilt the plant to produce pig iron and its byproducts—coal tar, ammonia, and coal gas—all of which could be used by other manufacturers in West Duluth. They also added a coal dock and began distributing coal. The company also had its own rail system to receive and deliver freight cars to both the Northern Pacific and Soo Line railways. (The 1902 plant is pictured above.) Wolvin left the company after a few years and credit for the plant's early success went to Fred C. Harris, who became general superintendent of Zenith Furnace in 1906. Additions to the facility in 1905 and 1908 created one of the largest industries in Duluth. In 1924 Zenith employed four hundred workers. In 1948 the company became a division of Interlake Iron Company and by 1955 was the country's largest producer of pig iron. But dramatic reductions in the demand for pig iron forced Zenith Furnace to close in 1962.

Interlake failed in 1964, the same year part of the complex was demolished. A portion of the facility became Hallett Dock #6. The site was declared a Superfund site in 1983 because of coal tar and chemical pollutants on the site and in the St. Louis River. Today the area is mostly vacant.

Iron Bay Works was a short-lived iron-and-steel manufacturing company which moved to Duluth from Marquette, Michigan, in 1889 and built a new brick facility at Fiftieth Avenue West and Ramsey Street along the St. Louis Bay (shown in sketch at right). The building was several stories high, seventy-five feet wide and two hundred feet long, and included a blacksmith shop, boiler shop, pattern room, drawing room, and storeroom. Prominent Duluthians D. H. Merritt, F. W. Merritt, and former mayor Clinton Markell became the company's officers, overseeing the production machinery for iron mines, many in which the Merritt family was heavily invested. As it did with other Merritt investments, the financial crisis of 1893 brought an end to the Iron Bay Works.

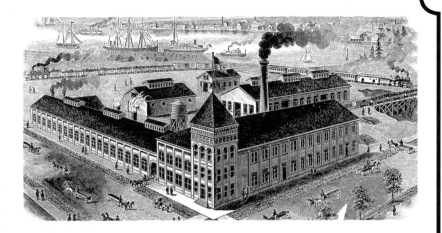

National Iron, founded in 1883 on Rice's Point along Garfield Avenue, purchased and moved into the Iron Bay buildings in 1902. National Iron grew quickly in its new location, expanding to manufacture machinery for mining, logging, and road construction and enjoying world-wide distribution of its machinery. In 1953 National Iron merged with Pettibone Mulliken Corporation of Chicago. An international downturn in the mining industry forced the facility to close in 1983, and Davidson Printing moved into the facility two years later. Davidson was forced to move out in 1993 when the complex was demolished to make room for the Interstate 35 expansion.

Founded in 1867 in Marinette, Wisconsin, by Dewitt Clinton Prescott (see page 27) the **Marinette Iron Company** moved to the blossoming Village of West Duluth in 1890. Developers imagined the new town as the future center of metal fabrication and other industrial concerns—the "Pittsburgh of the Northwest." Marinette built a foundry, machine shops, and carpentry shops—all served by a rail system—at 200 North Fiftieth Avenue West to produce sawmill machinery and marine engines. One of its engines, outfitted for the *Colgate* (designed by Captain Alexander McDougall), was said to be "the finest marine engine ever put into a whaleback steamer." Again the financial panic of 1893 cost West Duluth a business, with Marinette operating under receivership until 1898. Its last contract was to build the motors and pumps that operate Duluth's Lakewood Pumping Station. In 1900 Union Match Company moved into the facility (see page 154).

Metal Fabrication, continued...

Charles P. Craig, brothers James and Daniel Cass, and others—including future mayor Samuel F. Snively—formed the **Clyde Iron Company** in 1889 to smelt iron and other metals and to manufacture engines, boilers, and machinery "of all descriptions." (According to lore, "Clyde" refers to a river in Scotland.) They then hired Oliver Traphagen to design a facility at 304–108 South Lake Avenue. In 1902, after being purchased a year earlier by the Northwestern Supply Company, the firm's official name became the **Clyde Iron Works**.

That same year it began marketing its McGiffert Log Loader, which loaded logs onto railroad cars, and almost at once "completely revolutionized the log handling industry." The machine, which could be run by unskilled workers, eliminated a great deal of manual labor. Sales quickly expanded the operation, forcing Clyde to move to a new facility at Twenty-Ninth Avenue West and Superior Street in Duluth's West End. Clyde then began producing modern hoisting equipment, becoming the first company to use internal combustion engines for hoisting. Its hoists, derricks, and cranes built bridges, tunnels, and buildings, including the Grand Coulee Dam, the Boulder Dam, the Golden Gate Bridge, and New York's Empire State Building, Radio City Music Hall, and United Nations Building. They became best known for the Clyde Whirley Crane, which could revolve 360 degrees.

In the 1940s Clyde retooled for the war effort, but for the most part produced essentially the same type of equipment they had been specializing in for years, its four hundred employees working around the clock. Their efforts earned Clyde the Army-Navy "E" award for "outstanding machine production, engineering ability, efficiency and for the high character and workmanship of their products." Each Clyde employee proudly wore an "E" pin.

In 1961 the American Bridge Company ordered a portable hoist from Clyde to help build the Verrazano-Narrows Bridge in New York Harbor, the longest suspension bridge in the world at the time. The hoist itself was also believed to be the largest ever built. Throughout its entire history the ownership of Clyde traded hands time and again. In 1985 Clyde merged with the marine division of American Hoist & Derrick. Operations moved to St. Paul, Minnesota, and the firm was rechristened AmClyde.

The Duluth facility closed. After changing hands several times, local businessman Alessandro Giuliani purchased the property. While some of the complex has been demolished, several buildings survive, and Giuliani adapted the building shown at the bottom of page 142 for reuse and renamed the facility Clyde Park; the facility currently holds a restaurant and event venue and plans are in place for a brewery and bakery to open in the nearby surviving Duluth Brewing & Malting bottling house. The Clyde offices also survive as the home of Stewart's Sporting Goods and offices. Today much of the former Clyde Iron facility is occupied by the Duluth Heritage Sports Center.

In 1890 the *Duluth Daily Northwestern* reported that Colonel H. A. Frambach's **Atlas Iron & Brass Works** of Kaukauna, Wisconsin, had been purchased by members of the Duluth Business Men's Association. Frambach stayed behind to run his Eagle Paper Mill, and the new owners relocated the business's equipment in New Duluth, where Commonwealth Avenue ends at the St. Louis River (shown above), opening under the same name. While the colonel made a fortune milling paper (and was inducted into the Paper Industry International Hall of Fame in 2011), Atlas failed in the 1893 financial panic. Western Steel Products later moved into the Atlas Iron &

Brass Works building, which became part of the Coolerator company in 1935 (see page 159).

Organized in 1906, Edward G. Hilliard's **Duluth Brass Works** produced brass and copper castings for use in manufacturing under the management of W. F. Baile. Its complex (shown in the photo below), constructed at 5002 Ramsey Street in 1909, was made up of "commodious buildings" including a foundry and machine shop where it employed thirty men when it first opened. The West Duluth site was chosen because Duluth Brass made "brass castings of all kinds," most of which were used by other manufacturers in the neighborhood. The company, which sold its goods throughout northern Minnesota, expanded its facilities in 1916 and added bronze and copper castings to its product line. By 1926 they were casting aluminum, some of which was used to adorn the top of Denfeld High School's 120-foot clock tower. The company's name changed to Duluth Brass and Aluminum in 1968, the same year it moved out of the Ramsey Street site to a new facility at 6900 Polk Street. In 2001 it moved to 2301 Commonwealth Avenue, where it operates today as the last of Duluth's nineteenth-century metal fabricators. The original buildings were demolished for expansion of Interstate 35.

Metal Fabrication, *continued…*

Ever since mines operating on Minnesota's Mesabi Iron Range started shipping iron ore through Duluth to eastern markets in the 1890s, Duluthians envisioned a local plant to make steel in the Zenith City. Just after the turn of the nineteenth century, the idea of bringing a major steel plant to Minnesota became a major issue and was fiercely debated in the state's 1907 legislative session. From that debate a two-part bill was proposed to force the creation of a plant: first, a tonnage tax would be added to all ore shipped out of the state; second, that tax could be avoided by any company that built a plant in Minnesota. As the nation's largest steel-making concern, J. P. Morgan's United States Steel (U.S.S.) purchased a great deal of Misabi ore and balked at the idea of paying higher taxes on that ore, but resented being forced to open a plant in Minnesota. The company resisted at first, but later relented and in 1907 announced it would build a "monster plant in Duluth."

The project began in 1909, but construction progressed slowly and the factory did not produce an ounce of steel until December 1915. Meanwhile, U.S.S. built the nearby company town of Morgan Park for its officials and highly skilled workers (mostly Scandinavians) and developed land south of the plant as Gary and New Duluth, where many of its lesser-skilled employees of Serbian or African-American descent found housing (see pages 5 and 11).

U.S. Steel's huge complex on the St. Louis River, officially called the **Minnesota Steel Company**, included two blast furnaces, ten open-hearth furnaces, ninety coke ovens, a blooming mill, a rail mill, a power plant, a

pumping station, machine shops, a storage shed, a merchant mill that stretched over one thousand feet long, and other buildings—more than fifty in all. Most of the facilities were constructed of steel frames enclosed by concrete blocks. When it first opened, its two blast furnaces could produce 1,000 tons of pig iron every day.

In the 1930s the Great Depression forced U.S.S. to re-organize some of its struggling facilities, and the Duluth plant's focus turned to wire product. In 1932 the Minnesota Steel Company's holdings were placed under the umbrella of the American Steel and Wire company, another division of U.S. Steel. American Steel and Wire Company ran the Morgan Park facilities until 1964, when U.S.S. absorbed it under its Operations Division, and afterwards the company called their Minnesota plant the "**Duluth Works**."

The boom years of U.S.S.'s Morgan Park plant lasted until the 1960s. During World War I more than 3,500 workers were employed at the facility, increasing to over 5,000 during World War II. By the 1960s numbers had dropped, and through the decade anywhere from 1,700 to 3,000 people worked at U.S.S. in Duluth. During that time the plant's aging steel-making facilities—and the water and air pollution they produced—became major concerns. By 1971 only one blast furnace remained in operation and 1,600 employees were discharged, leaving less than 1,000 workers to operate the plant. The facility held on for eight more years, but in 1979 the coke plant closed and the last employees left. Some buildings were put into use by other Duluth companies and some were demolished. The last remnant of the plant was razed in 1988. The Morgan Park residential neighborhood remains as a Duluth historic residential district.

In 1984 the Pollution Control Agency placed the site on the National Priorities List for the federally funded "superfund" pollution clean-up program. U.S.S. was required to clean up heavily polluted portions of the site, and the process is ongoing, as are plans for the site's reuse. In 2009 the Duluth Port Authority received a $50,000 investigative grant from the State of Minnesota to determine if the former steel plant could be used for a warehouse and light industrial park designed to store electricity-producing windmills. The feasibility research continues.

Universal Portland Cement

Built along Commonwealth Avenue adjacent to the Minnesota Steel Company complex in 1915, the Universal Portland Cement plant converted granulated slag–a byproduct of steel manufacturing–into cement. The operation employed between 350 and 400 workers who could produce up to 4,000 barrels of cement daily. United States Steel opened a number of Universal Portland Cement plants across the country, next to wherever they operated a steel mill.

The cement factory's first client was its owner, United States Steel. The nearby "company town" of Morgan Park was created for U.S. Steel employees and named for the company's founder, J. P. Morgan. Like the steel plant itself, nearly every building and home in Morgan Park was made of concrete block, so in 1915 when the steel plant began producing steel–and slag–Portland took over from other cement providers. (The nearby neighborhoods of Gary and New Duluth were also populated by Minnesota Steel Company and Universal Portland Cement employees; see pages 5 and 11.)

In 1930 Universal Portland Cement merged with Universal Atlas Cement Company and assumed the latter company's name. When the steel plant stopped producing steel– and slag–materials for cement production were shipped from Gary, Indiana, to the Duluth plant, which proved to be impractical. In 1976 the Minnesota Pollution Control Agency pressured the steel company to arrest air pollution caused by cement dust. The necessary conversion to the already outdated facility was deemed cost prohibitive, and the cement plant closed, taking two hundred jobs with it. The plant was demolished In 1978; Duluth's Ikonics company now occupies forty acres of the site.

Inside the Minnesota Steel Company

After World War II, a wire mill was added to the Minnesota Steel Company plant, and focus turned to producing wire, barbed wire, nails, and staples (shown in a page from a company publication at bottom left) as well as fence posts, fences, springs, and concrete reinforcement bars. But just how did Minnesota Steel—and other steel manufacturers for that matter—make steel out of iron ore in the first place?

A steel company's blast furnace turned iron ore into pig iron—an iron-carbon mix—in a process called smelting. Essentially, the furnace extracted sulfur from the ore. The furnaces (huge chimney-like cauldrons lined with refractory brick) were loaded with ore, coke, and limestone, then preheated air was forced into the middle of the furnace—that's the blast. The mixture was heated in the middle for more even burning. Through this process, the unwanted materials formed a heavy liquid—called slag—which was poured out of the bottom of the furnace through a valve. Another valve allowed the pig iron, lighter than slag, to be removed separately. The brittle pig iron then had to be processed further to lower its carbon content. To accomplish this, the pig iron was placed in a special rotating container, which in turn was blasted with high-pressure oxygen. The impurities were removed from the pig iron, leaving behind both carbon monoxide and carbon dioxide. The purified pig iron was then used as wrought iron or converted to steel with the Bessemer process, wherein further impurities were removed by blowing air through the molten pig iron. The cooled steel was then shipped to various mills for processing into a variety of products.

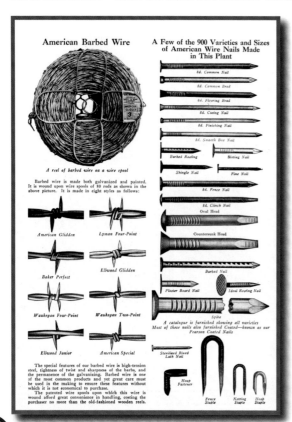

American Barbed Wire

A Few of the 900 Varieties and Sizes of American Wire Nails Made in This Plant

A reel of barbed wire on a wire spool

Barbed wire is made both galvanized and painted. It is wound upon wire spools of 80 rods as shown in the above picture. It is made in eight styles as follows:

American Glidden — Lyman Four-Point

Baker Perfect — Ellwood Glidden

Waukegan Four-Point — Waukegan Two-Point

Ellwood Junior — American Special

The special features of our barbed wire is high-tension steel, tightness of twist and sharpness of the barbs, and the permanence of the galvanizing. Barbed wire is one of the most common products and yet great care must be used in the making to ensure these features without which it is not economical to purchase.
The patented wire spools upon which this wire is wound afford great convenience in handling, costing the purchaser no more than the old-fashioned wooden reels.

8d. Common Nail
8d. Common Brad
8d. Flooring Brad
8d. Casing Nail
8d. Finishing Nail
8d. Smooth Box Nail
Barbed Roofing — Slating Nail
Shingle Nail — Fine Nail
8d. Fence Nail
8d. Clinch Nail
Oval Head
Countersunk Head
Barbed Nail
Plaster Board Nail — Ideal Roofing Nail
Spike
A catalogue is furnished showing all varieties. Most of these nails also furnished Coated—known as our Pearson Coated Nails.
Sterilized Blued Lath Nail
Hoop Fastener
Fence Staple — Netting Staple — Hoop Staple

THE IMAGES ON THESE PAGES COME FROM *HOW STEEL AND STEEL WIRE PRODUCTS ARE MADE*, PRODUCED BY THE MINNESOTA STEEL COMPANY. OPPOSITE, TOP: "THE BLAST FURNACE BOSH ENCIRCLED BY THE HOT-BLAST SUPPLY PIPE." OPPOSITE, BOTTOM RIGHT: "SIMPLIFIED DIAGRAM, WITH

GAS PURIFIERS AND PIPES OMITTED, SHOWING INTERNAL CONSTRUCTION OF THE BLAST FURNACE AND HOT-BLAST STOVES." THIS PAGE, TOP LEFT: "THE DRAWING ROOM OF THE WIRE MILL, SHOWING THE STEEL BEING PULLED THROUGH THE DRAWING BLOCKS." TOP RIGHT: "THE MACHINE MAKING NAILS." THE MACHINES WOULD TAKE COILED WIRE AND "AUTOMATICALLY STRAIGHTEN IT, CUT IT TO LENGTH, CUT THE POINT ON THE SHARP END, AND FORM A HEAD UPON IT, AT A RATE OF 125 TO 600 A MINUTE. OVER 900 DIFFERENT SIZES, SHAPES AND FINISHES OF NAILS ARE MADE HERE, THE TOTAL PRODUCTION BEING AT THE RATE OF 3 MILLION AN HOUR."
BOTTOM LEFT: "THE BOSH OF THE BLAST FURNACE AT THE LEFT, SHOWING MOLTEN IRON FLOWING THEREFROM. UPPER RIGHT HAND CORNER SHOWS DETAIL OF POURING THE METAL INTO ONE OF THE GREAT LADLES." BOTTOM RIGHT: "LADLES MOUNTED ON CAR TRUCKS, FOR TRANSPORTING MOLTEN METAL FROM THE BLAST FURNACE TO THE OPEN HEARTH FURNACES."

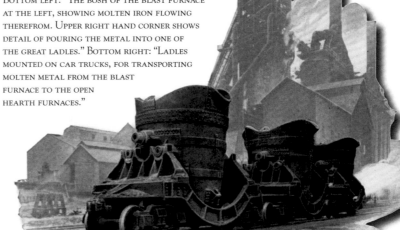

The Whaleback or "Pig Boat"

Born on Scotland's Isle of Islay, Alexander McDougall moved to Canada as a boy. In 1861, sixteen-year-old McDougall took his first job as a deckhand on a Great Lakes freighter; by twenty-five he had command of his own ship. For twenty more years he worked the Great Lakes, adopting Duluth as his home. In 1888 he dove head-first into the shipbuilding industry. He designed and built a steel boat with a flat bottom "designed to carry the greatest cargo on the least water." He rounded the top deck so water would run off and gave the bow a spoon shape to better cut through water; deck turrets allowed passage inside the ship's hull. The design earned the vessels the nickname "Pig Boats," but McDougall gave them a more noble title: whaleback. McDougall's American Steel Barge Company in Superior cranked out forty-three of them by 1898, when the last whaleback built, the *Alexander McDougall*, was launched. Twenty-five of the vessels had no engines: they were designed as barges meant to be towed. In 1890 American Steel Barge launched the *Colgate Hoyt*, the first whaleback steamer. The second self-powered whaleback was also the only passenger whaleback ever built, the *Christopher Columbus*, so named because it was intended to ferry passengers from downtown Chicago to the Columbian Exposition of 1893. Painted a "brilliant white," the *Christopher Columbus* launched in 1892 at 362 feet, making her the longest vessel on the Great Lakes at the time; she is said to have carried more passengers than any other vessel ever to sail the Great Lakes. McDougall had grander plans for his boats beside transporting goods on the Great Lakes, including building a transatlantic mail carrier and a man-o'-war, but the whaleback design lost popularity. Size limitation doomed the future of whalebacks, but many of McDougall's advances were employed in the modern ore boats that replaced his whalebacks. McDougall died in 1923. The last surviving whaleback, the *S.S. Meteor*, rests at Barker's Island in Superior, Wisconsin, and has been restored as a museum.

Ship Building (1869–1950s)

The Twin Ports' shipbuilding industry began in earnest in the winter of 1869–1870 when Lewis Merritt, his son Alfred, and Henry Ely built the *Chaska*, a seventy-two-foot-long, forty-nine-ton schooner—the largest ship built in Duluth at the time. Unfortunately, it was battered to pieces off the coast of Michigan's Upper Peninsula a year later.

Perhaps Duluth's most successful early shipbuilder was a French-Canadian named Napoleon Grignon, who arrived in Duluth in the 1870s and built the **N. Grignon Shipyard** on Minnesota Point at Buchanan Street. The firm later moved to the foot of Eleventh Avenue West. In 1880 Grignon incorporated his business as the **Marine Iron and Shipbuilding Company**; the company would go on to build many ships: fifty-seven of them between 1918 and 1940 alone.

While ships would be built in earnest in Duluth and Superior over the next eighty years, the industry peaked during the world wars. In Superior, ten tugs launched at the **Whitney Brothers Wharf** and nineteen 260-foot ocean freighters were built at the **Globe Shipyards** during World War I. In Duluth, Alexander McDougall (see sidebar at left) had revived his dormant **American Steel Barge Company**, renamed it **McDougall-**

Duluth Ship Builders, Inc., and moved across the St. Louis River to Duluth. His dormant facilities in Superior had opened under new ownership as the **Superior Shipbuilding Company** in 1900; during the war, it produced twenty-five freighters for England, France, and America.

McDougall's new shipyard (pictured at the bottom of page 148) went up at the foot of Spring Street on the St. Louis River in 1917 to build ships for the Allied war effort. The town of Riverside developed near the plant for the workers at the facility. More than thirty buildings, including machine, boiler, paint, and sheet metal shops—as well as three piers—were active in ship production until the war ended. Afterward, McDougall retired and the company became **Barnes-Duluth** with financier Julius Barnes as president, but the shipyards produced nothing.

As World War II began Barnes-Duluth and several other dormant shipyards sprang back to life in the Twin Ports. The facilities employed over ten thousand men and women, averaging ten ships a month while producing a fleet of 230 vessels. In Duluth, Marine Iron and Shipbuilding supplied the Coast Guard with eighteen cutters, and thirteen plane-rearming boats and four subchasers came out of **Inland Waterways**. **Zenith Dredge Company**, formed in 1905 at the foot of Thirteenth Avenue West as a harbor construction company, converted to shipbuilding and produced eight tankers and thirteen cutters. Duluth's **Scott-Graff Lumber Company** and **Industrial Construction Company** also got into the shipbuilding game, manufacturing one hundred landing barges. (The photo on this page shows a ship launching at the Barnes-Duluth yard.)

Across the bay in Superior, Globe delivered eight frigates and ten ocean-going tugs and **Butler** built thirteen coastal freighters, twelve frigates, and seven cargo carriers. On May 8, 1943, the Butler Yards became the first shipbuilder ever to launch five vessels in one day from the same shipyard. The launch was turned into a civic event when owner Robert Butler invited Canada's Dionne Quints, the world's first surviving quintuplets and argu-

ably the most famous children in North America at the time, to christen the cargo ships. Over fifteen thousand people showed up to watch the small pack of nine-year-olds, also born in May, take the stage carrying champagne bottles. They entertained the crowd by singing songs in their native *Quebecois* in honor of their mother's thirty-fourth birthday.

Nearly all shipbuilding in the Twin Ports stopped as World War II came to an end. The Marine Iron and Shipbuilding yard closed in the 1950s. Barnes-Duluth sold to Butler in 1943 and was closed in 1945 and sold for a marina. The rest of the Riverside shipbuilding complex was destroyed in 1976.

Jobbing Houses (1872–1958)

In the late nineteenth and early twentieth centuries, wholesalers were known as "jobbing houses" or "jobbers." At first, most jobbers did not manufacture the goods they sold. Many developed lines of products under different brand names. Some items these larger jobbers later manufactured themselves, but for the most part they paid other firms to manufacture under the jobber's brands. Duluth's own Jobber's Union formed in 1891.

William R. Stone founded what would become the **Stone-Ordean-Wells Company**—Duluth's first wholesale grocer—in 1872. Albert Ordean soon jumped on board, but it wasn't until 1896 that Benjamin Wells would join them to complete the firm's name. Three years earlier Stone and Ordean hired the well-used architectural firm of Traphagen & Fitzpatrick to design a four-story Romanesque building of brick and Port Wing brownstone at 203–211 South Fifth Avenue West (shown in sketch at bottom and in photo at top right). Built for $4,800, the building had a flat corner entrance and

arched windows on the top floor. It could ship and receive items from railcars along tracks on one side of the facility and from ships via a dock along Minnesota slip on another.

Stone-Ordean-Wells distributed mainly groceries with brand names of Nokomis, Hiawatha, Stone, Bluebird, and Express, but it also dealt with automobile tires, cigars, and wooden ware. They manufactured peanut butter and syrup, ground sugar, and at one point roasted and ground about 3.5 million pounds of coffee a year. The firm had three branch offices in North Dakota, four in Montana, and one in Minneapolis—which strictly handled tobacco products—and distributed in Michigan's Upper Peninsula, Wisconsin, Minnesota, the Dakotas, Montana, Wyoming, and eastern Idaho.

When the company closed in 1937, the building was occupied at various times by Alworth Woolen Mills, Western Electric Company, and Gershgol Food Stores, which used it as a warehouse. It was demolished in 1966 for the expansion of Interstate 35.

Six years before Stone-Ordean-Wells, Moses O'Brien and Joseph Knowlton had also hired Oliver Traphagen to design its Romanesque jobbing house, the O'Brien & Knowlton Block at 126–132 West Michigan Street (pictured in sketch at top left of next page). The four-story building had a large central entrance and two carved stone pediments above the fourth-floor arched windows. O'Brien had come to Duluth from Pennsylvania in 1870 and set up a livery service. In 1876 he became partner in the firm of **Pratt & Knowlton**. When Mr. Pratt died, O'Brien became full partner and the firm's name changed. Records are unclear about what exactly **O'Brien & Knowlton**

specialized in but it seems they made much of their income leasing the building. Over the years O'Brien & Knowlton rented space in its facility to **Duluth Coffee and Spice, Kelling Produce, Siepel & Huntley Printers, August Melander Bindery, Cudahy Packing**, and many others, including fellow wholesalers **Hartley-Chellew**. In March 1903 fire gutted one half of the building at 130–132 West Michigan Street, but it was repaired and continued to serve as a warehouse for many years. In 1961 the building was demolished for a parking ramp.

Guilford Hartley and Luther Mendenhall incorporated both **Duluth Dry Goods** and the **Duluth Shoe Company** in 1890 and had Traphagen & Fitzpatrick design a building to hold both firms at the foot of Sixth Avenue (pictured in sketch at lower right). Five stories of solid brick with arched windows on the third story, the building stood along the Sixth Avenue slip. Hartley and Mendenhall put Francis McIver in charge of Duluth Dry Goods, a clothing wholesale company, and made Robert Fitzgerald president of Duluth Shoe. The firm produced "every kind of shoe made" and Fitzgerald's team of fourteen salesmen sold throughout Minnesota, Wisconsin, Michigan, Iowa, the Dakotas, Montana, and Nebraska.

Duluth Dry Goods moved out in 1897 and Duluth Shoe planned to relocate when railroad industrialist James J. Hill purchased the building for

use as a passenger and freight dock for Northern Line Steamers. Hill gave up his plans when a severe fire in December 1899 destroyed the building. Duluth Shoe became the Phillips-Bell Shoe Company in 1905 (see page 157).

Michael Kelley, B. F. How, and A. D. Thomson pooled their resources in 1902 to form wholesaler **Kelley-How-Thomson**, setting up shop at 301–315 South Fifth Avenue West in a building designed by John J. Wangenstein (pictured next to Stone-Ordean-Wells at top right of previous page). Kelley-How-Thomson manufactured and sold tools for mining and lumber operations and supplied local hardware stores across the northern United States. The firm established its place in the history of the National Football League by sponsoring the league's Duluth Kelleys, the team that would become the legendary Duluth Eskimos. Its house brand "Hickory" competed directly with the "Zenith" brand of Duluth's Marshall-Wells. Apparently Zenith won, because in 1955 Kelly-How-Thomson became Marshall-Wells' subsidiary, operating under its own name until both companies closed in 1958. The buildings on South Fifth Avenue were used as warehouses until they were demolished in 1968 to make room for the Interstate 35 expansion.

In 1893 Albert Morley Marshall purchased Duluth's **Chapin-Wells** wholesale hardware business—first established in 1886 as **G. C. Greenwood & Company**—at 406 West Superior Street and renamed it **Marshall-Wells**. His business prospered, and soon he was shipping throughout the Midwest and Canada. Marshall-Wells got in on the manufacturing end as well, making everything from paint to appliances to tools under the "Zenith" house brand name. Business was going so well that in 1900 Marshall built a seven-story plant and warehouse at 325 South Fifth Avenue West (pictured below). The building was designed in two sections and straddled railway tracks.

A year later Marshall-Wells opened branches in Canada and the Pacific Northwest; nine years after that it became the largest hardware wholesaler in the United States, the third-largest in the world. Marshall-Wells grew to operate over one thousand retail stores in the United States and Canada and reached annual sales of $100 million. By 1950, sales dropped dramatically, and in 1958 the company liquidated. While Marshall-Wells is gone, its building has not been lost. Today the complex, known as the Meierhoff Building, has been divided into a hotel, restaurants, and offices.

Another building constructed as a jobbing house that remains in Duluth is the Gowan-Lenning-Brown Building, which went up at 525 South Lake Avenue in 1915. Designed by Frederick German, the building sits adjacent to Duluth's Aerial Bridge and was built as a grocery manufacturing and wholesale warehouse. **Gowan-Lenning-Brown** was considered Duluth's premier wholesale grocery at the time. Today it is the Paulucci Building.

Duluth entered the wholesale drug business in 1893 when Charles Sagar, Guilford Hartley, Frederick Patrick, and others incorporated **Sagar Drug**. Then, just as several other Duluth wholesalers had done, the firm hired Traphagen & Fitzpatrick to design its building at 225–227 South Fifth Avenue West. The five-story brick building (pictured in the illustration at right) featured an

entrance of three doors separated by sandstone columns. Sagar acted as the firm's first president. Leslie Walworth Leithhead, a native Canadian, learned his trade first in Montreal and then Winnipeg before arriving in Duluth in 1896, where he bought an interest in Sagar Drug and was named vice president. He immersed himself in Duluth society, joining the Kitchi Gammi Club, the Commercial Club, and Northland Country Club, and marrying Ophelia Sellwood, daughter of Captain John Sellwood. By 1898 the firm had reorganized as **Leithhead Drug** with Leslie Leithhead as president. It continued to sell wholesale drugs, lotions, and chemicals, and expanded with Leithhead's line of veterinary medicines. They served retailers in Minnesota, Michigan's Upper Peninsula, northern Wisconsin, and North and South Dakota, and their advertising boasted that the L. W. Leithhead Drug Company's label "has quickly become *an assurance of highest quality*."

In 1906 the company moved to a new building on Commerce Street, and six years later the firm became **Northern Drug**, which survived until 1997. The Fifth Avenue structure was renamed the Sweatt Building, eventually becoming part of the Kelly-How-Thomson Hardware wholesale complex. In 1966 the building—along with many of the wholesale buildings along South Fifth Avenue West—was demolished for the expansion of Interstate 35.

Cameron A. Rust arrived in Duluth in 1892 and joined the Wells-Stone Mercantile as a bookkeeper. He was eventually promoted to treasurer and general manager of Stone-Ordean-Wells. In 1910 he teamed up with Frank E. Parker, two of his brothers, and H. R. Ketchum and left Stone-Ordean-Wells to start **Rust-Parker-Martin**. That same year they retained the services of William Hunt to design a five-story brick building at 217 South Lake Avenue (pictured below), with railroad tracks running through the building's lower level. The business was later renamed **Rust-Parker Wholesale Grocery Company**.

Rust-Parker manufactured and/or packed spices, jams, jellies, syrups, vinegar, fish products, and roasted coffee under the Table Talk and Home Brand labels. Rust was struck with a heart attack at Northland Country Club in September 1916. According to historian Rachael Martin, the forty-eight-year-old businessman "left the links complaining of chest pain, and died in the locker room." Rust-Parker went on without him, and by 1922 it was one of the largest wholesale concerns in the region. But by the end of World War II its business had waned, and in 1947 Rust-Parker was liquidated. Other wholesale grocers occupied the building until 1980. The plant, which was then called the Viking Building, was demolished in December 1982 for the expansion of Interstate 35.

In 1922 A. Miller MacDougall, son of Captain Alexander MacDougall, began building a six-story warehouse at 824 Railroad Street, the foot of Ninth Avenue West. He named it the **MacDougall Terminal** for his father and backed his effort by bringing Marshall W. Alworth on as the concern's vice-president. Railroad tracks allowed trains to load and deliver food directly inside the building, which was constructed of reinforced concrete faced in brick with terra cotta trim.

Designed as a cold-storage warehouse by S. Scott Joy—the primary architect of Chicago's Manufacturing District—the McDougall Terminal was first served by two boats, package freighters each with a 2,300-ton capacity built by the Minnesota-Atlantic Transit Co. Business soon took off. Minnesota-Atlantic then purchased five small steel-hulled ships constructed for emergency salt water service in World War I. They nicknamed the newly acquired ships the "Poker Fleet," after a poker game inspired company executives to re-christen the boats—which had been named for lakes—after the highest five cards in a poker hand: *Ace, King, Queen, Jack,* and *Ten.* Each was refitted with refrigeration units to pack perishable food shipped to and from Duluth and New York. The Poker Fleet became the largest such operation in the world at the time. Success, however, was short-lived. By 1930 the business was placed in receivership. A group of Duluth businessmen purchased the building and renamed it the **Duluth Terminal**.

In the 1970s it was purchased by Jeno Paulucci and used to manufacture his Jeno's brand frozen pizzas. Jeno's left the building in 1983. It was demolished in 1987; the property remains vacant.

Miscellaneous Major Manufacturers

Since four unemployed young men opened a brewery in Portland Township in 1859, Duluth has been the home of a variety of manufacturing concerns. From Aroma Coffee to Zenith Broom, Duluthians tried their hand at just about everything. The Barsness Candy Company was the largest confectioner north of the Twin Cities, and the Ron-Fernandez Cigar Company introduced Cuban tobacco to the Upper Midwest. Puglisi Spaghetti Factory and Duluth Macaroni Company produced pasta while firms such as Elliott's Meats and Vokoven Sausage Company provided protein. One of Duluth's oldest manufacturers, Duluth Tent and Awning, is still in operation as Duluth Pack, and the DeWitt-Seitz Furniture Company lives on as the Happy Sleeper Mattress Company. Since cataloging all of Duluth's lost manufacturers would take a book of its own, we've narrowed the pool to those Duluth concerns whose products enjoyed nationwide distribution and employed the most Duluthians and Superiorites.

E. G. Wallinder Sash and Door opened its own doors at Fifty-Ninth Avenue West and Main Street in 1889 as Duluth's first manufacturer of windows, doors, mouldings, store fixtures, and a variety of metal work. By 1916 they had added buildings for planers, ripsaws, jigsaws, mortising machines, moulders, turning lathes, and polishers—along with storage sheds and a drying kiln—and the plant covered two city blocks. The company remained strong until 1944, when a fire in the paint shop spread to the entire facility. Forty-five-mile-an-hour winds fueled the flames, and the entire complex was

lost. Wallinder later resumed operations in Superior. Duluth Steel Fabricators later built a plant on the site.

After the Marinette Iron plant closed in 1900, the newly organized **Union Match Company** acquired and remodeled the Marinette facility and began to manufacture wooden friction matches in 1903. Each day the factory's ten match-making machines could take forty thousand feet of lumber and mill it into enough matches to fill two rail cars. In 1922 Union Match merged with **Minnesota Match** and a year later that firm was purchased by Deleware's **Federal Match Corporation**. In 1941 the firm became **Universal Match**. By 1950 the market for wooden matches had slumped and the match company closed. In 1950 Jeno Paulucci, Duluth's self-described "incurable entrepreneur," remodeled the plant to process his Chun King line of Chinese foods. Ten years later Chun King enjoyed an annual sales revenue of $30 million and sold more than half the prepared Chinese food in the United States. The food plant closed in 1973 and was demolished in 1986 for the Interstate 35 expansion.

Frederick A. Patrick learned the wholesale business at several prominent Duluth firms, including a stint as company secretary for Stone-Ordean-Wells, before starting **F. A. Patrick & Company** in 1900. The wholesale drygoods store sold its wares under the Northland brand. In 1903 Patrick had William Hunt design a seven-story brick building at 302 South Fifth Avenue West. A

year later it started manufacturing shirts and overalls. Patrick then acquired the Fosston Woolen Mills of Fosston, Minnesota. Other mills were added over the years, including Mankato Spinning and Knitting Mills in 1913. Later the firm added a mill in Duluth at 2900 West Superior Street. In 1922, the company reorganized as the **Patrick Duluth Knitting Mills**. Among the company's assets was Duluth's Glass Block store, which it purchased in 1911.

Patrick's became best known for its wool Mackinaw jackets, developed for lumberjacks but which became popular for men of all ages. In the 1920s the storied Duluth Eskimos wore customized Mackinaws on the sidelines. The Mackinaw (pictured in a detail of a catalog page at upper right) was said to be "a garment that has done much to spread the name 'Duluth' through the world!"

The Mackinaw was so popular that in 1928 Patrick launched a plan to sell directly to consumers. The timing was bad, and after the stock market crash of 1929—and with stiff competition from mills in New England—Patrick Duluth closed its operations. Patrick himself died in an automobile accident in 1931. After the Patrick company folded, the building functioned as a warehouse for several firms and was called the Kirk Building until it was demolished in 1965 for the Interstate 35 expansion.

One of the first companies to build in the Village of West Duluth as it developed in the late 1880s was the **Minnesota Iron Car Company**, which produced freight railroad cars. It built a plant along Central Avenue in 1888, and a year later added six more buildings. The facility (pictured in sketch below) stretched along the 200 and 300 blocks of South Central Avenue. The company made some of the first ore cars used to carry ore from the mines in Minnesota's Iron Range. Minnesota Car suspended operations in 1891 and became the **Duluth Manufacturing Company**, which continued to produce railway cars until 1896. The American Lumber Company occupied the site until 1907.

In 1898 an engineering publication announced that "if reports be true acetylene gas will shortly have a rival in carbolite." Not a rival, but an ally: carbolite, when burned, produced acetylene gas. A calcium, aluminum, and silicon carbide, carbolite was initially produced by mixing blast furnace slag and coke in an electric furnace in a process patented by Chicago chemist and metallurgist Herman Hartenstein. (The recipe later involved less-toxic limestone and coal.) The product, which resembled "crushed rock," was meant to produce acetylene gas for lighting, cooking, and generators. It was touted as being more "reliable, economical, and safe" than electricity or gasoline. Its most popular use was in welding and cutting torches and miners' headlamps.

Hartenstein opened **American Carbolite** in Constantine, Michigan, in 1899 to great success. Soon the Constantine plant was insufficient to fill orders. After considering Niagra Falls as the location for a new plant, he chose Duluth because of "the abundant power facilities available by harnessing the St. Louis River at the falls by the Great Northern Power Company." In 1908 American Carbolite took over the vacant Minnesota Car Company/Duluth Manufacturing plant. By 1910 it employed over 300 workers. For years it was one of the largest and most successful industries in West Duluth—the facility could produce 200,000 pounds of carbolite a day, enough to create twelve million cubic feet of gas. The plant became "the largest of its kind in the world" and its product was shipped as far way as South Africa and the Philippines. In 1928 American Carbolite was sold to Union Carbide, but in Duluth the company operated under the old name. In 1942 the company name was changed to **Electro Metallurgical Company**. Despite plant manager C. W. Knapp's assurance that "the change in name will not in any way change the nature or extent of operations at the local plant," it closed a year later.

During the 1950s **Zenith Concrete Products** occupied the site, but it was gone by 1964. Today a Coca-Cola Bottling plant and several building and scrap industries stand on the Carbolite site.

When A. W. Hartman became president of **Phillips-Bell Shoe**—which had evolved from the Duluth Shoe Company (see page 151)—in 1906, he reorganized the company as **Northern Shoe** and moved from a small facility on Michigan Street to a new factory which manufactured shoes and boots (some shown in the ad below) with names such as Gitche-Gamee, Duluth Hockey, Minnesota Hunter, Northern Maid, and Tamarack.

The firm built an eight-story brick building at 225–227 South Lake Avenue in 1907, complete with its own rail line and a dock for loading freighters. In 1910 Northern Shoe's four hundred workers produced 1,500 pairs of boots and shoes per day and sold over $1 million of footware a year. In 1918 Hartman again renamed the business, this time after himself. The **A. J. Hartman Shoe Company** closed for business in 1923. After the company closed, new owners changed the building's

name to the Industrial Building. Over the years a variety of businesses used the facility, including food producers and industrial machine dealers. By 1966 the building sat vacant; it came down in 1968 for the expansion of Interstate 35.

Blacksmith Otto Swanstrom invented a practical drive calk to be used with horseshoes, which smiths could easily remove and replace when damaged instead of reshoeing the horse. (A typical "sharp" calk is shown in the sketch at right.) Successful sales of Swanstrom's invention led to the 1907 incorporation of the **Diamond Calk Horseshoe Company**, originally operating on South Lake Avenue. In 1912 the firm moved to West Duluth and built a factory, office building, warehouse, and storeroom at 4702 Grand Avenue. For the next seventy-three years the company operated under the direction of the Swanstrom Family. It distributed its horseshoes and calks to all parts of the United States and was so successful that the plant required three additions before 1919. Eventually, as the popularity of the automobile grew and the need for horseshoes dwindled, Diamond Calk expanded into making hand tools and became known as **Diamond Tool**. In 1982 the company was purchased by Connecticut firm **Triangle Corp.**, which in turn was bought out by **Cooper Tools** in 1993. Cooper closed the Duluth plant in October 1994 and moved its operations to facilities in North and South Carolina. The buildings on Grand Avenue were razed in 1996 and replaced by a retail complex in 1998.

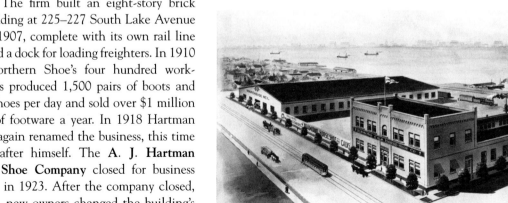

Miscellaneous Major Manufacturers, continued...

Duluth Boat Club financier Julius Barnes organized the **Western Rug Company** in 1909 (originally the **Western Linen Company**) to manufacture linen yarns from flax straw, which until then farmers considered waste product. In fact, the straw was burned in the fields before Western Rug found a way to use it. Afterward, farmers—mostly in Meadowlands, Minnesota, and Port Wing, Wisconsin—sold it to Western Rug. Barne's company developed the process and designed the machinery to spin straw into linen. In 1914 Western Rug installed that equipment in its brand new two-story steel-and-brick building at 6320 Grand Avenue and began producing rugs and carpets. Business boomed, and two years after the Grand Avenue facility opened, two more floors were added (shown above), followed by another two in 1918. The rugs, marketed under the Klearflax name, were successful in the United States and throughout the world. In 1924 its officers included Barnes' business partner, William Ames, and James Ten Eyck, the legendary coach of the Duluth Boat Club's national championship rowing squad. In 1939 **Klearflax**, as the entire company had come to be known, employed three hundred people. But postwar America found Klearflax struggling to compete with larger rug companies. The business sold to a competitor in 1953 and

the facility closed. The structure served as a warehouse until 1987, when it was imploded. The procedure took twelve seconds. The lot remains vacant.

In 1888 Canadian transplant Henry Bridgeman began a dairy in Duluth, selling his wares out of a horse-drawn wagon. When Newell F. Russell joined him as partner in 1892, the firm became the **Bridgeman-Russell Creamery**. The company expanded to produce dairy products in a building on East Superior Street and later on West First Street. By 1917 Bridgeman-Russell required a cold storage warehouse, so commissioned a design by John DeWaard and built it above the railroad tracks at 110–112 West Michigan Street. The brick building, trimmed in Bedford stone, stood seven stories tall; four stories rose above Michigan Street, but the building dropped three more stories to the railroad tracks behind it. Area farmers delivered fresh milk and cream to the creamery every day; there it was tested, pasteurized, and sealed in bottles marked with the Purity brand label. Henry Bridgeman acted as president until his death in 1924 and then Newell Russell ran the company until he died in 1935. By 1946 the ice cream–making process had moved to the Duluth Terminal building and the creamery was sold first to Land O' Lakes—who kept the Bridgeman-Russell brand—and later to Foremost Dairies. By 1960 the building sat empty. It was demolished in 1965; the site is vacant.

In 1902 Swedish-born Peter M. Carlson opened the **Duluth Showcase Company** to manufacture showcases and store fixtures for retail dealers, opening a sales floor and factory at 25 East First Street. Their cases were sold to druggists, jewelers, banks, and cigar stores. The firm also built iceboxes; the 1902 model was described in a 1955 *Duluth News-Tribune* article as "patterned after an Indian practice of wrapping meat as a means of preservation." It was lined with birch bark.

In 1921 the firm expanded, moving operations to a new building at Fiftieth Avenue West and Wadena Street (pictured below). Seven years later Duluth Showcase turned its complete focus to iceboxes, changing its name to **Duluth Refrigerator**. In 1932 the name changed again, this time to the **Coolerator Company**. Coolerator expanded again in 1935, acquiring the former Atlas Iron and Brass Works (see page 143) in New Duluth where Commonwealth Avenue meets the St. Louis River. (**Western Steel Products**, which specialized in the manufacture of tanks, culverts, fire escapes, and other metal products, occupied the site until 1935.) The collection of industrial buildings included the 1890 four-story Mansard-roofed office building (pictured at top right), an unusual style for an industrial complex.

During World War II, Coolerator made military products, including storage units, ammunition containers, and mess tables for the United States Army. The biggest plum in the pie was a $405,800 contract for large refrig-

eration units. After the war, Coolerator manufactured electric refrigerators and freezers and later expanded to include electric ranges and air conditioners. At its postwar peak, Coolerator employed 1,700 workers at the two plants and had eighty distributors across the country.

Coolerator was sold several times in the 1940s and '50s, first to Michigan's Gibson Refrigerator. While Coolerator shipped refrigerators as far away as Sweden, Gibson sold the Duluth plants to International Telephone & Telegraph in 1951 and held on four more years before closing in 1955. McGraw Electric purchased the plants' equipment and machinery.

In 1961 the West Duluth complex was remodeled and opened as Shoppers City. It later became a K-Mart and Country Store grocery before being converted to a Menards; the entire complex was destroyed in 2003 to build a new Menards superstore.

In 1958 Jeno Paulucci's Chun King foods moved into the New Duluth facility, staying until 1973. C. S. Lukovsky, owner of Gary Builders Supply, purchased the complex and used it as a storage facility. In September 1976 a fire was reported at the plant just after midnight. Eight fire companies fought the blaze until five in the morning as several hundred spectators watched. Besides heavy machinery, old furniture, sewing machines, and "as much as $150,000 in antiques" stored in the buildings were also lost in the fire, which was punctuated by exploding fuel oil tanks. The complex was a total loss; the site remains empty.

Miscellaneous Major Manufacturers, continued...

Founded in 1896 by George D. Lucore, the **Duluth Candy Company** was a wholesale candy manufacturer specializing in milk chocolate. The company initially leased space at 102 West Michigan Street. In 1900 Lucore built a three-story brick building at 20 East First Street.

Besides a wide variety of candies, Duluth Candy also supplied retailers with cigars, film for Kodak Brownie cameras, toys, and other non-candy products. Thanks to the Duluth Candy Company, Hunter's Park Grocery (better known to today's Duluthians as the old Snow White store) even stocked tam o' shanter hats for the neighborhood's predominately Scottish residents.

In 1916 Lucore sold his business to Milwaukee's **Zeiglar Candy**, after which it was operated under the management of E. J. Hutchinson. The firm was later bought out by the **Stratig Candy Company**. Owner Charles Stratig, a 1902 immigrant to Duluth from Greece, moved his company to the First Street building from his confectionery at 307 West Superior Street. Stratig Candy stayed in the building until the late 1950s, after which the building was used by a variety of tenants until its demolition in 2005. The building's site is now used as a courtyard and parking spaces.

In 1905 A. S. McDonald, R. B. Whiteside, and D. D. Murray organized the **Zenith Dredge Company**, a general dredging and harbor construction concern. The business was positioned at the foot of Thirteenth Avenue East along the waterfont, with docks for its various tugs. The tugs and crews of Zenith Dredge kept the harbor open for shipping traffic by removing the silt deposited by the St. Louis River and also built and repaired docks.

During World War II Zenith retooled and began building ships. The firm employed 1,500 workers who built thirty-two ships for the war effort, including tankers, cutters, and buoy tenders. (The photo below shows the Zenith facilities during war time.) After the war, dredges from Zenith helped create the St. Lawrence Seaway, which opened in 1959. In the 1950s the company began to diversify with subsidiaries including Superwood Corp., Zenith Concrete Products, and Superior Wood Systems, Inc. In 1994 Zenith Dredge was dissolved and sold to Marine Tech LLC which continues maintenance of Duluth and Superior's harbor channels and recycling of dredged materials. The former Zenith Dredge site is now owned by the Georgia Pacific Corporation.

PART FIVE

LOST PARKS, LANDMARKS & WATERFONT

The First Duluth Boat Club Building (1887 – ca. 1905)

Lost Parks, Landmarks & Waterfront

Duluth first invested in park space in 1870, setting aside a few acres along Clark House Creek for Cascade Park (see page 164), and since that time has developed over one hundred parks, giving Duluth more green space than most U.S. cities. At one time nearly all of Duluth's major parks included privately-operated pavilions. The Lester Park Pavilion, owned and operated by Mr. L. A. Fungerson, featured refreshment parlors, a dance hall, merry-go-round, small zoo, and shooting gallery. It remained a favorite amusement spot in the early 1900s until it was destroyed by fire. Nearby Harmonie Hall was also used for dances. Owned in part by John Busha, Harmonie Hall also featured carved Ojibwe designs similar to those on his Rustic Bridge (see page 165). Lincoln Park's original wooden pavilion was replaced in 1934 by the current stone structure built by the Works Project Administration. Chester Park's pavilion was gone by the time a 1924 structure for the Duluth Ski Club went up. That structure, along with toboggan slides and several ski jumps, are also gone from Chester Park, along with rustic bridges that once spanned Chester Creek (other parks along creeks and rivers had similar

bridges). Lester Park and Kitchi Gammi Park both had tourist facilities. Kitchi Gammi's Brighton Beach Municipal Tourist Camp even offered cabins for rent (pictured on the next page along with the other structures mentioned above).

Duluthians also built their own outdoor attractions, from horse-racing tracks to amusement parks. One unique facility was the Duluth Driving Park in Woodland, built by Guilford Hartley, which featured a grandstand designed by Traphagen & Fitzpatrick but only survived three years. Later the Boy Scouts built a soap box derby course on the site of Hartley's commercial farm, now Hartley Park and Nature Center.

The Duluth waterfront has been shifting and changing constantly since an outer breakwater was built in 1868. Due to the addition of railroads, changes in the shipping industry, and constant harbor development, the Zenith City has seen many landmark structures come and go, from the Citizen's Dock on the lake side of Minnesota Point in today's Canal Park Business District to the Arrowhead Bridge, which in 1927 first bridged West Duluth with Superior.

One "lost" landmark is still very much with us. Today's Aerial Lift Bridge began as Duluth's Aerial Transfer Bridge, built in 1905 (above). The bridge ferried people, vehicles, and goods across the ship canal in a gondola (left). In 1929 workers removed the gondola and its suspension truss and adapted the remaining superstructure into a lift bridge, adding a roadway for vehicle and pedestrian use. The aerial bridge's top span, a remnant of the ferry bridge, is not actually needed for the lift span to operate.

Lost Park Structures

Over the years Duluth's parks have seen many structures—from fieldhouses to footbridges—come and go, including (clockwise from top right) the then-new Chester Park fieldhouse in 1924, Portland Square water fountain shown ca. 1900, Lester Park Pavilion and Harmonie Hall, the Lincoln Park rustic pavilion in 1894, and the Brighton Beach Municipal Tourist Camp in Kitchi Gammi Park, date unknown (vehicles indicate the photo was taken in the 1940s, and the tourist camp is mentioned in the 1941 *WPA Guide to Minnesota's Arrowhead Country*).

Cascade Park's 1895 Pavilion

In 1870 the City of Duluth bought four acres of land near First Avenue West and Sixth Street through which ran Clark House Creek. Cascade Park, with the Clark House Creek running right through it, was plotted on those acres between Cascade Drive and Mesaba Avenue in 1886. Three years later Duluth's first superintendant of parks, William King Rogers, developed a plan for Duluth's park system that initially called for three parks to run along creeks starting at the proposed roadway between Miller Creek and Chester Creek that would become Skyline Parkway. As the scenic roadway expanded, more parks would follow along other creeks. Lakeshore Park, today's Leif Erikson Park, was also part of the plan's future and was intended to be much larger than it is today. Rogers envisioned many parks running along creeks from the boulevard to the shores of the lake and St. Louis Bay like "pearls on a string." When he announced his idea, Cascade Park was already in place along Clark House Creek. The other two he named for assassinated U.S. Presidents Abraham Lincoln and James A. Garfield: Lincoln Park along Miller Creek and Garfield Park (later renamed Chester Park) along Chester Creek. Of all of Duluth's early parks, Cascade was by far the grandest. Perched on a bluff above downtown Duluth's business section, Cascade Park held several meticulously tended gardens and carefully groomed pathways.

In 1895 the city added a sandstone pavilion and bell tower at the heart of the park, giving it a whimsical, castle-like atmosphere (shown at left under construction and above right in 1896). The structure had several levels and

picnic facilities and played host to many garden parties and social events. Clark House Creek flowed directly through the pavilion, cascading out an opening on the building's lakeside façade to a pond more than thirty feet below. (The creek was diverted below ground at First Avenue West.) The park quickly became a popular spot for picnickers and others seeking escape from the smoke and noise of Duluth's busy waterfront. Unfortunately, the bell tower was destroyed during a storm in 1897. More portions of the creek were altered to flow underground as the area surrounding the park developed. In the 1950s Cascade Park was reduced in size and most of its sandstone structures were razed.

Today only two-and-a-half acres of Cascade Park survive. When Mesaba Avenue was widened in 1975 to accommodate traffic heading toward Miller Hill Mall and surrounding retail developments, a large part of the park was sacrificed. The city demolished its remaining sandstone structures and forced Clark House Creek underground throughout the park. The city then built a concrete tower-like structure atop the bell tower's old sandstone foundation. That foundation, which holds a bronze plaque which reads "Cascade Park," and portions of the rock wall supporting Mesaba Avenue are all that remain of the original park.

Lester Park's 1898 Rustic Bridge

Green Bay, Wisconsin, native John Busha was born to an Ojibwe mother and a French-Canadian father in 1838. Busha served in the Civil War with Wisconsin's Twelfth Infantry, the "Marching, Fighting Twelfth," which in 1864 joined General William Tecumseh Sherman on his notorious March to the Sea. According to Ojibwe historian Christine Carlson, after the war Busha returned to Green Bay and married Rosalie Aino, and together they had seven children. Little is recorded about Busha's life in the 1870s and 1880s. In 1893 he moved his family to Duluth and found employment as Lester Park's first park policeman. Along with Frank Hodges, Busha ran the Harmonie Hall dance hall and a confectionary within the park. Busha's two oldest sons, Abraham and George, also worked in the confectionary.

After heavy rains in 1896 washed out many of the river's foot bridges, Duluth's Park Board commissioned Busha to build a bridge across the river. In the winter of 1897 Busha, along with Abraham and George, set to work felling Lester Park's cedar trees and using teams of horses to haul them to a site along the river. Then the Bushas started putting the unpeeled logs together until they spanned the river. Finally, Busha adorned the masterwork by carving Ojibwe embroidery designs into the wood. Their efforts earned the Bushas $345.68. The "Rustic Bridge," as it was called, became a popular tourist stop, with picnic tables on the bottom deck and lounging on the upper promenade. The lower deck even featured large square viewing holes (surrounded by rails) that allowed picnickers to look down on the Lester's roiling brown waters as they made their way to Lake Superior. Unfortunately, nature took its toll on the bridge, and the upper deck had to be removed in 1916 due to safety concerns. In 1931 the lower deck met the same fate. When the bridge came down, only Abe "Candy" Busha survived as one of its builders. He had earned his nickname running the confectionary at the White City amusement park; he later went to work for the city as a janitor.

Fond du Lac Winter Sports Center

The Fond du Lac Winter Sports Center included cross country ski trails, a toboggan slide, an alpine ski hill, and a 325-foot (60-meter) ski jump (pictured). In the summer, the cross country trails were used as bridle paths. Built by the Works Project Administration in 1940, the Winter Sports Center was accessed by an entrance at the convergence of East and West Mission Creek Parkway. It became a popular recreation site, and winter activities included skating and sleigh rides. It also became another home for the Duluth Ski Club which hosted tournaments at the site while continuing to train at Chester Bowl (see sidebar on the next page).

The ski jump was first used in a tournament in February 1941, when five thousand spectators turned out for the facility's dedication and an exhibition by famed Norwegian jumper Torger Tokle, who set the hill's initial record at 203 feet. The following year the national ski-jumping championships were held at Fond du Lac (the photos shown here were taken during that event). By 1949 the ski hill had been nicknamed the Ojibway Bowl. During a 1954 competition at Fond du Lac, Duluthian Joe Nowack jumped a record-setting 226 feet. His Ojibway Bowl record was tied in 1960 by Gene Kotlarek, also of Duluth.

In 1964 the ski jump was increased to 70 meters, but nature doomed the jump's future. The spring floods of 1972 eroded the land around the ski jump, making it dangerous to leave the jumps standing. The ski jump was removed and the erosion damage to the hill was filled; it was re-seeded and planted to prevent further erosion.

Duluth also had ski jumps at Old Maple Hill in West Duluth, Lincoln Park in the West End, and of course Chester Bowl in Chester Park, where the Duluth Ski Club started jumping in 1908.

Chester Bowl's Ski Jumps

According to the organization's papers, the Duluth Ski Club was formally organized on November 21, 1905, when club founders—including architect John J. Wangenstein—met at Duluth's St. Louis Hotel to create a ski club that would consist of mostly Norwegian immigrants, including legendary jumper Ole Feiring. The club held a few early tournaments on a hill in Hunter's Park, but by 1907 it had acquired land in today's Chester Park in an area known as Chester Bowl. There they built a ski jump. In 1908, Feiring set the U. S. record on the hill, jumping 112 feet. The slide blew over three times in the next ten years, and the club disbanded during World War I.

The ski club reorganized in 1922 and in 1924 built "Big Chester," a 115-foot slide that was the largest in the world at the time. By 1940 the sport was so popular that tournaments were moved to the new WPA faclity in Fond du Lac (see previous page). More slides were added over the years, including two training hills. In 1969 a 55-meter jump was added, as was a 35-meter hill that would later be named Little Chester. In the early 1970s Chester Bowl boasted five ski jumps. Over the years, many Olympic ski jumpers trained at Chester Park, including Jim Denney, Greg Swor, and Adrian Watt.

Duluth's enthusiasm for ski jumping had declined dramatically by the 1990s. Efforts have been made to revitalize the ski jumping program, but plans have proved too expensive. The top portion of Big Chester was removed years ago, and in 2011 the lower portions of Big Chester and Little Chester were removed for safety concerns. At the same time, what was left of the 20-meter Rabbit Ears and the 10-meter Bunny Ears training jumps and scoring booths were demolished.

SKI JUMPING, DULUTH, MINN.

Brautigan Gardens

Architect Karl Leurzer moved to Duluth in 1889, canoeing with his painting equipment and a friend all the way from Cleveland, Ohio. He had been lured to the Zenith City because his nephew Feodor von Leurzer, along with John Frey, had been hired by August Fitger and Percy Anneke to paint murals in their Fitger's Brewery Saloon (later renamed the Pickwick).

While in Duluth, Karl Leurzer married the daughter of Adolph Brautigan. Brautigan owned Duluth's first amusement park, Brautigan Gardens, which sat along the Lake Superior shore below London Road between Twenty-Ninth and Thirty-First Avenues East. The park became a popular gathering place for Duluth's social organizations, lodges, and churches. From downtown Duluth families rode in horse-drawn buggies, walked, and often pushed baby carriages through two-and-a-half miles of what was still wilderness to visit the Gardens. Brautigan's Gardens boasted an array of activities, including an outdoor bowling lane (pictured below), a variety of equipment for gymnasts, a shooting gallery, an open-air dancing pavilion, a German-style beer garden, and an outdoor theater. In the winter Brautigan set up an outdoor curling rink.

Leurzer built the Gardens' outdoor theater and painted beautiful murals inside several homes on the property. His talents were recognized throughout Duluth, and he was commissioned by the Robert B. Whiteside family to paint their famous grove of Redwood Trees (see page 22). Brautigan accidentally killed himself October 28, 1895, when he tripped while attempting to shoot a hawk. Shortly thereafter, the Gardens closed permanently, and Leurzer and his wife moved to Idaho.

White City

As early as 1900 a pavilion stood at Minnesota Avenue between Thirty-Ninth and Fortieth Streets, marking Oatka Park. ("Oatka" is Ojibwe for "an opening.") Still the park didn't see many visitors until 1905, when the Duluth Aerial Transfer Bridge began operating, allowing many more people access to Minnesota Point (prior to the bridge, the only way across the canal was in a ferry boat). Reports claim ten to fifteen thousand people enjoyed the park on the bridge's first day, even though it had little to offer at the time. Soon after the bridge opened the park became White City, an amusement park operated by the Duluth Amusement Company. On more than one Sunday in 1906, crowds using the aerial bridge to reach White City surpassed the record of 32,595 set the very first Sunday the bridge opened to the public.

White City, first envisioned by members of Duluth's Commercial Club, was patterned after amusement parks in large cities, especially the 1893 Columbian Exposition in Chicago, whose facilities were called White City because each of the wooden structures was covered in a white paint-

like material. Designed by St. Paul contractor Thomas H. Ivey, White City opened in the summer of 1906 with a circus, dancing pavilion, restaurant, merry-go-round, Ferris wheel, and water slide. Adults paid ten cents and each child was charged a nickel. Plans for the future involved more attractions, including a roller coaster and a $7,500 gasoline-propelled airship to be named *Duluth No. 1* (neither was built).

Some rides were added, including the "Mystic River" boat ride, a miniature railroad (operators claimed it had the smallest steam locomotive in the United States), the Old Mill, and the "Fun Factory," where ticket payers lost themselves wandering on twisted paths and "[ran] up against all kinds of funny and startling adventures." Other attractions included a corral of deer, a Gypsy Village (right), an automated baseball game, and free acrobats and burlesque performers, including "Rollo-Boy," pictured above. Facilities included sitting rooms (for the ladies), cafés and restaurants, and bathhouses. White City even offered swimming lessons in Lake Superior's chilled waters.

By 1908 financial problems forced the Duluth Amusement Company to sell, and the new owners changed White City to Joyland. But the new name helped little, and in April 1909 the park closed and most of its buildings were torn down. Oatka Park returned to picnic grounds with band concerts as its only form of entertainment. In June 1909 the only buildings left, the dancing pavilion and restaurant, burned in a suspected arson fire. Part of the property on which it stood became the home of Maggie McGillis—in fact, a portion

of McGillis's home, at 4010 Minnesota Avenue, is made from White City's old band shell. Today, most of the land White City sat on is now occupied by the Duluth Rowing Club and the Franciscan Health Center.

White City wasn't the only amusement park to operate on Minnesota Point. In 1938 the Minnesota Point Amusement Park opened near the entrance to the brand new Park Point Beach House and its surrounding facilities, which the city acquired in 1936. The park had a penny arcade, snack stand, kiddie cars, a chair-o-plane, and like White City, a miniature steam locomotive. Duluthian Charlie Willis earned fifty cents an hour at the park during the summers of 1960 and 1961, operating a 1906 Alan Herschel 36-horsepower carousel with hand-carved wooden horses suspended on brass poles and steam-powered when first built. Willis recalled on the public blog perfectduluthday.com that "The bumper cars were in terrible condition and the building was pretty dilapidated…If you bumped the cars, the steering chains would fall off the bottom, and two or three of us would have to tip the cars over on their sides and put on the chains." In 1964 Duluth Mayor George D. Johnson proposed closing the park because he thought the Point should remain natural and because the park drew crowds of "black jackets," likely young men with too much time on their hands. Johnson's proposal resulted in a failed petition to oust the mayor. The park closed that year.

Oneota Park Fairgrounds (aka Wheeler Racetrack)

The St. Louis County Agricultural Society organized in 1870 to exhibit the county's agricultural, mining, and industrial produce. The first St. Louis County Fair was held October 10–11, 1871, in downtown Duluth's Pendleton Block on Superior Street at First Avenue West. Five years later fairgrounds opened in Oneota Park, established on a parcel of land once owned by Henry Wheeler with an entrance at Thirty-Fourth Avenue West and East Third Street. The facility had just a few buildings and a gravel track for horse racing. In 1896 a new race track and buildings were constructed for that year's fair, and the facility became known as the Wheeler Racetrack. In 1911 the St. Louis County Fair moved to Hibbing. Wheeler continued to

be used as a racetrack and whenever a large space was needed for events such as circuses and carnivals. In 1924 the City of Duluth began proceedings to condemn Wheeler Racetrack and to convert it to a playground. Duluth acquired the land in 1926 and it has since been used as a public park known as Wheeler Field. Today the facility consists mostly of softball fields, a bocce ball court, and a historic field house. It also once held Peterson Arena, which was destroyed by a fire in December 2004 when a Zamboni exploded during a broomball game. Today that space is occupied by a skateboard park. (The photo at left shows Athletic Park behind the racetrack.)

Athletic Park

When the Duluth Cardinals entered the Northern League in 1903, they needed a place to play. So that April contractors hastily built a wooden ballpark with seating for 3,000 in the shadows of the DM&I ore docks. The next year the team became the Duluth White Sox, winning pennants in 1904 and 1905. Athletic Park later became the home field of the National Football League's Duluth Kelleys, who entered the league in 1923. Sportswriter and broadcasting legend Halsey Hall, who would become famous as

the radio voice of the Minnesota Twins, reported that Athletic Park had no locker rooms and that the playing field was an "uneven, coal-dust surface." It was actually iron ore dust. The Kelleys faced Curly Lambeau and his Green Bay Packers in 1924, the only time the Pack ever played in Duluth. Hall performed the referee duties, flagging Duluth's Bill Stein fifty-yards for "slugging," which helped a last-minute rally by the Packers. Despite the call, and a five-yard penalty for "stalling," Duluth hung on to win, 6–3. The Kelleys went on to become the Duluth Eskimos, a team that included Hall of Famers Ernie Nevers, Johnny "Blood" McNally, and Walt Kiesling. They only played one game at Athletic Park: because of Nevers' star power, the NFL made the Eskimos play every game except their first on the road in order to sell more tickets. In 1935 the Duluth White Sox were sold to Kansas City, who changed the team's name to the Duluth Dukes. In 1941 Athletic Park was destroyed and Wade Municipal Stadium became the home of the Dukes. The team changed names several more times until folding in 1970. (The 1993–2002 Duluth Dukes had no connection to the original franchise.)

Northland Country Club's 1903 and 1918 Clubhouses

When Northland Golf Club organized in 1899, one would have thought its members were unfamiliar with the game of golf, as their bylaws stated that: "No game for money shall on any account be allowed...No intoxicating liquors will be allowed...and no profane language unbecoming to a gentleman will be tolerated." With those and other rules in place, the club built itself a clubhouse on the former Howell estate, acquired for the golf course, at 3901 Superior Street. The Arts and Crafts–style club house (below) was built in 1903 at a cost of $17,000 and opened for the 1905 golf season. The building stood across a creek from what today is the first tee. In addition to golf events, the clubhouse provided space for dances, dinners, and teas. Early members included Guilford Hartley, Townsend Hoopes, and other prominent Duluthians. The club's membership all but mirrored that of the Kitchi Gammi Club.

Today the course sits below Skyline Parkway roughly between Glenwood and Superior Streets to the north and south and stretching from the easternmost edge of the Congdon neighborhood east to Fortieth Avenue East. Originally designed by Ward Ames, after a 1912 expansion the course included six holes on land now occupied by East High School. To play the Fifth hole, a three-hundred-yard par five, your tee shot had to clear Superior Street. Holes six, seven, and eight were located entirely on the lower side, and on nine you once again had to cross Superior Street from the tee box. But one's game was never disturbed by lawn maintenance equipment:

a herd of sheep was used to keep the grass down to playing level. According to the country club's website, "Each fall, the caddies would herd [the sheep] down Superior Street from the course, and then on to a West Duluth packing house when their work was done."

In 1956 Northland became part of golf history when it hosted the Women's USGA Open Golf Championship, which included the debut of Ann Gregory, the first African-American woman to play in a USGA event.

The 1903 clubhouse stood until 1918, when the infamous Cloquet/Moose Lake fire swept through eastern Duluth, and the clubhouse was caught in its path. That same year Northland built a new clubhouse (above). The 1918 clubhouse was remodeled after another fire in 1973 and demolished in 2006 to make room for a new clubhouse, similar in look, that opened in 2007.

A course redesign by Donald Ross, completed in 1927 after more land north of the course was acquired, positioned all the holes safely above Superior Street. Club member Albert Ordean bought the newly vacated land below Superior Street and donated it to the city for use as an athletic field. That land later became home to Ordean Middle School, soccer and football practice fields, and Ordean Stadium. In 2010–2011 the school was expanded into the new Duluth East High School. The former East High School, originally East Junior High, now operates as Ordean East Middle School.

Duluth Boat Club

On July 10, 1886, eleven Duluth sailing and rowing enthusiasts gathered to form the Duluth Boat Club, and by year's end their membership had grown to twenty-eight. The next year they built a clubhouse on Slip #1 in the harbor, located between Sixth and Seventh Avenues West, roughly where the stage of Bayfront Festival Park stands today. Designed by charter Boat Club member Charles M. McMillen, the boat house (below) stood three stories tall and was wrapped with verandas on its second and third stories; a square tower adorned one corner.

By 1895 the Boat Club boasted 193 members who enjoyed access to a fleet of fifteen rowing shells and more than twenty pleasure boats. By the turn of the century, membership growth and the club's inconvenient location adjacent to the canal's shipping lanes (shipping traffic and Boat Club activities often interfered with one another) forced the organization to find a new location. At the same time, Duluth had finally won approval to build a bridge over the ship canal. Since the bridge would give members easy access to Minnesota Point, Boat Club officers chose a site on the bay side of Minnesota Point at Tenth Street and St. Louis Avenue, building a new facility designed by John J. Wangenstein in 1903. The original Boat Club was demolished sometime after the second clubhouse opened.

Built for $5,000, the new Boat Club (above) boasted a larger boat house, a swimming pool, viewing stands, a café, tennis courts, and a dance floor. The two-story central building featured a tower at each corner and, like the original, many verandas for viewing club activities. Five hundred people attended its gala opening. The society columns of Duluth's newspapers called the dance floor "the most exclusive ballroom in the city."

To provide members with the experience of boating and vacationing at a resort, the Boat Club built another clubhouse on Spirit Lake in 1907. The facility (next page, lower left) included a pavilion with dance hall and dining room, cottages, and tents. The Spirit Lake clubhouse even had its own railroad depot, and members could arrive either by boat or train. In

1917 the Morgan Park Good Fellowship Club took over the facility. U.S. Steel employees remodeled the clubhouse, added a toboggan slide that extended onto the lake, and improved roads and sidewalks to make it easier for Morgan Park residents to access the lake and buildings. The Spirit Lake clubhouse remained active until the late 1920s when the buildings were abandoned and later demolished.

The Duluth Boat Club on Minnesota Point became Duluth's social center, hosting regattas, water carnivals, and national competitions. In 1912 club membership had swelled to 1,400 members, making it the largest such organization in the United States. Membership had received a boost in 1909 when the Boat Club merged with the Duluth Yacht Club, which had built a facility on Minnesota Point at Vine Street (today's Fourteenth Street). The newly expanded Boat Club then moved the former Yacht Club facility (right) to Oatka Park and placed it where the old pavilion once stood.

Boat Club president Julius Barnes, who had become a successful grain trader, hired James Ten Eyck to coach the Club's rowing squads. From 1911 to 1923, Duluth rowers dominated their national competitors, taking home twenty national championships. The club's "Invincible Four"—Max Rheinberger, Dave Horak, and brothers Doug and Phil Moore—did not suffer a loss between 1913 and 1916, taking home trophies from twenty-two na-

tional and international regattas. In 1922 Duluth Boat Club rower Walter Hoover became the world's best rower when he won the prestigious Diamond Sculls competition on London's River Thames. On his return to the United States, a flotilla of boats greeted the Duluthian in New York harbor. In the Zenith City, 65,000 people turned out to greet the returning hero.

Rowing's popularity declined sharply in the 1920s, about the same time many Boat Club members' enthusiasm shifted from watercraft to automobiles. By 1926 coach Ten Eyck had left and Julius Barnes was essentially financing the entire club. The club folded in 1926, and although Barnes—then the president of the United States Chamber of Commerce—convinced the City of Duluth to lease the club and operate it for the 1930–31 season, efforts to revive the club failed. The boat house was used to store boats until April 23, 1951, when an early morning fire destroyed the building and sixteen vessels stored within it. The former Boat Club became the site of the Duluth Yacht Basin and later the Lakehead Boat Basin. Winds of more than ninety miles an hour knocked down the Oatka clubhouse in 1964, when the building was owned by the American Legion.

The Boat Club was revived in 1955 as the Duluth Rowing Club and continues to this day.

Duluth Curling & Skating Club

With so many of its affluent residents hailing from Scotland or of Scottish ancestry, Duluth became a natural home for the sport of curling. In 1891 the Duluth Curling & Skating Club organized and began building Duluth's first curling rink on the foundation of Elevator A's ruins at Third Avenue East and Michigan Street. Curlers were so anxious to begin they couldn't wait for the facility—little more than two retaining walls and a tent—so they cleared some snow on St. Louis Bay at the foot of Eighth Avenue West and threw their first stone on Christmas Day 1891. The Third Avenue East rink hardly hosted a game; it was destroyed in an 1892 blizzard.

For the next twenty years curling in Duluth took place in several other buildings, including a makeshift facility at Wallace Avenue and Arrowhead Road. In 1897 the club built a rink at the foot of Fourteenth Avenue East and played there until the construction of its grand facility at 1338 London Road. Designed by Frederick C. German, the Duluth building was the largest curling club in the world when it opened on January 12, 1913. Its lower level boasted twelve sheets of ice and seating for three thousand spectators. The second level was open to ice skating and hockey in winter and roller skating in summer. The club had two kitchens, several dining rooms, a lunch coun-

ter, locker rooms, and a manager's living quarters. Besides curling, the facility hosted hockey tournaments, dances, and even a circus or two.

In 1976 the Duluth Curling Club moved into new facilities at the Duluth Entertainment and Convention Center's Pioneer Hall. It is the largest curling rink in the world, and the Duluth club itself is second only to the St. Paul club as the largest curling club by membership. Duluth won the men's national championship in 1964 and 2009 and the women's in 1984. Its junior women's team was best in the nation in 2004 and 2007, while the men's junior team won national championships in 2006, 2007, 2008, and 2009. Hibbing Curling Club president Francis "Fran" P. Befera was inducted in the Curling Hall of Fame for his efforts to build the 1976 facility in Duluth.

The 1912 building closed in 1976. It was saved from demolition for the expansion of Interstate 35, but lost in a spectacular fire on June 3, 1984. Its remains were demolished the next year. The space on which it stood is now a parking lot next to Leif Erikson Park's Rose Garden.

Amphitheater

The Duluth Hornets first formed in 1920 to play in the United States Amateur Hockey Association. The team went professional in 1924, the same year the Amphitheater at 1202–1206 East Superior Street was built as the team's arena. Designed by Frederick C. German, the brick-and-stone building measured 150 by 300 feet and held 5,000 spectators. The facility was used mainly by the Duluth Amateur Hockey Club. The Hornets dissolved in 1934. Two years later the Duluth Zephyrs formed and became the first team to join the International Amateur Hockey League. The Zephyrs won the league's inaugural season.

On February 12, 1939, the Amphitheater hosted a hockey game between Duluth policemen and Virginia firemen. A crowd of 3,000 gathered to watch, including many children invited as special guests: local Boy Scout and Girl Scout troops, school police patrol members, and residents of children's homes. During intermission loud cracks were heard throughout the arena, and the roof began to sag. Spectators panicked. Police and firefighters in attendance helped get people out of the building as large sections of the roof began collapsing. Organist Leland McEwan continued to play throughout the evacuation in an attempt to calm the crowd. Everyone got out safely minutes before the entire roof crashed to the ice. At first it was thought that heavy snow alone caused the collapse, but it was later determined that the building's design included roof trusses too weak to bear the extra weight of snow. When the roof collapsed, so did the Zephyrs; they folded the same year. The Amphitheater was damaged beyond repair and left vacant until it was partially demolished in 1941. The Plaza Shopping Center was built on the location in 1951; two of its walls are part of the old Amphitheater.

Frederick C. German

Born in Ontario in 1863, Frederick German attended the University of Toronto and later worked in New York City architectural firms before moving to Duluth. In 1889 he was employed as a draftsman for Oliver Traphagen before taking up partnership with several prominent Duluth architects beginning in 1892.

German's partnership with A. Werner Lignell, which began in 1905, resulted in many important Duluth buildings and homes, including the downtown YMCA and YWCA, Washington School, the Duluth Curling Club, Glen Avon Presbyterian Church, and St. Anthony of Paduah Catholic Church. From 1913 to 1923 German partnered with Leif Jenssen, and together they designed the Bradley Building and Pilgrim Congregational Church. After that partnership ended, German designed the Amphitheater. German also designed many grand East End homes, including the Henry and Amy Fee House at 2305 East Third Street and Highpoint, the home Bernard Silberstein built as a surprise fiftieth wedding anniversary gift to his wife Nettie at 21 North Twenty-First Avenue East.

Not everyone was pleased with German's work. In 1906 he and Lignell drew the original plans for Villa Scholastica (today's Tower Hall on the College of St. Scholastica campus). Mother Scholastica fired the pair of architects and the building contractor in 1908, citing faulty design and construction of the still uncompleted building (it was said to be in danger of collapsing). According to Scholastica historian Sister Agnes Somers, after being released German "tore up their plans" in disgust.

German "served continually" on Duluth's planning commission until he died in 1936 at his son George's house just after returning from a walk. He was seventy-three years old.

The Auditorium

Duluth's Curling Club commissioned the Union Rink Company to build a curling facility at 302 East First Street, but by the time the rink was completed in 1896, a contract disagreement had sent the curlers looking for another place to play. The building, a two-and-a-half-story wooden structure with a curling rink on the first floor and open ice skating on the second, opened in 1896 as the Union Ice-Skating Rink.

By 1900 the rink had closed and over the years the building was used for various purposes. In 1910 the Auditorium was faced with brick. In 1921 the L. Hammel Company purchased the building and converted its second floor into a hall with a seating capacity of 2,500. The company then renamed the building the Auditorium and advertised it as "well adapted for conventions, mass meetings, balls, assemblies, or any occasion for the gathering of a large number of people."

From 1965 to 1978 the building was home to the Hemlock Garage, an automobile repair shop that still operates at 110 East Fourth Street. In 1979 Krenzen's Cadillac-Pontiac-Honda was using the building as storage, renting a portion of it to future Duluth mayor John Fedo for his car refurbishing business. On March 6, 1979—three hours after Fedo moved his business out of the building—the Auditorium's roof collapsed under heavy snows. Several cars were crushed, and the building was so badly damaged it had to be demolished.

The 1908 YMCA Building

One of the oldest organizations in Duluth, the Young Men's Christian Association has been serving the community since 1882, when it set up a free reading room and library association at 18 East Superior Street. Since then the Y has grown and spread throughout the city. The 1908 building at 302–312 West Second Street, designed by Frederick C. German & A. Werner Lignell, was five stories of red brick in a classical design trimmed with Tennessee marble. Its amenities included two gymnasiums, a pool, locker rooms, game rooms, a library, classrooms, and a dormitory. Its lobby had a marble base and terrazzo floors and was trimmed in English Oak; the chairs were upholstered in Spanish leather. Adjoining the lobby was "The Alcove," offering "a retreat for reading, music, and social chats" and furnished with easy chairs, a piano, and a red-brick fireplace. The downtown YMCA was demolished in 1974 to make room for a new YMCA facility on the same site.

Railroads

Even before Duluth became a township, speculators had been eyeing the head of the lakes as an ideal spot for a railroad terminus. As early as 1853 Minnesota legislators created a railroad charter for a line to run from Lake Superior to Puget Sound, and in 1864 President Lincoln approved an Act of Congress that essentially created Jay Cooke's Northern Pacific Railroad (NP) along the planned line. The Lake Superior & Mississippi Railroad reached Duluth in 1871, and by 1926 nine railroads operated out of Duluth: Northern Pacific; Great Northern; Chicago, St. Paul, Minneapolis & Omaha (the Omaha Road); Minneapolis, St. Paul & Sault Ste. Marie (the Soo Line); Duluth, Winnipeg & Pacific; Duluth, South Shore & Atlantic; Duluth, Missabe & Northern; Lake Superior Terminal and Transfer; and the Duluth & Iron Range (see page 197). Others had come and gone or had been absorbed by other railroads. Their railyards took up considerable space along Duluth's waterfront, on Rice's Point, and between downtown Duluth and the wholesaler warehouse district that covered much of today's Canal Park Business District and the site of the Duluth Entertainment and Convention Center and Bayfront Festival Park. Freight and passenger stations could be found along the tracks from Lester Park to Fond du Lac.

Duluth's first railroad, the **Lake Superior & Mississippi** (LS&M), began construction in 1863 in St. Paul. It was designed as a portage railway to connect the Twin Cities to the **Northern Pacific** (NP). Jay Cooke was heavily invested in both concerns. Both Duluth and Superior wanted the railroad, knowing that it would bring success to the city in which it terminated. Because St. Louis County helped Duluth come up with more money than Superior could raise, LS&M's chief investor—Jay Cooke—chose Duluth. This must have infuriated LS&M president William L. Banning, who in 1867 told Duluth officials that "it is not possible to find room on the

North Shore either on the lake or bays, to build a railroad, lay out and build a town, or do any kind of commercial business."

While the railway began stretching north from St. Paul in 1862, building from Duluth southward did not begin until 1868. Starting in downtown Duluth, laborers laid track essentially alongside the St. Louis River to Fond du Lac and on to Thompson. It was in Thompson on August 1, 1870, that the final spike was driven, completing the road. Passenger service to Duluth began on August 22 of that year, with Banning eating crow as he hosted guests taking a specially-outfitted train to Duluth. By the end of the year, trains ran between Duluth and St. Paul every day.

The LS&M constructed Duluth's first railroad freight depot at 300 East Michigan Street (above) in 1870 next to grain Elevator A and the breakwater that protected it. The next year the LS&M built a five-stall roundhouse on Rice's Point east of Garfield Avenue (page 178, bottom). The first Union Depot, a passenger station serving LS&M and NP, went up

along Fifth Avenue West behind Michigan Street during this time (right).
The two-story building had just two rooms on the main floor and was likely
built in 1870. Cooke's continued investment in NP stretched his already
drained finances, and the great Philadelphia financier went broke in 1873,
the same year the NP reached Bismarck, North Dakota. The LS&M managed to hang on without Cooke's money, even adding ten stalls to its roundhouse in 1876. But the railroad failed the next year, reorganizing as the **St.
Paul & Duluth Railroad** (SP&D).

Sometime prior to 1884 the LS&M freight depot was enlarged, perhaps
when the railroad became the SP&D. (By 1890 the railroad leased the building to Duluth Iron and Metal, a scrap iron business; the company continued
to use the old depot until a fire on August 16, 1963, destroyed the historic
building.)

In 1892 a second and much larger Union Depot was built at Fifth Avenue West and Michigan Street to serve six railroads: SP&D, NP, the Duluth South Shore & Atlantic, the Duluth & Iron Range, Wisconsin Central,
and Duluth Winnipeg & Pacific. Before the century was out, Northern Pacific replaced the 1871 roundhouse with a new roundhouse located west of

Garfield Avenue (next page, top). A massive building, the second roundhouse included stalls for up to thirty-six engines. It came down in the 1970s.

Northern Pacific also either built or purchased
existing buildings for use as depots, including
freight stations at 114 South Fifth Avenue West
(next page, bottom right, pictured in 1951), and at
Hudson Boulevard and Commonwealth Avenue.
Passenger stations stood at 220 South Twentieth
Avenue West and 5400 West Wadena Street.

In 1886 SP&D built new lines from West
Duluth to Carlton to reduce the road's grade and
remove some turns, making it much easier on the
trains. The original line continued to provide com-
muter train service to Fond du Lac until the 1930s.
The SP&D became part of Northern Pacific at the
turn of the twentieth century. Northern Pacific was
succeeded by **Burlington Northern** (BN), today's
Burlington Northern Santa Fe (BNSF). Because
BN already had railways in place, much of the original LS&M line was considered redundant. Most of

the track was abandoned, and many segments have since been turned into "rail trails," including the Willard Munger Trail, named for long-time Minnesota Congressman and conservationist Willard Munger, which begins in West Duluth near the motel he owned for years.

The **Chicago, St. Paul, Minneapolis & Omaha Railway** (CMO) better known as the **Omaha Road**, served Nebraska, Iowa, Minnesota, Wisconsin, and South Dakota and created a direct link between Chicago and Superior in 1883. Until 1886, when the Great Northern Railroad built the St. Louis Bay Bridge, those who wanted to reach Duluth completed their journey by ferry boat. The CMO built a passenger station at 200 Fifth Avenue West (next page, bottom) and a freight depot next door at 232 Fifth Avenue West. The Northern Division main line to Duluth was abandoned by 1965, when both structures were demolished to make room for the Interstate 35 expansion. Another CMO depot stood at the foot of Eighth Avenue West; the Chicago & North Western Railway (C&NW) leased the Omaha Road in 1957; in 1972 the C&NW completely absorbed the Omaha Road.

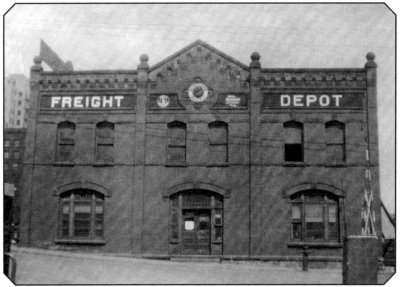

Major Railroads, continued...

The depots built by CMO were also used by the **Duluth, Winnipeg & Pacific Railway** (DWP), which began in 1901 as the Duluth, Virginia and Rainy Lake Railway and ran from Virginia to Silver Lake, west of the Twin Cities. The Canadian Northern Railway purchased the railway and renamed it the Duluth, Rainy Lake and Winnipeg Railway (DRL&W). In 1908 the line reached north to International Falls. The following year the railway was purchased by Canadian National and its name was changed again, this time to Duluth, Winnipeg & Pacific. It first connected to Duluth in 1912, using the CMO passenger and freight stations as well as its own freight depot at 5431 Grand Avenue, where Grand intersects with Central Avenue (right), which was demolished in 1965. The DWP also served a passenger depot at Spirit Lake, originally built for access to the Duluth Boat Club's Spirit Lake branch. Today the DWP serves the Canadian National as a link between Fort Francis, Ontario, and Duluth, where shipments are taken over by the Wisconsin Central Railroad.

First formed in 1888 from a conglomeration of existing railroads, the **Minneapolis, St. Paul, & Sault Ste. Marie Railroad**, commonly called the **Soo Line**, arrived in Duluth in 1910 in grand style. The Soo Line built a

large passenger depot designed by Charles E. Bell, William M. Tyrie, and Cecil B. Chapman at 602 West Superior Street (top right). The Neoclassical Revival–style building, faced in red brick with stone and terra cotta trim, stood one-and-a-half-stories tall along Superior Street but dropped two stories in back to reach Michigan Street. The depot's construction cost $250,000, but that wasn't the expensive part of bringing the Soo Line to Duluth. The company spent $2.5 million just getting the rail lines the final mile to the depot.

Most of the money went for the construction of a tunnel. By the time the Soo Line made plans to bring service to Duluth, much of the railroad right-of-way was in use and streets were in place, leaving little room for a new rail line. To make the Soo Line fit into Duluth without disrupting street traffic, the railroad had to create some room and found it under Michigan Street. Work on the tunnel was actually begun in 1908 by the Wisconsin

Central Railroad (WC). The Soo Line acquired majority interest of the CW that same year and took over the project. A small army of men used dynamite and rock drills to cut through the Point of Rocks. When completed, the tunnel ran sixteen feet below the Superior Street grade, measured 16 feet wide and 22.5 feet wide and stretched for 1,631 feet (The photo below shows workers and officials celebrating the tunnel's completion; the image at right was captured in the early 1960s.)

Including the cost of adding tributary lines to connect existing routes to Duluth, the Soo Line estimated it had spent $18 million. Passenger service began in October, 1910, offering passengers a variety of routes to destinations throughout the Midwest. The Soo Line's *Laker* ran an overnight service to and from the Twin Ports to Chicago's Grand Central Station. Soo Line also maintained two freight stations in Duluth, one at the foot of Ramsey Street (next page, bottom left) and another at the foot of Tenth Avenue West. In 1960 the Soo Line acquired the Duluth, South Shore & Atlantic Railway (DSS&A), a line first formed in 1888 to connect Duluth to Sault Ste. Marie and the eastern seaboard. The purchase made sense: the DSS&A had been using the Soo Line's track since they first opened, and both railroads were subsidiaries of Canadian Pacific. The relationship was short-lived, however;

Duluth service ended in 1961. The *Laker* was discontinued completely on January 15, 1965.

The Soo Line Depot was demolished in 1972 as part of Duluth's Gateway Urban Renewal Project. Gateway Towers, an apartment complex for seniors, now occupies the Soo Line Depot's former site. Redevelopment plans had at first called for the building to be saved and reused as the St. Louis County Heritage and Arts Center. Unfortunately years of neglect resulted in a completely flooded basement, which undermined the building's structural strength. The 1892 Duluth Union Depot at 506 West Michigan Street—originally slated for demolition—was instead saved for the Heritage and Arts Center and now includes the Duluth Playhouse, history museums operated by the St. Louis County Historical Society, and the Lake Superior Railroad Museum.

Including the 1892 Union Depot, the Zenith City is fortunate to have three former railroad depots still standing. The D&IR's Endion Station still exits, albeit not in its original location (see sidebar on page 104). The Lake Superior & Mississippi's Fond du Lac passenger station (bottom right), built in 1870 when the railroad first reached Duluth, is also with us but in a different location. After the railway line was abandoned, the depot was moved to 13308 West Third Street, where it still stands. It was used as a duplex until 1929, when it became the Olde Depot Inn restaurant. The Inn closed in 1985 and the building is now a private residence.

Other railroad depots that have come and gone from the Zenith City include a Great Northern freight station at 630 West Michigan Street; Duluth & Iron Range Railway (D&IR, see page 196) depots at 2700 West Railroad Street, 527 East Gary Street, on Forty-Seventh Avenue East near East Superior Street, and at Sixtieth Avenue East and Superior Street. (The station pictured above shows an unidentified NP station in Duluth).

Duluth's Street Railways

Authorization to build Duluth's first streetcar line—which by grant had to consist of at least one mile of track with rides on cars of "the best quality" costing no more than a ten-cent toll—was granted in October 1870, but no one rode on a Duluth streetcar until 1883. The **Duluth Street Railway Company** incorporated in 1881 and work began on tracks along Superior Street from Eighth Avenue West to Third Avenue East in September 1882. Small trolley cars or "dinkies" pulled by mules began service on July 6, 1883. The ride cost a nickel. The mules sometimes pulled the cars off the tracks; passengers had to help lift the cars back on track before the trolley could proceed. The company stored its cars and mules in a barn built along Superior Street at Eleventh Avenue West. By 1889 horses had replaced mules as the streetcar engines.

Those first small cars had open cabs, so early motormen had to dress for all kinds of weather, even if it meant covering their woolen uniforms with buffalo coats and slickers in the winter. The cars were soon adapted with closures, but that didn't make the job easier: a motorman was not allowed to sit, speak to patrons, nor smoke cigarettes while operating a dinky. And until 1922, when a token system was introduced, they had to make change for customers. The pay was low, and conductors (shown below in 1900) and those in the machine shops were often expected to work sixteen hours a day. Most employees were immigrants. During the winter, operators had to fight the cold and wet, as slush often clogged machinery. Operators of later electrified streetcars had to also contend with ice forming on wires, which reduced conductivity and therefore power. Along the way they had to constantly tend to the coal fire of the trolleys' heaters.

When Duluth regained its city charter in 1887, surrounding townships folded in to create a much larger city. As neighborhoods developed, the streetcar system developed with them. Often streetcar lines were built by land development companies who created the neighborhoods, but their operation would be handled by the Duluth Street Railway Company. In

1890 the dinkies were replaced with electrically powered cars (shown below towing a coach car). Overhead wires were strung along the tracks and a power station was built at the Eleventh Avenue West car barn. By 1892 the entire line was electrified, and the railway had increased from four to nearly thirty miles of track. Major arteries included lines along Superior Street, Fourth Street, and Eighth Street. They were extended to Twenty-Second Avenue East, Twenty-Third Avenue West, and later up Woodland Avenue to Hunter's Park and out to Lester Park. The Highland Park Tramway line, connected to the Incline Railway (see page 188), served Duluth Heights. Electrical substations sprung up along the lines to provide them with power. Land Companies added stations to their lines, including the Glen Avon station at 2102 Woodland Avenue (it is now a private home). But as it happened to

so many other businesses in Duluth and throughout the United States, the financial panic of 1893 put great financial strain on the streetcar operation. It had invested heavily during the boom, and now its revenues had suddenly been cut in half. The company reduced operations, leaving new

equipment idle. They tried cutting employee wages to stay alive, but that resulted in an employee strike, even though the work force was not organized in a union. The work stoppage resulted in the resignation of manager Fred S. Wardell. In 1898, the company entered receivership.

Meanwhile, the **Park Point Traction Company** had been operating a horse-drawn trolley (pictured, above) on Minnesota Point since it first organized in 1887 as the **Minnesota Point Street Railway Company**. Its line ran along what is today Minnesota Avenue, from the ship canal south, extending to Oatka Beach at Fortieth Street by 1899, the year it electrified and became the Park Point Company (it became **Interstate Traction** in 1912). Because of its location across the canal, which was not permanently bridged until 1905, Park Point was cut off from Duluth's fire department. So the trolley company outfitted one car with fire-fighting equipment and the city supplied a firefighter to operate it. The rig (pictured on next page, top right) was the only streetcar outfitted as a fire car in North America.

Street Railways, continued...

According to Duluth streetcar expert Wayne C. Olsen, it was the "moral obligation of any male citizen along the way to jump on the [fire] car to offer whatever assistance was needed." The trolley company also offered a freight service for its patrons.

The Duluth Street Railway Company absorbed the Park Point company in 1917. It had risen from receivership with an injection of cash from Luther Mendenhall and Guilford Hartley and new management provided by Herbert Warren. In 1900, the company teamed up with the Superior Rapid Transit Railway, itself in receivership, to operate a line between Duluth and Superior on the Interstate Bridge that connected the two cities (see page 194). During the next ten years, Duluth Street Railway experienced another boom, acquiring the lines owned by land companies and expanding its system. A line along Piedmont Avenue opened in 1910, followed by one along East Ninth Street to Thirteenth Avenue East two years later. A western line to Morgan Park opened in 1916 and was extended to Gary-New Duluth two years later. A line from East Eighth Street to Kent Road was completed in 1923. The streetcar system reached Lakeside's Crosley Avenue in 1926; it was the last line constructed in the Zenith City. Duluth Street Railway also operated the entire Superior system.

Besides extending its reach, Duluth Street Railway reinvested in its cars. The electric trolleys that had replaced the dinkies were themselves replaced in 1901. The new cars came from the Twin City Rapid Transit Company's shops in Snelling, and were large, sturdy vehicles (left). Their bright paint jobs inspired the nickname "Yellow Horse." Duluth Street Railway purchased 150 of them over the next twenty-five years, including the *St. Louis*, a private car outfitted with, according to Olsen, "elegantly upholstered chairs, thick rugs and ornate draperies...[and] an ice box stocked with a variety of refreshments." The cherrywood-paneled car was at the disposal of company officials to "show visiting dignitaries the city."

While it enjoyed financial solvency for a while, the going was hardly smooth. In 1912 employee conditions had not improved for the workforce, most of it made up of Scandinavian immigrants, and Herbert Warren did all he could to prevent union organization. According to historians Richard Hudelson and Carl Ross, Warren kept workers under surveillance trying to identify union organizers and fined them for "petty infractions." After the company fired nine men who had met secretly to discuss a new union, employees stopped work. They demanded that they be allowed to form a union, that their work day be

The streetcar system saw its peak in 1920, collecting 35,000,000 tolls. It saw its largest day the year before, when 178,700 riders used Duluth's transit system to attend Independence Day celebrations. Eventually, the popularity of automobiles and the introduction of buses dramatically dropped ridership, and Duluth simply didn't have a large enough population to support the system. The Great Depression didn't help, and in 1930 the company went bankrupt. Lines started shutting down, replaced by buses first used in the 1920s (below). First the Fourth Street Line shut down, then the Minnesota Point service. The Duluth-Superior Transit Company bought the Railway company's holdings in 1933. Soon the Lester Park line discontinued operation, and in 1935, service stopped on every line in Superior. The last piece of the railway to be dismantled was the Incline Railway, which came down the day after Labor Day 1939 (see next page). The Twenty-Sixth Avenue West streetcar barns survived until 1984, when they were demolished; Graybar Electric now occupies the lot. The Duluth Street Railway's office building at 2631 West Superior Street now serves as the Cartier Agency's offices.

cut to nine hours, and that their recently unemployed compatriots be given their jobs back.

The company refused and hired scabs. On September 9 three thousand people attacked the streetcar barns at Twenty-Sixth Avenue West and Superior Street (above). They derailed cars and mistreated scab workers. By the fourth day local papers were reporting 15,000 people at the site, and the violence increased. Strikers threw stones at scab crews, set up blockades on the tracks, and even overturned cars. On Friday, September 13, newspapers reported that shots had been fired at a scab motorman. Even with hired detectives along for the ride, attacks on scab conductors continued into October. Headlines declared the police helpless. But Warren dug in, refusing to negotiate. With the law of the day on the company's side, the strike failed.

Until World War I, all of Duluth's streetcar conductors were men. *Duluth News-Tribune* reporter Nathan Cohen, in a sentimental piece about the end of the streetcar line in 1939, asked readers if they remembered "the buxom lass on the steel plant route who used to drink beer with her lunch, and how the bottles used to roll all over the floor at every sharp turn?" Few women stayed on after the war, but two of them operated streetcars for at least ten years.

The Seventh Avenue West Incline Railway

William King Rodgers, Duluth's first parks superintendent and the man who first envisioned today's Skyline Parkway, was also an investor in the Highland Improvement Company, which first developed the Duluth Heights neighborhood. In 1890 he convinced his fellow investors—including fellow Ohioan and friend Rutherford B. Hayes—to build an incline or "furnicular" railway. It would run from Superior Street and Seventh Avenue West five hundred feet up the hillside to the top of what was called Beacon Hill along the developing Skyline Parkway (Boulevard Drive at the time, later Rodgers Boulevard). At the top the company built the Highland Park Tramway, a short-line streetcar system to serve Duluth Heights residents. The incline allowed those living in Duluth Heights to get to and from downtown, where they could transfer to a streetcar heading toward their jobs.

The Seventh Avenue West Incline consisted of two tracks built into a 2,975-foot superstructure. Two specially designed streetcars weighing twenty-nine tons a piece were pulled along cables driven by a hoisting engine powered by 400 horsepower boilers in a powerhouse at the top of the railway. The cars—which carried both people and horses—were positioned on the track to provide counterbalance: when one car was at the top of the railway, the other was at the bottom; they passed at precisely the middle.

The conductors called out "East car clear!" and "West car clear!" before the cars were engaged in operation. Both going up and coming down, the railway offered spectacular views of downtown, the harbor, Minnesota Point, and, later, the aerial bridge. Along Superior Street the company built a small depot that later doubled as grocery (it enjoyed several incarnations over its lifetime). Once complete, the Highland Improvement Company immediately turned operations over to the Duluth Street Railway Company.

At the top of the hill, the railway took advantage of the incline's growing reputation for its pleasant ride and views. So to increase ridership, in 1892 the company built a grand pavilion adjacent to the powerhouse. Designed by Traphagen & Fitzpatrick, the

Beacon Hill Pavilion—at the time considered a "resort"—would make the top of the incline a destination. The large Shingle-style building measured one hundred by three hundred feet and featured a square tower. Over twenty windows across the building's front façade offered views of the harbor. It became more popularly known as simply the Incline Pavilion.

Open from May until late autumn, the Incline Pavilion included restaurants, an amusement center, and the Pavilion Theatre, which was run by Matt Kussell and could seat two thousand spectators. Patrons paid twenty-five cents to see dramatic works as well as vaudeville acts, though as one advertisement assured customers, "the best talent is engaged, and the class of entertainment is suitable for ladies and children as well." Diners could be satisfied at the Palm Garden, a restaurant operated by J. L. Travers, who also ran the pavilion itself. Pavilion guests were entertained by orchestral and military band performances and attended dances at the building. The grounds were used for picnics and hot air balloon flights by Professor Baldwin, a "daring aeronaut" whose acts included ascents and descents in his balloon. Independence Day celebrations of 1892 drew 16,000 people to the pavilion.

The Beacon Hill Pavilion graced Duluth for less than a decade. On May 28, 1901, a fire broke out in the powerhouse and quickly spread to the pavilion. The east car sat just outside the power-house while the west waited at the bottom of the hill. The intense heat of the flame literally melted the rail system's cables, releasing the flaming east car, sending it racing toward Superior Street. Luckily the Superior Street station attendants anticipated the situation and did as much they could to get people, horses, and street cars out of the way. The car smashed through the railway's Superior Street depot, crossed Superior Street, and came to a halt in the railyards near the Union Depot. No one was injured. The car was destroyed.

The Beacon Hill Pavilion, heavily damaged in the fire, was never rebuilt. The incline was hastily reconfigured with just the west car operating with a counterweight for balance taking the place of the east car. An electric engine replaced the steam boilers, but the railway did not receive a proper overhaul and new cars until 1911. Meanwhile, four small bridges were built over the east track at street intersections so passengers could get on and off at different points along the railway and had better access o the west car, which only had one door. When the incline finally returned to two-car operation in 1912, with brand-new trollies, the bridges were removed and replaced by small stations containing stairs that led to the street.

The Seventh Avenue West Incline, the last of Duluth's streetcar system to be dismantled and sold for scrap, served Duluth until Labor Day 1939.

Duluth Beltline Railway

Much like the Seventh Avenue West Incline, the Duluth Beltline Railway was built to help a developing neighborhood. First operated in 1889, the "West Duluth Incline," as it came to be known, ran from a station at Sixty-First Avenue West and Grand Avenue (below left) up to the newly developing neighborhood of Bayview Heights at Vinland Street and Seventy-Seventh Avenue West (below right). A one-car operation, the incline rose six hundred feet during the twenty-four minutes it took for the car to travel from the bottom to the top (one report claimed it was the longest funicular in the world when built). Despite early success, the incline ceased operation in 1916 due to lack of ridership. Most of those who settled in Bayview Heights worked in nearby Proctor railyards and so did not require the incline's services often enough to keep it profitable. To this day children living in Bayview Heights attend school in Proctor. Powerlines now mark the railway's former location.

Minnesota Point Lighthouse and Keeper's Home

The Soo Locks on the St. Mary's River at Sault Ste. Marie opened in 1855, making it possible for larger vessels to enter Lake Superior from Lake Michigan and Lake Huron and opening ship traffic from New York to the Head of the Lakes. Seeing the natural Superior Entry between Minnesota and Wisconsin Points as the best way to enter safe harbor, the federal government commissioned a lighthouse and keeper's residence at the southern end of Minnesota Point to help mariners find the entry.

The Minnesota Point Lighthouse was placed atop mile marker zero, set there by George Stuntz and used for all surveys mapping Lake Superior. Stuntz, the first non-native to settle on Minnesota Point, operated a trading post near the lighthouse. The tower stood fifty feet tall when it was first built in 1858. German stonemason Adam Dopp used red Ohio brick to construct the tower and the keeper's home, later coating the tower with a limestone whitewash.

R. H. Barrett, its first keeper, lived with his wife Stella and their four children in the simple house shown at right. When thick fog rendered the light useless, Barrett used his own lungs to blow a warning through a logging camp dinner horn. Local residents called it "Barrett's Cow." Barrett was succeeded by Horace Saxton, J. B. Greenfield, Patrick McCann, G. M. Grover, and Robert Sanborn.

The lighthouse constantly needed repairs; it leaked, and plaster fell off in chunks. The ever-changing sand bar also created a problem: the location of the natural entry shifted; within a year of the tower's construction, it no longer stood close to the water (today it is about a half mile away). The lighthouse was all but rendered useless in 1871, when Duluth completed the first cut of its ship canal; within the next two years most shipping traffic at the Head of the Lakes came through the Duluth Ship Canal, bypassing the Superior Entry altogether. Because traffic through the Superior Entry became so rare, the federal government shut down the lighthouse on August 6, 1885.

In 1889 a wooden pierhead beacon was built on the north timber pier that was under construction in the Superior Entry and fitted with the lens from the Minnesota Point light, and the Keeper's House was refurbished to serve the new Superior Entry Pierhead Light. Unfortunately, that light was destroyed in the *Mataafa* Storm of 1905. The keeper's house was abandoned after a new facility was built in Wisconsin in 1895 and torn down soon after. The lighthouse still stands, albeit in ruins. It currently reaches less than thirty feet high and is protected by a broken fence.

Duluth's Nineteenth-Century Waterfront

Almost as soon as the dredging tug *Ishpeming* finished its initial cut of the Duluth Ship Canal in 1871, work began on wooden piers that would frame the canal along the dig site and expand its length on the lakeward side. The pier was in constant need of repair from the start. Some portions of the cribbing sunk to support the piers had gone in crooked and were never properly aligned, causing problems throughout the wooden piers' entire existence. Further, a storm in November 1872 severely damaged the piers, requiring $25,000 worth of work in 1873, the same year the financial panic caused by Jay Cooke's collapse struck the nation. The federal government helped pay for the repairs, and the next year unofficially took control of the canal from the financially drained city.

In 1875 a large section of the north pier had tilted and many feared it would fall into the canal. It took over three hundred cords of stone riprap to bolster the pier once it had been put back in place. As Duluth prospered from its railroads and ship canal, the canal's piers needed frequent attention. In 1879 ice damage forced engineers to replace 250 feet of cribbing; in 1880, 325 feet of the north pier were completely rebuilt, along with 190 feet of the south pier. In 1882 workers finally placed decking on the piers.

The natural flow of water through the canal also undermined the piers—literally. Originally dredged to a depth of fourteen feet at the time the workers laid the piers' cribbing, by 1882 portions of the canal near the piers had been naturally scoured to a depth of eighteen feet. With its feet washed out from under it, the north pier again listed toward the canal. Workers pulled the pier back and bolstered it with large iron rods fastened to the face of the cribbing. Each spring the same problems arose: damage from ice and log rafts had battered the piers. The canal's engineers thought spending money on further repairs was far from practical, so only absolutely necessary work was done on the piers throughout the 1880s.

The canal hadn't been sufficiently wide since 1881, when the locks at Sault Ste. Marie were enlarged. The iron ore industry arrived in the early 1890s by way of the newly opened Mesabi Iron Range, creating more shipping traffic through Duluth. The canal and harbor's shallow depth prevented bigger ships from carrying more profitable loads. So in 1893 Captain Alexander McDougall set about forming the Duluth-Superior Harbor Improvement Committee, which petitioned Congress for funds to improve both the Duluth and Superior Harbors. In 1896 Congress "appropriated $3 million...to make Duluth-Superior harbor the most modern in America." Between 1896 and 1902 the old wooden piers (left) were removed, the canal was widened to three hundred feet, and substantial concrete structures replaced the rickety, crooked wooden piers that once lined the canal.

The 1871–1896 wooden pier included

two lights and a fog signal. In 1872 contractors hired by the Corps of Engineers built a wooden pyramid tower on the outer end of the south pier and capped it with an octagonal cast-iron lantern housing a fifth order Fresnel Lens (a lens developed specifically for navigational lights by French physicist Augustin-Jean Fresnel). The light, which cast a red beacon visible 12.5 miles away, was lit for the first time on June 2, 1874. In 1877 the light was upgraded with a fixed red fourth order Fresnel lens. Lighthouse keepers reached the South Pier Light by walking over a trestle walkway, so the keeper could reach the light even when the pier was submerged by large waves (above).

Duluth had already gained a reputation for extremely thick fog. So in 1880 engineers installed an automated fog bell inside the tower of the South Pier Light, but it proved inadequate. Five years later it was replaced with tin steam-powered fog whistles housed in a small structure near the light. Duluth experienced one of the foggiest seasons on record in 1895, and the fog-signal whistle screamed for over 1,000 hours, gobbling forty-five tons of coal in the effort. The whistles not only sent a warning to mariners on the lake, they also bounced off Duluth's rocky hillside, creating a cacophony Duluthians couldn't bear. To remedy the problem, the signal's horns were relocated to the roof and covered with a parabolic reflector. The reflector not only directed sound away from the city, it nearly doubled the signal's reach.

While the South Pier Light helped mariners find the canal, another light was needed to provide a focal point by which to guide them through. In 1880 the Lighthouse Board recommended appropriating $2,000 for another light at the south pier's western (or inner) end. The light would stand taller than the South Pier Light; when used together, the two lights helped navigators establish range, as lighthouse historian Terry Pepper explains: "By maintaining a line in which these two lights were constantly oriented one above the other, a direct course could be followed to the opening between the two piers." Placed atop a wooden pyramid, the South Breakwater Light shined for the first time in September 1889. The beacon boasted a red fourth order Fresnel lens, but instead of a continuous beam, it flashed a signal every six seconds. It wasn't foolproof: just sixteen days after the light commenced flashing, the steamer *India* collided with the pier at the base of the light itself, damaging the foundation.

Building the new concrete piers at the turn of the twentieth century meant tearing down the shaky old wooden piers—and everything on top of them. The 1901 South Pier Light was outfitted with steam-powered twin fog whistles. In 1916 these were replaced by locomotive whistles, which in turn were replaced in 1923 by electrically powered twin Type F diaphone horns whose deep "Bee-Oh" tone could be heard for twenty miles. Almost immediately Duluthians complained. The horn was much too loud and rattled windows; in the hillside neighborhood, the horn disrupted conversation and woke the sleeping. In 1968 the Coast Guard retired the horn, replacing it with a much quieter single-tone horn. While some Duluthians rejoiced, others dearly missed the old horn's deep bellow and felt the city had lost part of its very identity. They called the new signal a "peanut whistle."

Other elements of Duluth's old waterfront have been lost, including the wooden breakfront that protected ships docked at Elevator A at the foot of Third Avenue East and Citizen's Dock, which was owned by the city and reached into the lake from Morse Street. Both structures were gone by 1900.

The Interstate Bridge

Until the Interstate Bridge was stretched between Duluth and Superior in 1897, the only way to get to and from the cities was by ferry boat. While Congress had passed a bill allowing a toll bridge between Duluth and Superior in 1890, disagreements between the two cities delayed construction for years.

The bridge, designed by A. P. Boller and built by the Duluth-Superior Bridge Company, spanned 1,094 feet between Duluth's Rice's Point and Superior's Connor's Point. The swing-arm bridge was built in three spans; the 486-foot center span swiveled to allow shipping traffic to pass. The Interstate Bridge "opened" on April 23, 1897, with Mayor C. S. Starkweather of Superior calling the event the "marriage of Helen and Troy." Like the Trojan horse itself, the opening was a deception—in this case, to give the appearance of compliance to the bridge's charter. Work hadn't actually been completed on the Superior side, much to the chagrin of a farmer from Tower, Minnesota, who tried to cross in an ox-drawn wagon. When it was first placed in operation the bridge welcomed pedestrians and horse-drawn vehicles and carried two railroad tracks and a streetcar line. Everyone paid a toll: five cents for pedestrians and bicycles, fifteen cents for wagons, and a dime for each head of cattle.

The first hours of August 11, 1906 were rough on the bridge, as well as the steamer *Troy* and her captain, Robert Murray. Around one AM the *Troy*—all 398 feet and 3,665-tons of her—slammed into the still-opening swing span, knocking a two-hundred-foot piece of steel into the bay and buckling the northern span, which collapsed, blocking all traffic on the bay and trapping thirty-three ships inside the upper harbor. Clearing the channel took almost a week, costing each trapped vessel's operators about $1,000 a day. Engineers spent nearly two years restoring the bridge while a tug and barges transported pedestrians and wagons across the harbor. Over the years the bridge was refitted for automobile traffic; the streetcar line was removed in 1938 and by 1949 only one railway track was in use. The Blatnik Bridge was built in 1961 to replace the Interstate Bridge so longer ore carriers could navigate in the harbor. The Interstate Bridge was dismantled in 1971; its northern span, off Rice's Point, was retained as a fishing dock.

St. Louis Bay once had three swing arm bridges: the Interstate Bridge, the 1887 Grassy Point Railroad Bridge (which still operates), and the Northern Pacific Railway's 1885 St. Louis Bay Bridge (shown in the photo above to the left of the Interstate Bridge), which was dismantled in 1986.

The Arrowhead Bridge

As the automobile became more popular, the Interstate Bridge became more congested—and its location was hardly convenient for those in Duluth's and Superior's western environs. Plans for the Arrowhead Bridge took shape in 1925 when the War Department issued a permit for a bridge over a narrow stretch of the St Louis River. Superior's Arrowhead Bridge Company began construction in 1926 and finished a year later. The Arrowhead, technically a rolling lift bridge, was built entirely of wood except for its steel 300-foot center lift span. It stretched eight hundred feet from Lesure Street on Grassy Point in West Duluth to Superior's Belknap Street, extending U.S. Highway 2 across the state line. The center span was actually two spans that met in the middle; each lifted on a pivot to allow marine traffic to pass; it took ninety seconds for the spans to open or close.

The Arrowhead Bridge's opening on July 16, 1927, was a gala event. Celebrations took place on both sides of the St. Louis River, in West Duluth at Memorial Park and along Superior's Tower Avenue. Each celebra-

tion led a parade onto the bridge, stopping at either side of the new bridge's lift span. While the crowd waited, the spans lifted and the replica Viking ship *Leif Erikson*, which had just arrived in Duluth, was escorted between the spans by the fire tug *McGonagle*, which sprayed huge spouts of water along the way. After the watercraft cleared and as the spans lowered, Duluth mayor Sam Snively and his Superior counterpart, Fred Baxter, met in the middle and clasped hands just as the spans closed. Fireworks were launched, the United States Naval Reserve Band and the Superior American Legion's drum-and-bugle corps played, and ships and boats and industrial plants all sounded their whistles. The Duluth marchers then paraded in Superior as the Superior paraders passed through West Duluth. A time capsule containing souvenirs of the event was encased in one of the bridge's piers.

Superior's Walter Buch claimed to be the first person to cross the bridge in a car—and thereby first to pay its toll. In 1963 the bridge became jointly owned by Minnesota and Wisconsin and the toll was dropped. The bridge itself came to an end in 1985 after being rendered obsolete with the construction of the Richard I. Bong Memorial Bridge. It cost $700,000 to demolish the bridge, $200,000 more than the original construction cost.

Duluth's Ore Docks

Construction of Duluth's first ore dock began in 1884 in anticipation of iron ore from Charlemagne Tower's mines on the newly opened Vermillion Iron Range. Unfortunately for Duluth, work was forced to stop after Tower announced he would ship his ore through Agate Bay, today's Two Harbors. The Duluth dock was finally completed in 1893, after Duluth's Merritt brothers opened mining on the Mesabi Iron Range. The wooden dock, built by the Duluth, Missabe & Northern Railway, stretched into the bay at Thirty-Third Avenue West, had a capacity of 57,600 tons, and received its first load of ore on July 22, 1893. A second wooden dock went up west of the first in 1896, a third in 1900, and a fourth in 1906, the year after the first dock closed due to its insufficient size. At 2,304 feet in length and a capacity of 76,800 tons, Dock #4 (below) was the largest wooden ore dock ever built. Duluth's fifth ore dock—made of steel—went up in 1914. The Zenith City's final ore dock was built in 1918. The largest ore

dock in the world, Dock #6 was made of steel and had a capacity of 153,600 tons. Duluth's row of storage and loading structures stretched from Thirty-Third to Thirty-Fifth Avenues West.

The first two docks were simple affairs, and ore was simply dumped from train cars into vessels for shipment to eastern steel plants. The later docks were specifically designed to take ore from train cars, store it if need be, and load it into ore boats. At the dock, the carloads of ore were dumped into pockets along the dock; a chute carried the ore from the pockets into the cargo holds of ore boats (next page, bottom). When the ore-laden boats reached steel-making centers along the Lake Erie rust belt, Hulett ore off-loaders would pull ore from the ships' holds ten tons at a time. A Hulett unloader could empty ore boats like the *Edmund Fitzgerald*, which held 25,000 tons of ore, in five to ten hours; before Huletts came along in 1900, the process would take days. When the last Great Lakes ore boat was converted to a self-

unloader in 1992, the Huletts became obsolete.

By 1938 ore demand had lessened and the DM&N was down to two docks, #5 and #6, and the railroad merged with the Duluth & Iron Range Railway to become the Duluth, Missabe & Iron Range Railway in 1938. That same year U.S. Steel merged the DM&N with the Duluth & Iron Range Railway to form the Duluth, Missabe & Iron Range Railway. U.S. Steel had acquired the DM&N in 1901 from John D. Rockefeller, who had taken control of it when the

Merritt Brothers' finances went sour; that same year the firm purchased the D&IR from Illinois Steel, which had acquired the railroad from Tower's Minnesota Iron Company in 1887.

Ore demand increased dramatically during World War II, and in 1944 the DM&IR docks in Duluth and Two Harbors broke loading records three times. The docks set a forty-eight-hour loading record by filling sixty ships with 649,275 tons of ore between Sunday, May 28, and Tuesday, May 30. And they didn't stop. The following day they broke the seventy-two hour record when the loading total reached 859,959 tons. And from that Wednesday morning at 7 A.M. until the same time Thursday morning, crews loaded 406,484 tons, setting the single-day record in the process. (The previous twenty-four hour record was set in 1942 with 337,180 tons.)

The docks were built or dismantled according to demand. The two smallest docks went first: Dormant since 1905, Dock #1 came down in 1913; Dock #2 closed two years later. Despite a 1905 expansion, Dock #3 lasted only until 1919. Dock #4 served until 1927. Docks #5 and #6, both built in 1918 due to increased demand in iron ore to build ships for World War I, remain today, although Dock #5 is no longer in use. The docks are now owned by Canadian National Railway.

Duluth's Coal Docks

Duluth received its first cargo of coal in June 1871, much to the confusion of local residents. Why, they asked themselves, would anyone in Duluth need coal for fuel—after all, you could cut all the firewood you want for free, or pay someone just a few dollars for an entire winter's supply.

Officials from the Delaware and Hudson Canal Company didn't see it that way when they sent that first shipment of coal from its deposits in Pennsylvania. They were thinking about the arrival of Jay Cooke's Lake Superior & Mississippi Railroad and the sprouting of commercial buildings in Duluth and indeed the entire region: coal would drive the locomotives and heat those buildings. Soon Duluth was supplying coal, most of it a high-sulfur grade mined in Pennsylvania and Ohio, to Minneapolis, St. Paul, and cities in at least seven other states.

Jack Lewis received the first contract for unloading coal in the Zenith City. Lewis had no modern machinery, and his crew shoveled coal from the ships' holds into baskets, which were hoisted to a tramway by horse, where their load was transferred to wheelbarrows. Later giant cranes (pictured) were used to unload the coal boats. Eventually steam replaced horsepower, and bigger baskets were employed. Between 8,000 and 20,000 tons were shipped to Duluth that first year.

In 1875 Northwestern Fuel built Duluth's first dedicated coal dock; it remained Duluth's only coal company until 1881, bringing in 60,000 tons of coal for use in the Twin Ports in 1880. Eventually a system of giant coal docks and their support machinery lined the waterfront from Rice's Point to Seventh Avenue West; another cluster of docks later rose around Grassy Point between Fiftieth and Fifty-Sixth Avenues West. Beginning in 1881 docks were built for use by the Lake Superior Coal and Iron Company, New Pittsburgh, Clarkston Coal (pictured), Ohio Central Coal, St. Paul & Pacific Coal and Iron, Pioneer Coal, Little and Company, and Lehigh Coal. In 1886 over 735,000 tons were brought to the Twin Ports for use in homes and businesses in Duluth and Superior—and that doesn't include coal loaded onto rail for other destinations.

As the century turned, Duluth received more than 2.5 million tons of coal; ten years later, 8.3 million tons. By 1921 Duluth alone was home to twenty-two coal docks with the capacity of 11,305,000 tons of coal. Dozens of coal docks operated out of Superior as well. Coal shipments hit their peak just two years later, when 12.6 million tons passed through the Duluth-Superior Harbor. At this time the coal industry provided 3,600 full-time jobs, 5,000 during peak periods.

As people and businesses turned to cleaner-burning oil and gas to heat their homes and offices, the demand for coal dropped dramatically. Half as much coal passed through the Twin Ports in 1936 than did in 1923; by 1972 tonnage had dropped below 100,000. Then the market reversed. Montana and Wyoming began mining cleaner-burning low-sulfur coal in the 1970s. Instead of loading it from ships onto trains bound elsewhere, Duluth's coal now arrived on trains from the west and was loaded onto ships bound for the east—and beyond. The first load shipped out of Duluth in 1973, aboard the British ship *Gloxinia*, bound for Scotland. Duluth has no more coal docks, and Superior's Midwest Energy Resources is the only functioning coal dock in the Twin Ports.

Passenger Steamships

Literally thousands of ships, boats, and other vessels have called on the Port of Duluth since before there even was a Port of Duluth. From native and voyageur canoes to sail-powered freighters, side-wheel steamers, small fishing vessels, whalebacks, and the 1,000-foot-long ore boats that navigate the Great Lakes today, Duluth has hosted just about every kind of watercraft made. Salt water vessels began calling on Duluth in 1959, after the opening of the St. Lawrence Seaway. Cataloging just the ore carriers would be a tall order. Perhaps the most romanticized vessels ever to ply the Great Lakes were the passenger steamers popular during the first half of the twentieth century, which brought people and goods to and from Duluth and Buffalo, New York, and ports of call in between.

The Canadian Steamship Lines sister ships **Noronic, Huronic,** and **Hamonic**, originally built for the Northern Navigation Company, steamed along the course shown in the company's promotional poster, above right. When Northern Navigation and Richelieu & Ontario Line merged to form the Canadian Steamship Lines, the sisters became the new company's Northern Navigation Division.

Named for Lake Huron and the oldest of the sisters, the *Huronic's* maiden voyage took place in May 1902. On November 21 of that same year she passed the steamer *Bannock-burn*—now known as the "Flying Dutchman of the Lakes"—which sank that night. During the Great Lakes Storm of 1913, also called the "White Hurricane" for its hurricane-force winds, which blew from November 7–10, she ran aground on Whitefish Point, Michigan. In 1928 she beached on Lucille Island, southeast of Lake Superior's Pigeon Point. Late in the 1930s her cabins were removed from the upper deck, and passenger service ended. She was scrapped in Hamilton, Ontario in 1950.

The *Hamonic* (pictured), named for Northern Navigation president H. C. Hammond, first launched in 1908. Considered the most beautiful passenger and freight ship to ever run the Great Lakes, her dining room had a vaulted ceiling and featured a mural of natives and French explorers meeting at the shores of a lake. She came to a fiery end in the early morning hours of July 17, 1945, at Point Edward, Ontario, in a blaze originating at a warehouse along the pier. All four hundred aboard the *Hamonic* lived to tell tales of daring rescue, including the efforts of a coal crane operator who lifted fifty passengers from the bow of the burning ship to the shore. Others jumped into the water—including the last man off the ship, Chief Engineer James Nielson—and were plucked from the water by the *Hamonic's* captain, William Taylor, who had commandeered a small boat. A total loss, the *Hamonic* was scrapped in Hamilton, Ontario.

The last and largest of the Canadian Steamship sisters, the *Noronic* hit the water in 1913. Her name was derived by combining "No" for Northern Navigation and "ron" for Richelieu & Ontario, the two companies who

Passenger Steamships, continued...

had merged to form the Canadian Steamship Lines. Measuring 362 feet long and weighing 6,095 gross tons, she had five decks that held six hundred passengers and two hundred crew. Like her sister the *Hamonic* before her, when first launched the *Noronic* earned the label of the Great Lakes' most beautiful passenger ship and was nicknamed "The Queen of the Lakes."

From 1914 to 1949 the *Noronic* ran from Detroit and Windsor, Ontario, to the "Lakehead"—the Twin Ports of Duluth and Superior. Like the Hamonic before her, the *Noronic's* fate would be sealed by an early-morning fire. While the ship was docked in Toronto in September 1949 during a post-season cruise, a passenger awoke at 2:30 A.M. and smelled smoke. A locked linen closet was burning; when it was unlocked, it exploded. Half of the *Noronic's* decks were on fire by the time anyone could sound an alarm. By 4:41, when firefighters first arrived, the entire ship was ablaze. Many passengers were trapped; those who weren't jumped into the bay. Newspapers reported that the screams of the dying were heard over the inferno's roar and the wail of whistles and sirens. The ship sunk; 139 people died, some still in their beds. The *Noronic's* salvaged hull was later sold for scrap.

The Anchor Line Triplets **Octorara**, **Juniata**, and **Tionesta** were sister ships built in Cleveland, Ohio, by the American Shipbuilding Company for the Anchor Line, a subsidiary of the Pennsylvania Railroad. The ships made regular runs between Duluth and their home port of Buffalo, New York, where the Pennsylvania Railroad terminated. Their names come from Pennsylvania rivers. In 1916 all three were purchased by the Great Lakes Transit Corporation of Buffalo.

The first of the Anchor Line triplets, the *Tionesta* first steamed toward Duluth in 1903. Like her sisters, she was a 346-foot-long propeller-driven steamship that carried 350 passengers and 3,500 tons of cargo at a top speed of eighteen knots. Due to a drop in passengers during the great Depression, she was taken out of service in 1936 and scrapped at Hamilton, Ontario, in 1940. In 1910 the *Octorara* (pictured) launched as the last of the Anchor Line triplets. Like the *Tionesta* she was forced to lay up in 1936, but found temporary reprieve from the scrapyard when she was called to duty by the U. S. Army in 1942 and served as a troop transport in the Hawaiian Islands. She was scrapped in San Francisco in 1952. The *Octorara's* brass bell hangs at the Dossin Great Lakes Museum at Belle Isle, Detroit, where it is rung each year during the annual blessing of the fleet in memory of ships and sailors lost to the Great Lakes.

The best known of the Anchor Triplets is still afloat. The *Juniata*, launched in 1904, also served the Great Lakes before being retired in 1936. Before the army could take her the *Juniata* was restored and renamed the *Milwaukee Clipper*. From 1941–1970, the *Milwaukeee Clipper* ran between Milwaukee, Wisconsin, and Muskegon, Michigan. In 1977 she was purchased and converted to a museum ship named simply *Clipper*, but the business went sour and a year later she steamed to Chicago and docked at the Navy Pier as a "boutique-flotel." In 1990, the ship moved to Hammond, Indiana, and was renovated as a tourist attraction with retail and office space.

Steamers **North American** and **South American** (above) were built in Ecorse, Michigan, in 1913 and 1914 for the Chicago, Duluth & Georgian Bay Transit Company of Detroit. The *North American* had a history of running aground as she sailed the Great Lakes. On tow for Piney Point, Maryland, for use as a training vessel, the ship suddenly sank about twenty-nine miles northeast of Nantucket Island on September 13, 1967, in two hundred feet of water. The *South American* sailed the Great Lakes until 1967, when ownership transferred to the Seafarers' International Union of Piney Point, Maryland. It then steamed to Newport News, Virginia, where its engines were removed and it was converted into a dormitory for the Lundberg School of Seamanship. After many failed attempts to return the *South American* to the Great Lakes as a museum or restaurant, she was scrapped in 1992.

St. Louis River Excursion Boats

In the late 1880s steamships that made the daily run delivering mail and goods (and commuters) to Fond du Lac began to offer "pic-nic cruises" and the excursion trade was born. Taking an excursion boat from the Duluth harbor to Fond du Lac and back became widely popular after the century turned, with the steam vessels *Plow Boy, Chicora, Columbia,* and *News Boy* steaming up and down the St. Louis River. Fond du Lac offered picnic sites, fine hotel dining, and even some entertainment, including shows featuring native ceremonies billed as the "Chippewa Indian Medicine Dance." In 1919, Duluth's Clow & Nicholson Transportation Company purchased the sidewheeler *A. Wehle Jr.* and brought her to Duluth for the Fond du Lac route (the company also owned the Fond du Lac Inn, a popular restaurant). Company owner David Clow, president of the local rotary club, then renamed her *Rotarian.* The *Rotarian,* which docked at Fifth Avenue West on the Duluth waterfront, ran to Fond du Lac twice a day, charging sixty cents for the round trip. She also ran a special "Around the Horn" route out the ship canal and into Lake Superior, south along Minnesota Point to the Superior Entry, through the Entry, and north along Minnesota Point back to its berth; the ride cost thirty-five cents. Despite a capacity of six hundred passengers, the *Rotarian* proved so popular that Clow & Nicholson purchased the paddlewheeler *Mauntauk* (below) in 1924 to keep up with demand. The *Rotarian* was sold in 1927, leaving the *Mauntauk* as the last of the Fond du Lac steamers. By 1930 the *Rotarian* was tied up in Chicago and used as a floating restaurant and dance hall; she sank at her moorings that year. The *Mauntauk* ran the Duluth-to-Fond du Lac route for nearly fifteen years before being sold, stripped of her cabins, and converted to a barge. There are no records for her past 1947.

Tugboats: Workhorses of the Harbor

While giant ore boats and graceful steamships have drawn tourists to the Duluth Ship Canal for over a century, the harbor they call on couldn't function without the work of the small, ungraceful tugboats that handle the bulk of the waterfront's dirty work. Countless tugs have served the Duluth-Superior Harbor over the years, guiding much larger vessels to dock and pulling them free when they beached. A severely cold winter can easily freeze over the bay, sometimes even the lake. Before the Coast Guard began supplying the harbor with ice-breaking vessels, it was up to privately-owned tugs such as the **Record** and **James R. Sinclair** to keep shipping lanes open. The *Record* came to Duluth in 1887 as part of the Inman Tug Line, later Union Towing & Wrecking Company. The *Record* had a record of sinking. She first sank after colliding with tug *Joe D. Dudley* in 1895, and she crossed the *Robert Fulton's* bow during a heavy storm and went down in 1898, taking three lives with her. She was raised only to be rolled and sunk again in 1899 after the whaleback *James B. Nielson* increased speed while the *Record* was towing her; another life was lost. Even at rest she was at risk: in 1902 while docked in Superior, she was struck by the *Bradford* and sank, costing another life. She was moved to Michigan in 1927 and scrapped in 1975. Duluth's Union Towing & Wrecking Company acquired the *James R. Sinclair* in 1907. She served the Twin Ports until 1938.

Since the steam dipper dredging tug **Ishpeming** first dug the Duluth Ship Canal in 1871, dredging tugs have served to keep the St. Louis Bay and canal navigable by removing silt deposited by the St. Louis River. They have also played instrumental

roles helping free grounded ships. In 1985, when the *Socrates* ran aground off Minnesota Point during a November storm, the work of dredgers and seven tugboats directed by Dorocher Dock and Dredge Company refloated the vessel. The **William Saphanco** performed dredging duties in the 1880s. The most famous of the dredgers was the 116-foot long **Col. D. D. Gaillard**, built in 1916 by the U.S. Army Corps of Engineers and responsible for most of the work widening the St. Lawrence Seaway. The *Gaillard* was named for Lieutenant Colonel D. D. Gaillard, who oversaw the Duluth Ship Canal Pier reconstruction of 1896–1902 and helped build the Panama Canal. Two years after he died in 1913, President Woodrow Wilson ordered the Panama Canal's Culebra Cut renamed Gaillard Cut in the Lieutenant Colonel's honor.

Built in 1908 for the Duluth, Missabe & Iron Range Railroad Company, the **McGonagle** (named for DM&IR president William McGonagle) was a 110-foot fire tug. She served the Twin Ports until 1935, not only putting out fires but helping in celebrations, such as the arrival of the *Leif Erikson* replica Viking boat and the opening of the Arrowhead bridge, both in 1927.

Many Duluthians still remember the **Essayons** (left), built in 1908 for the Army Corps of Engineers and famously the first vessel to pass under Duluth's Aerial Lift Bridge in 1930. She was sold to Duluth's Zenith Dredge Company in 1950. After the vessel was retired, its engine was removed and put on display at the Lake Superior Marine Museum. Now privately owned, the *Essayons* was gutted in preparation to be converted to a floating bed and breakfast. It sank at its dock site in the spring of 2009, the victim of vandalism, and currently rests at the bottom of the bay.

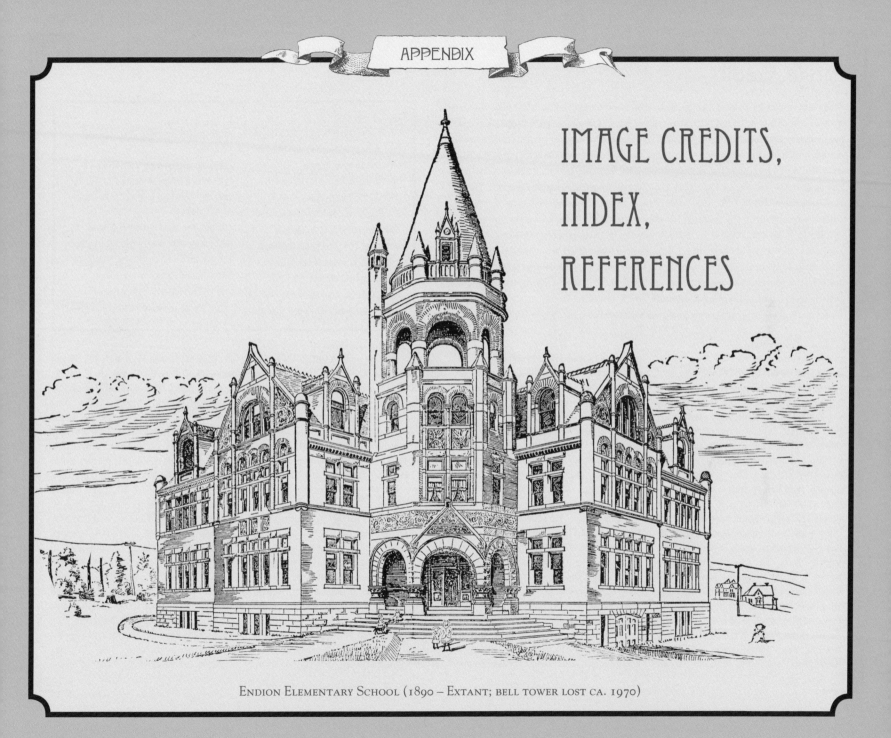

APPENDIX

IMAGE CREDITS,
INDEX,
REFERENCES

ENDION ELEMENTARY SCHOOL (1890 – EXTANT; BELL TOWER LOST CA. 1970)

Image Credits

Nearly all the photos and sketches that appear herein have been cropped, and many have been touched up in some way, mostly to clean up dust, tears, water damage, etc., in order to make their subjects more visible. We have artificially sepia-toned the portraits, added color to select advertising images, and printed the sketches in maroon. Most of this book's images were scanned from public domain books at the Duluth Public Library, many from the following works (full citations appear in the Reference section): *Duluth Illustrated in Photo Etching from New and Original Plates* (date unk.); *Duluth Illustrated: Historical, Descriptive, Picturesque* (1887); *Illustrated Duluth, 1901* (1901); *Duluth and Environs: A Historical, Biographical, Commercial and Statistical Record* (1895); *O.G. Traphagen Successor to Traphagen & Fitzpatrick, Architects* (date unk.); and *The Booster Book: West Duluth in 1916* (1916). Most of the portraits came from *Men of Minnesota: a Collection of the Portraits of Men Prominent in Business and Professional Life in Minnesota* (1902). Many of the building sketches came from Illustrated Annual Edition of the *Duluth Daily News* (1888, 1889, 1891). The caricature portraits came from *Duluthians in Cartoon: Being a Most Successful Attempt at Portraying Representative Business Men of Duluth, Minnesota, in their Respective Professions and Trades* (date unk.). Digital images obtained by scanning will be given to the Duluth Public Library for its archives.

Page ii: The Duluth National Bank, DPL. Page iii: Duluth Ship Canal's Original Wooden Pier, DPL. Page iv: Scene at the Northern Pacific Docks, DPL. Page v: Manhattan Building, DPL. Page vi: Looking east from the Duluth hillside, DPL. Page vii: Duluth Outer Waterfont, 1871, TD. Page viii: *Picturesque Duluth* cover, DPL. Page 1: Minnesota Point Lighthouse and Keeper's Cottage, TD. Page 2: Duluth 1850s Townships Map, TD. Page 3: Duluth Township 1865 Map, TD. Page 4: Jay Cooke, DPL. Page 5: "No Man's Land," DPL. Page 7: East Hillside 1887, DPL. Page 9: Canal Work 1890s, LSMC. Page 10: Downtown Duluth 1905, LoC. Page 14: Alexander House , DPL. Page 15: Jefferson House, DPL. Page 16: Roger Munger portrait, TD; Munger House, DPL. Page 17: William Sargent portrait, DPL; Sargent House, DPL. Page 18: Charles Johnson portrait, NEMHC; Johnson House, NEMHC; canal bridge sketch, DPL. Page 19: J. D. Ensign portrait, DPL; Ensign House, DPL. Page 20: Melvin Forbes portrait, DPL; Forbes House photo, sketch, DPL. Page 21: J. D. Ray

portrait, DPL; James D. & Caroline Ray House, DPL; Robert C. & Helen Ray House, DPL. Page 22: Markell House, DPL. Page 23: William Sherwood portrait, DPL; Sherwood House, DPL; Loeb House, DPL. Page 24: Edward Bradley sketch, DPL; Bradley house, DPL; McLean House, DPL. Page 25: Spalding House, DPL; Harrison House, DPL. Page 26: Guilford Hartley portrait, DPL; Hartley House sketch, photograph, DPL. Page 27: Prescott House, NEMHC. Page 28: Alonzo Whiteman portrait, DPL; Whiteman House, DPL. Page 29: Jed Washburn portrait, TD; Washburn House, DPL. Page 30: Hoopes House, gazebo, DPL. Page 31: Hamilton Peyton sketch, DPL; Peyton House, DPL. Page 32: Marshall H. Alworth Portrait, DPL; Alworth House, porch, DPL. Page 33: John Sebenius portrait, DPL; Sebenius House, DPL. Page 34: Roy Halvorson portrait, DPL; Halvorson House, MCN. Page 35: Ashtabula Flats, DPL; Oliver Traphagen Portrait, MCN, Traphagen & Fitzpatrick business card, DPL. Page 36: Gray Terrace, DPL; Alva Bradley portrait, DPL; Bradley Townhouses, DPL.

Page 37: Park Terrace, NEMHC; Philadelphia Terrace, DPL. Page 38: Northern Pacific Immigrant House, DPL (both images). Page 39: Soumalainen Boarding House, DPL; St. Croix Avenue scene, DPL. Page 40: The Glenn, DPL (both images). Page 41: Merritt Hotel, DPL. Page 42: Twenty-Seventh Avenue West Birdge, DY; Slabtown houses, DY. Page 43: Kayo Hotel, Vi-Kar diner, Garfield Avenue scene, GM. Page 44: Sargent cabin, DPL; trolley postcard, TD. Page 45: Franklin Elementary sketch, DPL. Page 46: U.S. Thrift Stamp Sub Treasury, NEMHC. Page 47: Post Office, DPL; County Jail, DPL. Page 48: U.S. Federal Building, DPL. Page 49: West Duluth Public Library, DPL. Page 50: John Darling portrait: DPL, Darling Observatory, DPL; Darling at telescope, DPL. Page 51: Oneota Township School, DPL; Oneota Elementary photo, sketch, DPL. Page 52: Adams Elementary, DPL. Page 53: Duluth High School/ Washington School, DPL. Page 54: Franklin Elementary, DPL; Jackson Elementary, DPL. Page 55: Longfellow Elementary, DPL; ELy Elementary,

DPL. Page 56: Lincoln Elementary, DPL; Bryant Elementary, TD. Page 57: Monroe Elementary, JL; Ensign Elementary, TD. Page 58: 1892 Lester Park Elementary, NEMHC; 1918 Lester Park ELementary, DPL. Page 59: Whittier Elementary, DPL; Glen Avon Elementary, DPL. Page 60: Hardy Hall, DPL. Page 61: Duluth Normal School, DPL; WIlliam Hunt, DPL. Page 62: Charles Salter portrait, DPL; 1888 Bethel, DPL. Page 63: 1892 Bethany Children's Home, TD; 1922 Bethany Children's Home, NEMHC. Page 64: First St. Luke's Hospital, DPL; 1883 St. Luke's Hospital, DPL. Page 65: 1888 St. Mary's Hospital photo, sketch, DPL. Page 66: Morgan Park Hospital, TD; Morgan Park Goodfellowhip Club, DPL. Page 67: St. Paul's Episcopal, DPL; First Presbyterian, DPL. Page 68: Pilgrim Congregation, DPL; Merritt Memorial Methodist, DPL. Page 69: 1871 First Methodist, DPL; 1893 First Methodist front, NEMHC; 1893 First Methodist back, TD. Page 70: First Evangelical Lutheran, DPL; Bethesda Norwegian Lutheran, NEMHC. Page 71: Sacred

Heart Roman Catholic, DPL; St. Stephen's Lutheran, DPL. Page 72: 1885 St. Jeane-Baptiste Catholic, JRM; 1904 St. Jeane-Baptiste Catholic, DPL. Page 73: St.Peter's Catholic CHurch, JRM; St. Clement's Catholic, TD. Page 74: Tifereth Isreal, DPL. Page 75: Spalding Hotel, DPL. Page 76: 1885 Board of Trade, DPL. Page 77: Clarkhouse Hotel, DPL. Page 78: Bayview House, TD; Merchant's Hotel sketch, photo, DPL. Page 79: 1882 St. Louis Hotel, DPL; 1894 St. Louis Hotel, DPL. Page 80: William Spalding portrait, DPL, Spalding Hotel, DPL; Ladies Writing Room, TD. Page 81: Spalding Hotel Lobby, Ladies Parlor, Sun Room, and Palm Room, TD. Page 82: Cody Hotel, NEMHC; Hotel Grand, DPL. Page 83: Lester Park Hotel sketch, photo, DPL. Page 84: Holland House exterior, DPL; Holland House lobby, lounge, and dining room, TD. Page 85: Hotel McKay exterior, TD; McKay Hotel interior, TD; Lenox Hotel, TD. Page 86: View of demolition from Union Depot, DF; Lyceum demolition, DF; Classy Lumberjack, GM. Page 87: Lincoln Hotel, TD; interior, TD. Page 88: Clarendon Hotel, DPL; 1908 Garfield News, TD. Page 89: Metropole Hotel, DPL; Joe Huie, WYH. Page 90: 1930 Flame, MP; 1946 Flame, DPL. Page 91: Jack's Café, TD; Miller's Cafeteria, TD, King Leo's, GM. Page 92: Grand Opera House, DPL; Grand Opera House stage, DPL. Page 93: Grand Opera House sketch, DPL. Page 94: Temple Opera House exterior, DPL, Temple Opera House entry, DPL. Page 95: Temple Opera House Scottish Rite, stage scene left, and strongman act, DPL. Page 96: Lyceum sketch, photo, DPL. Page 97: Lyceum stage photos, DPL. Page 98: Orpheum Theatre exterior, stage, JH. Page 99: Orpheum Theatre balcony, 1929 entrance, JH. Page100: Grand, DPL; Lyric, DPL; New Lyric, JH. Page 101: New Lyric entry, balcony, and stage, JH. Page 102: Metropolitan Opera, DPL; Empress, DPL. Page 103: Garrick, TD; Sunbeam, DPL; Zelda, DPL. Page 104: Branch's Hall, DPL; Endion Station, DPL. Page 105: Fargusson Blocks, DPL; H. F. Williamson

Block, DPL. Page 106: Costello Block, DPL; Miles Block, DPL; Alexander Miles portrait, DPL. Page 107: 1885 Board of Trade, DPL; George Wirth Portrait, DPL. Page 108: American Exchange Bank sketch, lobby, and offices, DPL. Page 109: Duluth National Bank, DPL; Luther Mendenhall Sketch, DPL. Page 110: Michael Pastoret sketch, DPL, Pastoret-Stenson Block, DPL; Benz Block, TD. Page 111: Manhattan Building, DPL; Manufacturer's Bank, DPL. Page 112: Palladio Building, DPL; Palladio Building entry, NEMHC. Page 113: C. H. Oppel Block, NEMHC; Phoenix Block, DPL. Page 114: Howe Building, DPL; Glass Block, DPL. Page 115: Bradley Building, DPL; Edwin S. Radcliffe sketch, DPL. Page 116: French & Bassett, DPL; Columbus Block, DPL. Page 117: Burrows Block, DPL; Metropolitan Block, DPL. Page 118: Odd Fellow's Hall, DPL; Modern Woodmen's Hall, TD. Page 119: Iron Bay Works, DPL. Page 120: Aston Fur Post front, back, TD. Page 121: Aston Fur Post ruins, DPL, Fur post reconstruction, TK. Page 122: A. Booth & Sons, DPL; Sam Johnson & Sons, DPL. Page 123: Fishing village, TD; Steamer *America*, TD. Page 124: Scott-Graff, DPL. Page 125: Mitchell & McClure, DPL. Page 126: Merrill & Ring, DPL; Huntress & Brown, DPL. Page 127: Lumberjacks, TD; Fitger's bottle, SV. Page 128: Fitger's complex postcard, TD; Fitger's bottle, TD. Page 129: Royal 58 can, TD; Duluth Brewing & Malting, D.PL. Page 130: Duluth Brewing & Malting sketch, DPL; Regal Supreme can, TD. Page 131: People's Brewing, DPL. Page 132: Fond du Lac Quarry, DPL. Page 133: Chambers House ruins, DPL. Page 134: Elevator A, MHS. Page 135: Elevator D, DPL; Consolidated Elevator row, DPL. Page 136: Imperial Mill Sketch, DPL; Duluth Imperial Flour advertisement, TD. Page 137: Universal Mill, DPL. Page 138: Imperial Mill exterior, boiler room, and grinding floor, DPL. Page 139: Imperial Mill bolting machinery, spouting floor, packing floor, and warehouse, DPL. Page 140: Duluth Iron & Steel

Works, DPL; Zenith Furnace, DPL. Page 141: National Iron Works, DPL; National Iron Works, DPL. Page 142: Clyde Iron sketch and photograph, DPL. Page 143: Atlas Iron & Brass, DPL; Duluth Brass Works, DPL. Page 144: United States Steel, DPL. Page 145: Universal Portland Cement, TD. Page 146: All Minnesota Steel Company images, DPL. Page 147: All Minnesota Steel Company images, DPL. Page 148: Whaleback steamer, TD; McDougall-Duluth, DPL. Page 149: McDougall-Duluth, DPL. Page 150: Stone-Ordeansketch, DPL; Stone-Ordean-Wells, DPL. Page 151: O'Brien & Knowlten, DPL; Duluth Dry Goods, DPL. Page 152: Marshall-Wells, DPL; Leithead Drug, DPL. Page 153: Rust-Parker-Martin, TD; McDougal Terminal, DPL. Page 154: Wallinder Sash & Door, DPL, Union Match, DPL. Page 155: F. A. Patrick offices, DPL; Mackinaw Ad, DPL. Page 156: Minnesota Car Company, DPL; American Carbolite, DPL. Page 157: Northern Shoe building, DPL; Northern Shoe advertisement; DPL; horse calk sketch, DPL; Diamond Horseshoe sketch, DPL. Page 158: Klearflax, DPL; Bridgeman-Russel, DPL. Page 159: Coolerator Plant #1, NEMHC; Coolerator Plant #2, DPL. Page 160: Duluth Candy Co. Logo, TD; Zenith Dredge, DPL. Page 161: Duluth Boat Club, DPL. Page 162: Duluth Aerial Transfer Bridge, LSMC; Duluth Aerial Transfer Bridge ferry car, LoC. Page 163: Brighton Beach Municipal Tourist Camp, TK; Chester Park Field House, TK, Portland Square Fountain, TK, Lester Park Pavilion, DPL; Lincoln Park Pavilion, DPL. Page 164: Cascade Park Pavilion, DPL, pavilion construction, DPL. Page 165: Lester Park Rustic Bridge, DPL. Page 166: Fond du Lac ski jump, TK. Page 167: Fond du Lac entrance; parking lot, DPL; Chester Park ski jump, TD. Page 168: Brautigan's Gardens, SV; White City water slide, DPL. Page 169: White City rollerskate jumper, gypsy village, DPL. Page 170: Athletic Park, TD; Wheeler race Track, DPL. Page 171: 1903 Northland Country Club, DPL; 1918 Northland

Country CLub, TD. Page 172: 1887 Boat CLub, DPL; 1903 Boat CLub, DPL. Page 173: Oatka Boat CLub facility, TD; Spirit Lake Boat CLub facility, TD. Page 174: Curling Club, TD; curlers, TK. Page 175: Amphitheater, DPL; Frederick German, DPL. Page 176: Auditorium, DPL; Y.M.C.A., DPL. Page 177: LS&M freight depot, MHS. Page 178: LS&M roundhouse, MHS; NP roundhouse, LoC. LS&M roundhouse, MHS; First Duluth Union Depot, LSRM. Page 179: NP roundhouse, LoC. NP Freight Depot, LSRM. Page 180: DWP depot, LSRM; CStPM&O depot, DPL. Page 181: Soo Line Depot, TD; Soo Line Depot interior, LSRM. Page 182: Soo Line tunnel construction, DPL; Soo Line from tunnel, DF. Page 183: West Duluth Soo Line Depot, DPL; Fond du Lac Depot, LSRM, ; unknown NP depot, LSRM. Page 184: Streetcar Conductors, LSRM. Page 185: Minnesota Point streetcar, LSRM; Duluth Street Railway car, LSRM. Page 186: Park Point fire trolley, LSRM; Yellow Horse trolley car, TD. Page 187: Duluth Street Railway car barns, LSRM; bus and trolley, DPL. Page 188: Incline railway car, DPL; Seventh Avenue West Incline, DPL. Page 189: Incline Railway Superior Street station, DPL; Beacon Hill Pavilion, DPL. Page 190: Duluth Beltline Railway car, DPL; Duluth Beltline Railway's Grand Avenue station, NEMHC; Duluth Beltline Railway Vinland Street station, DPL. Page 191: Minnesota Point Lighthouse and Keeper's Cottage, DO. Page 192: Duluth Ship Canal and Piers, LSMC. Page 193: First South Pier Light, LSMC; First Inner Pier Light, LSMC. Page 194: Interstate Bridge, DPL; St. Louis Bay Bridge, TD. Page 195: Whaleback Steamer and tug at Ore Dock #4, DPL. Page 196: Bird's-eye view of ore docks, DPL; ore boats loading at docks, DPL. Page 197: Clarkson Coal Docks, TD. Page 198: Steamer *Hamonic*, LoC; Canadian Steamship Lines advertisement, TD. Page 199: Steamer *Octorara*, LoC. Page 200: Steamer *South American*, TD. Page 201: Steamer *Mauntauk*, TD. Page 202: Tug *Essayons*, NI.

Index

References

Books, Periodicals, and Online Resources

Alanen, Arnold R. *Morgan Park: Duluth, U.S. Steel, and the Forging of a Company Town.* University of Minnesota Press. Minneapolis: 2007.

Aubut, Sheldon T. & Norton, Maryanne C. *Images of America: Duluth Minnesota.* Arcadia Publishing. Chicago: 2001.

Azema, Michel. "Duluth, Seventh Avenue West Incline." Funimag Photoblog. http://www.funimag.com/photoblog/index.php/20081206/duluth-7th-avenue-west-incline-solution-of-quiz-25-part1/ (Accessed September 14, 2012)

Bovie, Kevin J. "Duluth's First Lighthouse." *Northern Wilds.* Spring, 2007.

Bowen, Thomas E. *The Duluth Yearbook: A Review for the Year 1892.* LeTourneau: 1893.

Brissett, Jane. "Starting the Second Century." *Duluthian.* January/February 2008.

Carlson, Christine, ed. *Fond du Lac, Wa ye Kwaa Gichi Gamiing, End of Great Body of Water, & a Visual Feast.* Insty Prints. Duluth: 2000.

Carey, John R. *History of Duluth & Northern Minnesota.* Duluth News Tribune. Duluth, Minn.: 1898.

Carlson, Christine. "John Busha: Civil War veteran and Creator of a Masterpiece." *Nah gah chi wa nong Di bah ji mowin nan Translation: Far End of the Great Lake; Narrating of Story.* October 10 2010.

Catalog of Men's Furnishings. FA Patrick & Co. Duluth, Minnesota: 1909.

"Chester Bowl Park." Skisprungschanzen Website. http://www.skisprungschanzen.com/EN/Ski+Jumps/USA-United+States/MN-Minnesota/Duluth/0718/ (Accessed November 18, 2012)

"Christmas Trees from the Top of the World." *The Soo-Liner.* July-Aug.-Sept., 1958.

The City of Duluth with a Review of its Trade, Commerce and Industries. Duluth Journal of Commerce Company. Duluth, Minn.: 1886.

Cody Wetmore, Helen. *Last of the Great Scouts: the Life of Col. William F. Cody "Buffalo Bill."* University of Nebraska Press. Lincoln, Neb.: 2003.

Cooley, Jerome Eugene. *Recollections of Early Days in Duluth.* Duluth, Minn.: Published by the Author, 1925.

Coventry, William D. *Duluth's Age of Brownstone.* St. Louis County Historical Society. Duluth, Minn.: 1987.

de Kruif, Paul. *Seven Iron Men: The Merritts and the Discovery of the Mesabi Range.* University of Minnesota Press. Minneapolis: 2007.

Dierckins, Tony. *Crossing the Canal: An Illustrated History of Duluth's Aerial Bridge.* Duluth, Minn.: X-comm, 2008.

––. *Zenith: A Postcard Perspective of Historic Duluth.* Duluth, Minn.: X-comm, 2006.

Dorin, Patrick C. *Great Lakes Ore Docks & Ore Cars.* Iconografix. Hudson, Wisc.: 2007.

Drenning Holmquist, June. *They Chose Minnesota: A Survey of the State's Ethnic Groups.* Minnesota Historical SOciety Press. St. Paul., Minn.: 1981.

du Bellet, Louise Pecquet, et al. *Some prominent Virginia families, Volume 2.* J. P. Bell Company. Lynchburg, Virg.: 1907.

Duluth Commercial Club. Duluth, Minnesota. Duluth Commercial Commercial Club. Duluth, Minn.: date unk.

Duluth Illustrated in Photo Etching from New and Original Plates. James P. Craig and Duluth Book and Paper Co. Chicago: date unk.

Duluth Illustrated: Historical, Descriptive, Picturesque. Art Publishing Co. City unk.: 1887.

"Duluth, Minnesota: The Zenith City of the Northwest." *North American Industrial Review.* Duluth, Minn.: date unk.

"Duluth's Pine Knot Cabin on Minnesota Point – Everything you wanted to know about its removal, history, etc." Perfect Duluth Day, http://www.perfectduluthday.com/2010/12/08/the-pine-knot-cabin-on-minnesota-point---everything-you-wanted-to-know-about-its-removal-history-etc/ (accessed November 8, 2011).

Early Days in Duluth, Minn.: The City, the People, the Changes. Stewart-Taylor Co. Duluth, Minn.: date unk.

Eckert, Kathryn Bishop. *The Sandstone Architecture of the Lake Superior Region.* Wayne State University Press. Detroit, Mich.: 2000.

El-Hai. *Lost Minnesota: Stories of Vanished Places.* University of Minnesota Press. Minneapolis, Minn.: 2000.

Ensign, J. D. *History of Duluth Harbor.* Duluth News Tribune. Duluth, Minn.: 1898.

Farnsworth, Nan. "Moving Experience." *Duluthian.* July-August, 1992.

"Fate of Oppel Building." *Preservation Matters.* Vol. 3, no. 4 (April, 1987).

Federal Writer's Project. *The WPA guide to the Minnesota Arrowhead Country: 1930s Minnesota.* Minnesota Historical Society Press. St. Paul, Minn.: 1988.

Federal Writer's Project. *The WPA guide to the Minnesota Arrowhead Country: 1940s Minnesota.* Minnesota Historical Society Press. St. Paul, Minn.: 2008.

Flower, Frank A. *The Eye of the Northwest.* Publisher Unknown. Superior, Wisc.: 1890.

Frederick, Chuck. *Leatherheads of the North: the True Story of Ernie Nevers and the Duluth Eskimos.* X-Comm. Duluth, Minn.: 2007.

Fritzen, John. *The History of Fond du Lac and Jay Cooke Park.* St. Louis County Historical Society. Duluth, Minn.: 1978.

Ginger Magazine, Bound Volume 5. Stone-Ordean-Wells, May 1915–June 1916. Duluth, Minn.: 1916.

Good Shepherd Church: Dedication Book. Good Shephard Church. Duluth, Minn.: 1960.

Hall, Stephen P. and David A. Walker. *Duluth-Superior Harbor Cultural resources Study.* Minnesot Historical Society. St. Paul, Minn.: 1976.

Harmsberger, John L. "Jay Cooke and Minnesota: the formative years of the Northern Pacific Railroad, 1868-1873." Ph.D. Thesis, University of Minnesota, 1956.

Hecht, Arthur. "The Evolution of the Duluth Post Office." *Minnesota History Magazine*. Spring 1955.

Hedges, James B. "The Colonization Work of the Northern Pacific Railroad." *The Mississippi Valley Historical Review*. Vol. 13, no. 3. (Dec. 1926).

Heed, Sandra and Bruce. *Duluth, Minn.: Past & Present*. Published by the authors. Duluth, Minn.: 1972.

Historical Review of Sacred Heart Cathedral. Duluth Diocese. Duluth, Minn.: 1935.

Hofferbert, Richard I. "Socio-economic, Public Policy, and Political Data for the United States, 1890-1960." [Computer file] Cornell University Center for International Studies.. Ann Arbor, Mich.: 1971.

Hollister, Louise. "History of the High School." *The Tiger*. Central High School. Duluth, Minn.: 1894.

Horwitz, A. B. *Land Platting History of Duluth, Minnesota, 1856–1939*. Duluth City Planning Department. Duluth, Minn.: 1940.

– –. *Newspaper Record of The Physical Growth of Duluth, Minnesota, 1888–1928*. Study by Duluth City Planning Department. Duluth, Minn.: 1939.

Hoverson, Doug. *Land of Amber Waters*. University of Minnesota Press. Minneapolis, Minn.: 2007.

How Steel and Steel Wire Products are Made. Minnesota Steel Company. Duluth, Minn.: date unknown.

Huch, Ronald K. From *Blacksmith Shop to Modern Hospital: The Story of St. Luke's in Duluth, 1881–1981*. University of Minnesota Press. Minneapolis, Minn.: 1983.

Hudelson, Richard and Carl Ross. *By the Ore Docks: a Working People's History of Duluth*. University of Minnesota Press. Minneapolis, Minn.: 2006.

Illustrated Annual Edition of the Duluth Daily News. Duluth Daily News. Duluth, Minn.: 1888, 1889, 1891.

Illustrated Duluth, 1901. Publisher unk.: 1902

In the Wake of the Voyageur. Glass Block. Duluth, Minn.: date unk.

Karni, Michael G., Ed. Finnish Diaspora II: United States. The Multicultural History Society of Ontario. Toronto, 1981.

Kaups, Matti. "North Shore Commercial Fishing, 1849–1870." *Minnesota History Magazine*. Summer, 1978.

Kennedy, Roger G. *Historic Homes of Minnesota*. Minnesota Historical Society Press. St. Paul, Minn.: 2006.

King, Frank. *Minnesota's Logging Railroads*. University of Minnesota Press. Minneapolis, Minn.: 2003.

Koutsky, Kathryn and Linda Koutsky. *Minnesota Eats Out: an Illustrated History*. Minnesota Historical Society Press. St. Paul, Minn.: 2003.

Kramer, Carol A. *Calavaras Big Trees*. Arcadia Publishing. Mount Pleasant, SC.: 2010.

Krueger, Andrew. "Hemlock Garage Collapses, 1979." Duluth News Tribune Attic. http://attic.areavoices. com/2008/05/16/hemlock-garage-collapses-1979/ (Accessed June 8, 2011)

–– "Lennox Hotel, 1957." Duluth News Tribune Attic. http:// attic.areavoices.com/2010/09/01/lenox-hotel-1957/ (Accessed January 21, 2011).

–– "Remembering Slab Town and Below the Tracks." Duluth News Tribune Attic. http://attic.areavoices.com/page/18/ (Accessed December 16, 2010).

Lapinski, Patrick. "Beacon of Change: Minnesota Point Lighthouse." *North Star Port*. Summer, 2005.

––. "Going with the Grain: Duluth's Board of Trade." *North Star Port*. Summer, 2006.

Larson, Agnes M. *The White Pine Industry in Minnesota: A History*. University of Minnesota Press. Minneapolis: 2007.

Leggett, William. *Duluth and Environs: A Historical, Biographical, Commercial and Statistical Record*. Leggett & Chipman. Duluth, Minn.: 1895.

Lovett, C. E. "Early History of West Duluth, New Duluth, and Their Environs." (Undated and unpublished manuscript, SA file, NEMHC).

Lubetkin, M. John. *Jay Cooke's Gamble: the Northern Pacific Railroad, the Sioux, and the Panic of 1873*. University of Oklahoma Press. Norman, Oklahoma: 2006.

Lueck, John C. *The Northern Pacific in Minnesota*. Grenedair Publications. St. Paul, Minn.: 2005.

Lydecker, Ryck and Lawrence J. Sommer, eds. *Duluth: Sketches of the Past, a Bicentennial Collection*. Duluth American Revolution Bicentennial Commission. Duluth, Minn.: 1976.

MacDonald, Dora Mary. *This is Duluth*. Duluth, Minn.: published by the author, 1950.

Macrae, Jean M. *Development of the Glen Avon-Hunter's Park Area of Duluth*. St. Louis County Historical Society. 1961.

Marquis, Albert N., ed. *The book of Minnesotans: a Biographical Dictionary of Leading living Men of the State of Minnesota*. A. N. Marquis & Company. Chicago: 1907.

Martin, Rachael A. "North Country History" (column). *Senior Reporter*. Duluth, Minnesota.

––. "Cameron R. Rust." Rotary Club of Duluth Website. http://www.clubrunner.ca/CPrg/DxProgramhome/ programhome.aspx?cid=1307&pid=49854 (accessed October 22, 2012).

Meyers, Cecil H. "Financing a Frontier City: the Pioneer Banks of Duluth." *Minnesota History Magazine*. Vol. 37 (September 1960).

Miller, E. C., ed. *Duluth Trade News*. Miller Printing CO. DUluth, Minn.: 1921.

Morrison, John L. *The Booster Book: West Duluth in 1916*. Published by the author. Duluth, Minn.: 1916.

"Northland Country Club is Rich with History Beginning in 1908." Northland Country Club Website. http:// northlandcountryclub.com/?page_id=2 (accessed November 20, 2012),

The Northland Country Club Story. Publisher unk. Duluth, Minn.: date unk.

The Northwestern Industrial Souvenir. F. C. Bliss & Co. St. Paul, Minn.: 1887.

Nylander, Enid Pearce. *A History of the Duluth Public Library System*. Published by the author. Duluth, Minn.: 1962.

O. G. Traphagen: Successor to Traphagen and Fitzpatrick. Photo Tint Engraving Co. Chicago: date unk.

Pen and Sunlight: Sketches of Duluth, Superior and Ashland. Phoenix Publishing Co. Chicago: 1892.

Pepper, Terry. "North Pier Lighthouse; Duluth North Pierhead Lighthouses; Duluth Rear Range Light; Duluth Sound Breakwater Light; Minnesota Point Lighthouse;." Seeing the Light, http://www.terrypepper.com (accessed December 10, 12, and 17, 2007).

Rascher Fire Insurance Maps: City of Duluth. Chicago: Rascher Map Publishing Company, 1892.

R. L. Polk's & Co.'s Duluth City Directories. Duluth, Minn.: Duluth Directory Co. (1

Rocchio Moran, Jacqueline. "The Italian-Americans of Duluth." (Masters Thesis.) University of Minnesota Duluth: Duluth, Minn. 1979.

Ryan, J. C. "Buzz." *Early Loggers in Minnesota, Volume I.* Duluth, Minn.: Minnesota Timber Producer's Association, 1973.

– –. *Early Loggers in Minnesota, Volume II.* Duluth, Minn.: Minnesota Timber Producer's Association, 1976.

Saint Peter's Italian Church Dedication. Congregation of Saint Peter's Italian Church. Duluth, Minn.: 1927.

Sanborn Fire Insurance Maps: City of Duluth. Pelham, New York: Sanborn Map Company, 1883–1954.

Scott, James Allen. *Duluth's Legacy, Volume 1: Architecture.* City of Duluth. Duluth, Minn.: 1974.

Sommer, Lawrence. *Duluth Historic Resources Survey: Final Report.* St. Louis County Historical Society. Duluth, Minn.: 1984.

– –. *Landmark Structures of Duluth, Minn.: Their History and Architecture, Volumes 1–2.* Published by the author. Duluth, Minn.: 1971.

Souvenir of Duluth. Panton and White. Duluth, Minn.: date unk.

Souvenir of Duluth. S. H. Knox and Co. Duluth, Minn.: 1906.

Souvenir of the City of Duluth. C.P. Gibson. St. Anthony Park: 1909.

"Special Extra Number Descriptive of and Illustrating Duluth Minnesota." *American Journal of Progress.* New York: 1898.

Stensaas, Mark "Sparky." "The Old Lighthouse of Park Point." *Northlife.* July, 1999.

Tour of Historic Buildings. Junior League of Duluth. Duluth, Minn.: 1972.

Tour of Historic Buildings. Junior League of Duluth. Duluth, Minn.: 1982.

Souvenir Book of the Tenth Annual United Commercial Travelers of America Convention. United Commercial Travelers of America. Duluth, Minn.: 1903.

Statistical Abstract of the United States: 2012 (131st Edition). U.S. Census Bureau Website http://www.census.gov/compendia/statab/. (Accessed June 8, 2011)

Upham, Warren. *Minnesota Geographic Names: Their Original and Historic Significance.* Minnesota Historical Society. St. Paul, Minn.: 1920.

Van Brunt, Walter. *Duluth and St. Louis County, Minnesota: Their Story and People, Vols. 1–3.* The American Historical Society. New York: 1921.

Views of Duluth, Minnesota. S.H. Knox & Co. Duluth: date unk.

Vukelich, Joe. *Come Back Home: A History of Denfeld High School.* Published by the author. Duluth, Minn.: 2010.

Vigliaturo, Robert J. and Keppers, Jerry M. *Fire and Ice: A History of the Duluth Fire Department.* Taylor Publishing Co. Duluth, Minn.: 1993.

A Visit to the Minnesota Steel Plant, Morgan Park, Duluth, Minnesota. Minnesota Steel Company. Duluth, Minn.: date unknown.

Wasastjerna, Hans R., ed. *History of the Finns in Minnesota.* Duluth: Minnesota Finnish-American Historical Society, 1957.

Waters, Thomas F. *The Superior North Shore: a Natural History of Lake Superior's Northern Land and Waters.* Universoty of Minnesota. Minneapolis, Minn.: 1987.

Wharton, Joe. "Welland Canal Classics: Jack" Welland Canal Website. http://www.wellandcanal.ca/shiparc/misc/jack/jack.htm (accessed November 23, 2012)

"White City, Duluth's 1906 Amusement Park." St. Louis County Historical Society Newsletter. Fall, 1998.

West Duluth Centennial Memory Book. Western Area Duluth Business and Civic Club. Duluth, Minn.: 1994.

West Duluth, Minn.: Centennial Edition. Budgeteer Press. Duluth, Minn.: 1995.

West Duluth, the Pittsburg of the Northwest. West Duluth Chamber of Commerce. West Duluth, Minn.: date unk.

Wirth, George. *Residences, Business and Public Buildings, Erected from 1881-1884, Upon the Designs and Under the Supervision of George With, Architect and Superintendent.* The Pioneer Press Publishing Company. St. Paul, Minn.: 1884.

Woodbridge, Dwight E. and John S. Pardee, eds. *History of Duluth and St. Louis County, Volumes 1 and 2.* C. F. Cooper & Company. Chicago: 1910.

Newspapers

Brainerd Dispatch, Brainerd, Minnesota

Duluth Budgeteer News, Duluth, Minnesota

Duluth Daily Northwestern, Duluth, Minnesota

Duluth Evening Herald, Duluth, Minnesota

Duluth Herald, Duluth, Minnesota

Duluth Minnesotian, Duluth, Minnesota

Duluth Morning Call, Duluth, Minnesota

Duluth News Tribune, Duluth, Minnesota

Duluth Weekly Herald, Duluth, Minnesota

Hillsider, Duluth, Minnesota.

Milwaukee Journal, Milwaukee, Wisconsin.

Milwaukee Sentinel, Milwaukee, Wisconsin

Minneapolis Tribune, Minneapolis, Minnesota

St. Paul Pioneer Press, St. Paul, Minnesota

THE AUTHORS

Writer, publisher, and book designer **Tony Dierckins** has authored or co-authored over a dozen books, including the *Duct Tape* books and calendars, *The Mosquito Book*, *Zenith: A Postcard Perspective of Historic Duluth* and *Crossing the Canal: An Illustrated History of Duluth's Aerial Bridge*, a finalist for the Minnesota Book Award. A native of St. Paul, Dierckins has lived in Duluth since 1984.

Historian and Minneapolis native **Maryanne C. Norton** has made her home in Duluth since 1987, where she has worked as assistant director of the St. Louis County Historical Society and currently volunteers at the Duluth Public Library, helping others with historic and genealogical research. She is co-author of several books, including *Images of America: Duluth, Minnesota*, and worked as an archivist and librarian for the Marathon County Historical Society in Wausau, Wisconsin.

X-comm has become...

Zenith City ONLINE

CELEBRATING HISTORIC DULUTH, WESTERN LAKE SUPERIOR & MINNESOTA'S ARROWHEAD

At *Zenith City Online*, you'll find...

- A *FREE* regional history publication updated monthly, weekly, and daily
- A *FREE* researchable public archive of historic information and images
- A *FREE* guide to heritage tourism lodging, attractions, and events
- A *FREE* guide to resources for renovating your historic property
- *Zenith City Trading Post:* apparel, drinkware, & other sundry items

...and we're still crafting fine books, now under the name

zenithcity.com

Josiah D. & Rose Ensign House

504 East 2nd Street
Architects: McMillen & Stebbins
Built: 1884 | Lost: 1933

A native of New York, Josiah Davis Ensign (pictured at left) was educated in Ashtabula, passed the Ohio bar exam, served as clerk of court of Ashtabula County, and practiced law there. He arrived in Duluth before 1870, wearing "a light-colored coat and a low-crowned, broad-brimmed leghorn hat," according to *Duluth News Tribune* founder Robert C. Mitchell. He married Rose Watrous of Bay City, Michigan, in 1872. (Rose was his second wife; his first, Kate Jones of Jefferson, Ohio, died in 1868 after they had been married ten years.) A voracious reader, Ensign's personal library was considered one of the largest in the city.

Ensign was instrumental in the legal fight concerning the Duluth Ship Canal, which lasted from 1871 to 1877 and involved both the state of Wisconsin and the city of Superior. His 1898 history of the Duluth Harbor development in the 1860s and 1870s is the seminal work on the topic. Ensign served as Duluth's mayor from 1880 to 1884, as the St. Louis County Attorney, and spent thirty-two years (1889–1921) as a district court judge.

He also served as Duluth's first "juvenile judge" and reportedly loved children. Duluth's Ensign Elementary in Piedmont Heights was named for him in recognition of his service of many years on the city's school board, and it became a tradition for the Ensign Elementary schoolchildren to send him bouquets of flowers on his birthday. President William Howard Taft, after an encounter with Ensign, told friends, "It was worth crossing the continent to meet him."

The Ensign House (shown here in 1891) had a typical Queen Anne round corner tower with a witch's hat roof, a third-story balcony, gables, and patterned brick chimneys. It is not clear when the Ensigns moved from Ashtabula Heights, but at the time of his death (Josiah died in 1923, Rose in 1924) they were living at 2244 Woodland Avenue. By the late 1920s the mansion had become a boarding house. It was demolished in 1933 for construction of Miller Memorial Hospital, which became Miller-Dwan Medical Center.

Melvin & Ida Forbes House

Melvin Forbes was born in Bridgewater, Massachusetts, in 1848 and came to Duluth in 1870 to run a book and stationery store, but soon turned his attention to the grain trade. By 1874 he was working as a bookkeeper for George Spencer & Co. and later became a partner in the firm. In 1882 George Spencer became the first president of the newly formed Duluth Board of Trade.

530 East 2nd Street
Architect: OLIVER G. TRAPHAGEN
Built: 1886 | Lost: 1966

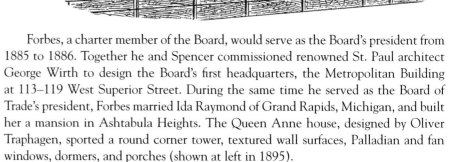

Forbes, a charter member of the Board, would serve as the Board's president from 1885 to 1886. Together he and Spencer commissioned renowned St. Paul architect George Wirth to design the Board's first headquarters, the Metropolitan Building at 113–119 West Superior Street. During the same time he served as the Board of Trade's president, Forbes married Ida Raymond of Grand Rapids, Michigan, and built her a mansion in Ashtabula Heights. The Queen Anne house, designed by Oliver Traphagen, sported a round corner tower, textured wall surfaces, Palladian and fan windows, dormers, and porches (shown at left in 1895).

Before he married, Forbes—like so many other single men of means in 1880s Duluth—lived at the St. Louis Hotel on Superior Street and was a charter member of the Kitchi Gammi Club. Forbes also belonged to Northland Country Club, the Duluth Curling Club, and the Duluth Boat Club. He continued in the grain commission until 1894, when he became president of the Consolidated Elevator Company.

Forbes died in 1907, but Ida continued to live here until her death in 1934. By 1936 the house was subdivided into apartments. It was demolished in 1966 to make room for the Nat G. Polinsky Rehabilitation Center (now the Polinsky Medical Rehabilitation Center) next to Miller Dwan Hospital.